C A R L **AUER**

Carl Auer: Geist oder Ghost

Gunthard Weber und Fritz B. Simon, eds.

1990

Einband Gestaltung: Ulrike Pollmeier
Satz: Angelika Fisher
Printed in Germany 1990
Gesamtherstellung: Druckerei Zimmermann, Balve

Erste Auflage, 1990

CIP-Kurztitelaufnahme der Deutschen Bibliothek

Carl Auer: Geist oder Ghost : Merkwürdige Begegnungen /
GunthardWeber ; Fritz B. Simon (eds.). - 1. Aufl. -
Heidelberg : Auer, 1990
ISBN 3-927809-02-0
NE: Weber, Gunthard [Hrsg.]

Table of Contents

Inhalt

How to Five

Editors' Preface

Probably no other personality of our time has divided opinion so sharply as Carl Auer. It is indeed possible to split up the human species into those who love und revere him and those who don't. And this second group can in its turn be divided into those who would love and revere him if they knew he existed and those who probably, or quite definitely, wouldn't. Although Carl Auer has always been a declared enemy of the appalling oversimplification that such binary oppositions represent, he in fact signals his agreement in this particular instance when he remarks: "I have always loved and revered the second group."

We thus had no occasion to be surprised by the difficulties we encountered in coming within hailing distance of the Carl Auer phenomenon. He had after all spent all his life combating the idealization of personalities in whatever form and crusading with equal acrimony against the personalization of ideas. And to say that we received any kind of cooperation or encouragement from him in our intention of publishing a book on the man and his ideas (if it is indeed possible to separate the two) would be a wilful misrepresentation of the facts. We wanted him to tell us everything he didn´t want to tell us anything. Only very reluctantly did he finally agree to withdraw a court order prohibiting any kind of homage to, or appreciation of, his merits and achievements. Unpredictable as ever, he made his ultimate acquiescence conditional upon having the establishment publishing the *festschrift* in honor of his 90th birthday named after him. If this ultimatum was designed to deflect us from our purpose, then it failed to achieve the desired result, as the present volume attests. Instead, Carl Auer has once again been responsible for a new departure. Alongside all his other pioneering ventures, he has

How to fünf?

Vorwort der Herausgeber

Wohl an keiner Persönlichkeit dieser Zeit scheiden sich die Geister in gleichem Maße wie an Carl Auer. Man kann die Menschheit einteilen in diejenigen, die ihn wertschätzen und lieben, und diejenigen, die es nicht tun. Diese zweite Gruppe läßt sich noch einmal unterteilen in diejenigen, die Carl Auer schätzen und lieben würden, wenn sie nur von ihm wüßten, und diejenigen, die es auch dann nicht tun oder gerade dann nicht tun würden. Obwohl Carl Auer sich immer als ein Feind der schrecklichen Vereinfachung solch binärer Unterscheidungen gezeigt hat, dieser Aufteilung stimmt er zu, wenn er bemerkt (im doppelten Sinne): „Ich habe stets die zweite Gruppe geliebt und wertgeschätzt."

So durfte es uns nicht wundern, daß sich auch unser Versuch der Annäherung an das Phänomen Carl Auer schwierig gestaltete; schließlich hat er ein Leben lang gegen jede Form der Idealisierung irgendwelcher Personen wie auch der Personalisierung irgendwelcher Ideen gekämpft. Daß er unser Vorhaben, ein Buch über ihn und seine Ideen (falls beides überhaupt zu trennen ist) zu publizieren, kooperativ unterstützt hätte, können wir beim besten Willen nicht behaupten. Wir wollten alles von ihm wissen, und er wollte nichts von uns wissen. Nur widerwillig erklärte er sich bereit, den Antrag auf ein gerichtliches Verbot einer jeden Würdigung und Ehrung seiner Person zurückzuziehen. Immer für eine Überraschung gut, bestand er darauf, daß - wenn schon, denn schon - auch der Verlag, in dem die von uns geplante Festschrift anläßlich seines 90. Geburtstags erscheinen würde, seinen Namen tragen sollte. Falls es seine Hoffnung gewesen sein sollte, uns so von unserem Vorhaben abzubringen: er hat sich - wie man sieht - getäuscht. Stattdessen wirkte Auer wieder einmal innovativ: Neben allem anderen wurde er auch noch zum Vater und Namensgeber eines neuen Verlages (ob dies

now become the initiator of a new publishing press bearing his name (whether posterity will reckon this among his achievements is arguable given the glut of printed matter on the market and the consequent disorientation of the potential reader).

If we decided to persevere in our intention of publishing a volume devoted to Carl Auer, then largely because of his outstanding significance for our own personal development and that of many others as well. In critical situations encountered in our private and professional lives we knew that Carl Auer was there to proffer advice and assistance. Even if he usually appeared somewhat absent on such occasions, it was his way of thinking and feeling, sometimes the suspicion of unashamedly tasteless humor and invariably the creative spark he communicated that showed us the way out of some apparent impasse, opened up new avenues or inspired us to feats of visionary, innovative thinking accompanied by loud cries of "eureka!". In short, our debt to Carl Auer is immense, he has been our guiding light.

Since the publication of his *magnum opus* "Between Fear and Sex", his influence on the development of western culture and academic and scientific endeavor has been palpable indeed. Carl Auer has done as much to query and shake the very foundations of western thought as he has to confirm its significance and extend its frontiers. His publications, and even more so his own life, have been devoted to revealing the absurdity of distinctions hitherto taken for granted, such as those between raw and cooked, man and woman, sensory and extra-sensory, intellect and emotion, body and soul, German and English, abstract and concrete, future and time, right and space, all of them polarizations which he has passionately and radically shown up for the fictions they are.

His has been a life full of contradictions. At home in many languages, Auer has always rebelled against the restrictions imposed by dictionaries and grammar books, exploring with inimitable gusto the limitless semantic freedoms afforded by a multilingual approach to meaning and thought. Himself a major thinker, he began at the tender age of 14 to preoccupy himself with all conceivable and apperceptible phenomena of *Geist*, more specifically with the interrelations that exist between the various meanings of that word, Geist as mind, spirit and spectre. Was this, as some historians have

einmal zu seinen Verdiensten gerechnet werden wird, steht allerdings noch offen, angesichts der sowieso schon viel zu vielen Bücher, die den Markt überfluten und dem potentiellen Leser die Orientierung rauben).

Daß wir trotz all dieser Widerstände an der Idee festhielten, ein Buch über Carl Auer zu veröffentlichen, liegt an der überragenden Bedeutung, die er - wie sicher für viele andere auch - für unsere persönliche Entwicklung gewonnen hat. Immer wieder konnten wir uns in kritischen Situationen unseres privaten und beruflichen Lebens darauf verlassen, daß Carl Auer uns mit Rat und Tat zur Seite stand. Auch wenn er dabei meist ein wenig abwesend wirkte, so waren es seine Art zu denken und zu fühlen, manchmal die Spur von geschmacklosem Humor (dessen er sich nicht schämt), immer aber der von ihm überspringende kreative Funke, der uns den Weg aus der vermeintlichen Sackgasse, neue Optionen, den von einem freudigen „Heureka"-Ruf begleiteten, rettenden oder alles erklärenden Einfall bescherte. Kurzum: Wir schulden Carl Auer viel, er ist unser großer Lehrer.

Seit dem Erscheinen seines (bislang leider immer noch nicht ins Deutsche übersetzten) Opus magnum „Between Fear and Sex" ist sein Einfluß auf die Entwicklung der westlichen Kultur und Wissenschaft nicht zu übersehen. Carl Auer hat die Grundlagen des abendländischen Denkens gleichermaßen in Frage gestellt und in ihren Grundfesten erschüttert, wie auch bestätigt und zu neuer Blüte geführt. Die bislang so selbstverständlich scheinenden Unterscheidungen zwischen roh und gekocht, Frau und Mann, sinnlich und außersinnlich, Vernunft und Gefühl, Körper und Geist, deutsch und englisch, abstrakt und konkret, Zukunft und Zeit, rechts und Raum hat er radikal durch seine Veröffentlichungen, mehr aber noch durch seine Lebensweise ad absurdum geführt.

Ein Leben voller Widersprüche: In vielen Sprachen zu Hause, akzeptierte er niemals die Beschränktheit von Grammatiken und Lexika, sondern schöpfte die Weiten vielsprachiger Bedeutungsräume nach Lust und Laune aus. Selbst ein großer Geist, beschäftigte er sich bereits im Alter von 14 Jahren mit allen denk- und erfahrbaren Phänomenen des Geistes, speziell mit den Wechselbeziehungen von Geist (englisch: mind) und Geist (spirit) und Geist (ghost). War dies - wie manche Historiker behaupten - die Geburtsstunde der Selbstbezüglichkeit? Oder lassen sich all seine begeisterten, manch-

claimed, the birth of self-referentiality? Or are these enthusiastic, albeit occasionally no more than spirited, reports of his sensory and extra-sensory experiences traceable to the inspiriting influence of alcohol? What relation exists between body and *Geist* (in all its forms)? Is there in fact such a relation at all?

This of course is a question that we as editors of this volume have been constantly preoccupied with. The spirit of Carl Auer is all-pervasive and yet Auer himself is always on the verge of disappearing like a spirit in the mists of impenetrable contradiction. As we felt incapable of broaching the question of the truth about Auer on our own, we elected to make a virtue of necessity and request prominent personalities who have encountered Auer to give an impression of their experiences with him. We should like to express our gratitude for the promptness with which they acceded to this request. The result is a mosaic, a coruscating, multi-faceted compendium of glimpses and vignettes, made up of sketches, letters and anecdotes all reflecting Auer´s major interests and concerns, a collection of accounts covering the whole gamut of feelings between fear and sex, full of passion and adventure, intellectuality and worldly wisdom, banality and genius, unconventionality and conformity, revealing Auer as a unique blend of the subversive and the survivor.

As Auer himself put it quite recently: "True greatness reveals itself in the acceptance of one´s own mediocrity!" It was on the basis of this conviction that he insisted that he was one of the greatest figures of his age. He has always been extremely reticent on the point, however, for, as he has often said, if there is one thing he is proud of it is his humility.

Auer's own response to the existential question that he poses in his major work ("What comes between fear and sex[1]?") finds him crossing the boundaries of language again. His answer is: "fünf!" (="five").

Where a more conventional mind would be tempted to concentrate on the dark animal impulses of human nature, Auer suddenly brings in the quantitative, precisely mathematical element. Here we have the quintessential Auer, the wanderer between psychoanalysis and mathematics. It is thus that he shakes us out of the deceptive security of a complacent, impermeable, cut-and-dried system of blind self-satisfied specialism. He forces us to cross boundaries and face up to contradictions.

mal auch nur geistvollen Berichte über sinnliche und außersinnliche Erfahrungen auf den inspirierenden Einfluß von Alkohol zurückführen? In welcher Beziehung stehen Körper und Geist (in all seinen Formen)? Gibt es sie wirklich?

Eine Frage, die sich auch uns als den Herausgebern dieses Buches immer wieder stellte. Der Geist Carl Auers ist überall zu spüren, und trotzdem verschwindet Auer selbst immer wieder wie ein Geist im Nebel unauflöslicher Widersprüche. Da wir uns allein der Aufgabe, die Wahrheit über Auer zu ermitteln, nicht gewachsen fühlten, haben wir aus der Not eine Tugend gemacht und prominente Persönlichkeiten, deren Lebensweg sich mit dem Auers kreuzte, gebeten, ihre Begegnungen mit ihm zu schildern. Für ihre spontane Bereitschaft dazu sei ihnen an dieser Stelle ganz herzlich gedankt. Entstanden ist so ein Mosaik, schillernd und bunt, zusammengesetzt aus Skizzen, Briefen und Erlebnisberichten, in denen sich Auers Lebensthemen widerspiegeln. Geschichten, die das ganze Spektrum zwischen Fear und Sex umfassen: voller Leidenschaft und Abenteuer, Intellektualität und Weltläufigkeit, Banalität und Genialität, Eigensinn und Kon-Formismus, subversiv und angepaßt zugleich.

„Wahre Größe zeigt sich", so formulierte Auer erst kürzlich, „wahre Größe zeigt sich darin, sich mit seiner Mittelmäßigkeit abzufinden!" Aus diesem Grunde bestand er stets darauf, einer der Größten seiner Zeit zu sein. Er machte allerdings nie irgendein Aufhebens deswegen, denn, so erklärte er, seine Demut sei sein ganzer Stolz.

Die Antwort auf die uns alle existentiell betreffende Frage aus Auers Hauptwerk („What comes between fear and sex?"), die Auer selbst gibt, lautet: „Fünf!"

Gerade an dem Punkt, an dem jeder in Versuchung gerät, seine Aufmerksamkeit auf die nicht gebändigten, triebhaft-animalischen Qualitäten der menschlichen Natur zu richten, bringt Auer die quantitative, mathematisch-exakte Saite ins Spiel und zum Klingen. Das ist so typisch und kennzeichnend für ihn: Er ist der Wanderer zwischen Psychoanalyse und Mathematik. So bewahrt er uns davor, uns der trügerischen Sicherheit unseres in sich geschlossenen, alle Beunruhigungen abwehrenden und ausschließenden Fach-

For this reason we have refrained from imposing a spurious consistency on the apparent logical or temporal contradictions that obtain between some of the reports and interpretations of the authors assembled here. All we have done is to compile the (admittedly incomplete) data on Auer in the form of a table of facts and figures. But it may well have been the deeper motive behind Auer's signal lack of cooperation to force the reader to draw his own conclusions. Our Auer is not everybody's Auer. His true nature was, is and will perhaps remain an enigma, spectral, impalpable.

For all its apparent obviousness, his insistence that five comes between fear (four) and sex (six) is no real aid to comprehension. Does this really represent the synthesis (in Hegel's sense) of the conflict between quantity and quality? This would only be the case if we knew what "5" really means for Auer. What does fiving imply for him, how does one actually go about it? This is a topic which we may safely predict, will be preoccupying critics and academics throughout the decades to come. Carl Auer's own answer to the question of "how to five" was in many ways typical: "Just five in at the deep end!"

Heidelberg, summer 1990
Fritz B. Simon and Gunthard Weber

[1] *vier* (pronounced as "fear") and *sechs* (pronounced "sex") in German are the words for "four" and "six" respectively.

idiotentums hinzugeben. Er zwingt uns, Grenzen zu überschreiten und uns mit Widersprüchen zu konfrontieren.

Aus diesem Grunde haben wir auch nicht versucht, die scheinbaren logischen oder zeitlichen Kontradiktionen zu bereinigen, die sich zwischen manchen der Berichte und Deutungen unserer Autoren ergeben. Wir haben uns damit begnügt, die über Auer vorliegenden (zugegebenermaßen lückenhaften) Daten in einer kommentierten Zeittafel zusammenzustellen. Doch das war womöglich der Hintersinn von Auers mangelnder Kooperation: Der Leser wird sich seinen eigenen Reim machen müssen, unser Auer ist nicht aller Auer. Seine wahre Natur war, ist und bleibt womöglich immer ein Geheimnis, geisterhaft, nicht zu greifen.

Denn auch seine unmittelbar evidente Antwort, daß zwischen fear und sex fünf kommt, hilft uns nicht weiter. Ist damit - wie zunächst scheint - wirklich der Gegensatz zwischen Quantität und Qualität (im Sinne Hegels) aufgehoben? Das wäre nur der Fall, wenn wir wüßten, was für Auer „5" bedeutet. Konkret: Wie macht er, wie macht man das? Ein Thema, das Exegeten und Seminaristen in den nächsten Jahrzehnten sicher noch intensiv beschäftigen wird. Carl Auers eigene Antwort auf die Frage „How to fünf?" - „Five drauf!"

Heidelberg, im Sommer 1990
Fritz B. Simon und Gunthard Weber

Acknowledgements

All those persons who have time and again encouraged and energetically supported us in daring this first attempt at an estimation of Carl Auer deserve our special thanks. The constant flow of unexpected information made the typing and desk-top-publishing tasks of Ms. Syska and Ms. Fisher especially wearisome; their contribution deserves our thanks as well. Sally and Bernd Hofmeister and Andrew Jenkins helped some of the texts to "speak two languages." Neither do we want to leave unmentioned all those souls whose colorful contributions we could not include for the sole reason that these accounts did not stand up to rigorous academic investigation. This was the case, for example, with a resident of a home for the aged in the north of Baden, S. C. Hertz, who used to play in a sandbox with Carl Auer, as well as a Carl-Auer-infatuated woman who was vacationing in Greece.

Heidelberg, October, 1990
The Editors

Danksagung

Allen, die uns immer wieder ermutigt und tatkräftig unterstützt haben, diesen ersten Versuch einer Würdigung Carl Auers zu wagen, gilt unser besonderer Dank. Durch die vielen immer wieder unerwartet auftauchenden Informationen war die Schreib- und Satzarbeit von Frau Syska und Frau Fisher besonders langwierig und verdient ebenfalls unsere Anerkennung. Sally und Bernd Hofmeister und Andrew Jenkins haben einigen der Texte zur Zweisprachigkeit verholfen. Nicht unerwähnt möchten wir aber auch all die lassen, deren farbige Beiträge wir nur deshalb nicht aufnehmen konnten, weil sie sich einer strengen wissenschaftlichen Überprüfung entzogen. Das bezieht sich z. B. auf die in einem nordbadischen Altersheim lebende S. C. Hertz, die schon im Sandkasten mit Carl Auer gespielt hat und auf eine von Carl Auer schwärmende Griechenlandurlauberin.

Heidelberg, im Oktober 1990
Die Herausgeber

Inner Formation
Instead of Information

Innere Formation statt Information

Watersheds of Understanding

Ernst von Glasersfeld

> The droplet frosting cleaves the mountains' night,
> Thus wisdom's word the world refashions quite.
> Pang-Chi-Yu (17th century)[1]

The news that Carl Auer will be celebrating his ninetieth birthday this autumn came as a considerable shock. For some fifty years now he has played the role of an inadvertent but extremely influential mentor to me. I say inadvertent because he is presumably oblivious of any kind of relationship between us, influential because, looking back, I see that my encounters with him, although not initially understood as such, were encounters of a kind that mark one for life.

My first reaction to the invitation to contribute to this *festschrift* was the chastening reflection that, as both of us are now well-stricken in years, it becomes less and less likely as time passes that the future will hold any further "chance" encounters with this unique personality. This was soon compounded with the paralyzing diffidence that befalls one upon being actually confronted, for the first time, with an all but mythical figure one has hitherto revered from a safe distance. So this is probably the last opportunity I shall have of giving anything like an unself-conscious account of the circumstances in which contact with Carl Auer has been the source of entirely novel insights.

I

The first encounter, though I failed to recognize it as such, took place in impenetrable fog. For two years it was to remain as unforgettable as it was incomprehensible. When I was a student in the mid-1930s, I took every available opportunity to go on skiing expeditions in the glacier regions of the Austrian Alps. On such excursions it is by no

Scheidewege des Verstehens

Ernst von Glasersfeld

> Wie Frost mit einem Tropfen Wasser Felsen spaltet,
> hat das Wort eines Weisen meine Welt umgestaltet.
>
> Pang-tschi-yü (17. Jahrhundert)[1]

Die Mitteilung, daß Carl Auer in diesem Frühling 90 Jahre alt wird, war für mich ein gehöriger Schock. Im Laufe von fünf Jahrzehnten hat Carl Auer für mich die Rolle eines unabsichtlichen, aber überaus wichtigen intellektuellen Mentors gespielt. Unabsichtlich, weil er wohl nichts von einer Beziehung zu mir wußte; wichtig, weil meine Begegnungen mit ihm jedesmal einen zunächst unverstandenen, im Rückblick aber ganz erheblichen Einfluß auf mich hatten.

Zunächst erweckte die Einladung, zur vorliegenden Festschrift beizutragen, den ernüchternden Gedanken in mir, daß es, da sowohl er als auch ich nun ein recht ansehnliches Alter erreicht haben, von Tag zu Tag unwahrscheinlicher wird, daß die Zukunft mir noch weitere „zufällige" Begegnungen mit diesem einzigartigen Menschen bescheren wird. Dazu kam die lähmende Schüchternheit, die einen befällt, wenn man einer sozusagen mythischen Figur, die man sein Leben lang aus sicherer Entfernung bewundert hat, zum ersten Mal tatsächlich gegenüberstehen soll. Drum ist dies nun wohl die letzte Gelegenheit, einigermaßen unbefangen die Umstände zu schildern, unter denen Carl Auer mir zu unverhofften Einsichten verholfen hat.

I

Die erste Begegnung, die ich freilich nicht als solche erkannte, fand in dichtem Nebel statt und blieb mir zwei Jahre lang ebenso unvergeßlich wie unverständlich. Mitte der dreißiger Jahre war ich Student und ging, sooft es möglich war, zum Skifahren auf die Gletscher der österreichischen Alpen. Da das Wetter bei solchen Fahrten ja nicht

means unusual for the weather to play tricks on one, and thus it was that, in the course of an ascent to one of those Alpine shelter huts that one has to cross the glaciers to get to, Irene, my companion at that time, and I found ourselves suddenly shrouded in fog. Only someone who knows the mountains can have so much as an inkling of what fog at that altitude can do. It creates a world in which all visible distinctions and outlines are lost, one can literally see no further than the end of one's skis. The driving snow forms a completely uniform expanse of whiteness in which the sky above and the earth beneath are as one and there is no discernible horizon or any other landmark from which to take one's bearings. The situation is comparable to that of those unfortunate animals that experimental psychologists observe to see how they react when a translucent sphere similar to a giant ping-pong ball is tied around their heads, allowing the passage of light but not the usual perception of contours, let alone "objects."

I made my way forward with small, regular steps, my sole concern being to proceed in as straight a line as possible. Suddenly, only a few yards in front of me a shadow emerged from the white, swirling, broth-like element around me, a man on skis, coming in our direction. His sudden appearance was so startling that we almost collided.

"Noli tangere circulos meos," he called cheerily and without coming to a halt. Like ourselves he had the hood of his ski parka well down over his eyes and was wearing snow-goggles. No face was discernible. He negotiated the obstacle we represented with a skating step before continuing his descent in the tracks we had left and seemed to hesitate for an instant and then called over his shoulder: "As long as we come full circle we have not lost our way!" The next moment he was swallowed up by the mist in the direction we had come from.

Astonishment had taken our breath away. As I was occupied in taking out two apples from my rucksack, we experienced one of those moments which make one suddenly forget the rigors of such an ascent. In a blinding flash of sunlight the white void around us was suddenly riven, and before we could bite into our apples the fog miraculously lifted and disappeared. The broad expanse of the glacier lay before us, the peaks reared like monuments of ice that we could reach out and touch, the sky arched like a vault of deep blue above us.

It was then that we saw the broad circle, as yet hardly snowed over, that the stranger had left in the expanse of virgin snow all

immer mitspielt, kamen Irene, meine zeitweilige Gefährtin, und ich eines Tages beim Aufstieg zu einer jener alpinen Schutzhütten, deren Zugang über einen großen Ferner führt, in den Nebel. Wer das Hochgebirge nicht kennt, kann sich von der Welt, in der man sich da befindet, kaum eine Vorstellung machen. Es ist eine Welt, in der es keine sichtbaren Unterschiede gibt, denn man sieht buchstäblich nichts als die eigenen Skispitzen. Der treibende Schnee bildet ein vollkommen homogenes weißes Medium, in dem Boden und Himmel nahtlos miteinander verschmelzen, so daß es weder Horizont noch den geringsten anderen Anhaltspunkt gibt, an dem man Fortbewegung oder Richtung ermessen könnte. Man fühlt sich wie eines jener armen Versuchstiere, denen Experimentalpsychologen eine einem großen Pingpongball ähnliche, lichtdurchlässige Kugel um den Kopf schnallen, um ihm zwar Licht, aber keinerlei visuelle Wahrnehmung von Konturen, geschweige denn „Gegenständen", zu gewähren.

Mit kleinen, regelmäßigen Schritten spurte ich vorwärts, nur darauf bedacht, gerade zu gehen. Plötzlich tauchte wenige Meter vor mir ein Schatten aus der weißen Suppe auf - ein Mann auf Skiern, der uns entgegenkam. Die Erscheinung war so unvorhergesehen, daß wir fast ineinander rannten.

„Noli tangere circulos meos", sagte er mit fröhlicher Stimme, ohne stehenzubleiben. Wie wir hatte er die Kapuze tief über die Stirn gezogen und trug eine Schneebrille. Kein Gesicht war zu sehen. Als er mit meisterlichem Schlittschuhschritt an uns vorbei und hinter uns in unsere Spur glitt, zögerte er einen Moment und rief über die Schulter zu uns: „Solang man den Kreis schließen kann, hat man sich nicht verirrt!" Im nächsten Augenblick war er in der Richtung, aus der wir gekommen waren, im Nebel verschwunden.

Das Staunen hatte uns den Atem verschlagen. Während ich dann zwei Äpfel aus dem Rucksack holte, geschah, was einen in den Bergen mitunter die scheußlichen Aufstiege vergessen läßt. Wie ein blendender Blitz flog eine Sekunde Sonnenschein durch das weiße Nichts um uns, dann noch einmal, und bevor wir in den Apfel beißen konnten, hatte sich der Nebel in wunderbarer Weise aufgelöst. Der breite Gletscher lag nun vor uns, die Gipfel standen wie eisige Monumente in greifbarer Nähe, und der Himmel wölbte sich tiefblau über uns.

Nun sahen wir den großen, kaum verwehten Kreis, den der Fremde mit seiner Spur in den sonst unberührten Schnee gelegt hatte

around, a circle to which our own tracks stood as an accurate tangent. He had obviously been going around in that circle for some time as there was no vestige of any track that might have shown how he got there.

But the most astounding thing of all was yet to come. We discovered it as we were about to resume the ascent. With his skiing-pole he had written something in the snow, in large letters along the circumference of the circle. I almost fell over myself in my eagerness to decipher what I was convinced would be an important message. And there, still legible, stood the words: "From night to night, a ladder from nowhere to nought."

When we finally resumed our course we repeated to ourselves those enticingly arcane words until they merged into the very rhythms of our motion. Although we had no notion of their profounder significance, they became as it were the refrain of our ascents and the brief span of our togetherness.

II

Almost exactly two years later, Hitler had just marched into Austria, I was passing through Zurich. I decided to phone Irene. I had not seen her for some time but there had been a cordial, if occasional, change of letters.

"Hallo," she said and then, after recovering from her initial suprise, "I know you've been worried about me, but there's no need now"; then, after a slight hesitation, "As long as we come full circle, we have not lost our way: I'm getting married next week."

I was touched and gladdened by this news, wished her much joy and repaired to the dentist's where I had contrived to get myself an appointment at short notice. Listlessly thumbing my way through one of the so-called "radical" literary journals of the time in the waiting-room, I suddenly came upon the very same words we had stumbled across in the mountain snows two years before.

My heart began to thump in a most unruly manner. Here were those very words, as part of a poem quoted in the course of a book-review. The relevant section read as follows:

> The young scientist Carl Auer who relinquished his research post in Austria a year before the anschluss in order to devote himself to studies of a private nature in Hintertüpfli near Appenzell has published a volume of delightful parodies.

und den die unsere wie eine saubere Tangente berührte. Offenbar war er da geraume Zeit im Kreis gegangen, denn von seiner Anfahrt war keine Spur mehr zu sehen.

Das Erstaunlichste aber sahen wir erst, als wir uns wieder auf den Weg machen wollten. Längs der Kreisspur hatte er mit seinem Stock in großen Buchstaben etwas in den Schnee geschrieben. Ich konnte gar nicht schnell genug der Kreisspur folgen, um zu entziffern, was - ich hatte nicht den geringsten Zweifel - eine wichtige Botschaft sein würde. Und da stand noch ganz gut lesbar: „Die lange Leiter eurer Schlüsse stuft sich zwischen Nichts und Nichts."

Als wir endlich weitergingen, wiederholten wir diese verführerisch esoterischen Worte und sie schmolzen in den Rhythmus unserer Fortbewegung. Obschon wir keine Ahnung von ihrer tieferen Bedeutung hatten, wurden sie zum Refrain unserer Aufstiege und unseres kurzen Zusammenseins.

II

Fast genau zwei Jahre später, Hitler war gerade in Österreich einmarschiert, rief ich bei der Durchfahrt in Zürich Irene an. Ich hatte sie lange nicht mehr gesehen, aber wir hatten uns ab und zu freundschaftlich geschrieben.

„Hallo", sagte sie, und dann, nach überraschter Begrüßung, fuhr sie fort: „Ich weiß, du hast dir Sorgen gemacht um mich, jetzt brauchst du das nicht mehr", und nach kurzem Zögern: „solang man den Kreis schließen kann, hat man sich nicht verirrt, ich werde nächste Woche heiraten."

Ich war gerührt und erfreut, wünschte ihr viel Glück und eilte zum Zahnarzt, wo ich nach einigen Anstrengungen einen kurzfristigen Termin bekommen hatte. Im Wartezimmer blätterte ich unlustig durch eine der damals „radikalen" literarischen Zeitschriften. Unversehens fiel mein Blick auf eben jene Worte, die wir damals im Schnee gelesen hatten.

Mein Herz begann ungehörig zu klopfen. Hier stand der gleiche Satz mitten in einem Gedicht, das Teil einer Rezension war. Ich las:

> Der junge Wissenschaftler Carl Auer, der bereits ein Jahr vor dem Anschluß seine Forschungsstelle in Österreich aufgab, um sich in Hintertüpfli bei Appenzell privaten Studien zu widmen, hat soeben einen Band erquicklicher Parodien ver-

Instead of the usual analysis we have chosen to reproduce one of these confections here, entitled by Auer, "Sonnet to Prometheus, after R. M. Rilke":

Tethered and blind,
with futile tools
fools grope to find
a soothing truth in rules.

No one attains a rhyme
to weave a world together,
to last forever
against the blast of time.

From night to night
the ladder grows.
Thought upon thought

into the darkness reason throws,
from nowhere to nought,
but a transient spark of light.[2]

I tore the page out of the magazine and took it away with me, of course with the intention of looking for the book. I was convinced that this Carl Auer and the man in the fog were one and the same person. The following evening, however, in the third-class compartment of a crowded train to Paris, I suddenly started having doubts. The man in the fog might have been a friend of Carl Auer's, who, upon being shown the budding poet's efforts had said with the typical heartlessness of youth: "My dear Carl, this is no good at all. You can pass it off as a Rilke parody if you like, but you can't publish it as a poem of your own."

III

Anyone who ever travelled overnight by train in those years will remember that reading was anything but easy. Even the long-distance trains had to economize on electricity and the light from the grimy light-bulbs in the third class was murky indeed. Soon after we left Zurich my fellow passengers lapsed into deep slumber. My thoughts

öffentlicht. Statt der üblichen fachmännischen Analyse drucken wir hier eines der Kunststücke ab, das Auer - frei nach Rainer Maria Rilke - „Sonett an Prometheus" nennt:

Ihr sucht so seicht,
den Tiefen seid ihr blind,
und ihr erreicht
nichts, das dem Wind
der Zeiten widerstände;
und niemand fand
was seine eignen Hände
und der Gedanken Wandern band.

Die lange Leiter
eurer Schlüsse
stuft sich zwischen Nichts und Nichts,
die Spanne wächst ein wenig weiter,
vom Unbekannten in das Ungewisse,
doch Nacht umrahmt den Kreis des Lichts.[2]

Ich riß die Seite aus dem Heft und steckte sie ein, denn ich wollte mir selbstverständlich das Buch besorgen. Ich hatte nicht den geringsten Zweifel, daß dieser Carl Auer und der Mann im Nebel ein und derselbe waren. Erst in der folgenden Nacht, als ich in einem Abteil 3. Klasse im überfüllten Zug nach Paris saß, wurde ich unsicher. Der Mann im Nebel hätte ja auch ein Freund von Carl Auer sein können, dem der angehende Dichter seine lyrischen Produkte zeigte und der ihm herzlos, wie junge Leute so oft sind, sagte: „Mein lieber Carl, das geht nicht. Das kannst du vielleicht als Rilkeparodie verkaufen, aber nicht als eigenes Gedicht."

III

Wer in jenen Jahren nachts mit der Eisenbahn gefahren ist, wird sich erinnern, daß das Lesen da nicht so leicht war. Selbst die internationalen Züge mußten anscheinend Strom sparen, und die verrußten Glühbirnen in der dritten Klasse gaben herzlich wenig Licht. Meine Mitreisenden waren bald nach der Abreise in Zürich in ein tiefes

revolved around the man in the fog and his poem. In order to reread it I had to hunch myself forward and hold the crumpled page up before my eyes. The fourth or fifth time I did this, I noticed that the man next to me was awake. "Carl is a wizard!" he said, in a hoarse whisper addressed more to himself than to anyone else. Without waiting for any affirmation on my part he carried on in broad Swiss dialect, manifestly at pains not to awaken any of the sleepers. Not once did he raise his voice, and yet he evinced an enthusiasm that I had never encountered before from the inhabitants of that region on any subject. Although I had difficulty understanding his dialect after all those years, I was still able to glean from this whispered outburst details that I could hardly have learned from any other source.

The first thing I was told was that my fellow-traveller was a member of the Cantonal Council of Appenzell and that this Council had just decided to make Professor Auer a freeman of the canton. "Because he's so good at writing parodies?" I asked, amazed. (Having spent much of my youth in Switzerland I knew by experience how unlikely it was that that country's smallest canton should feel moved to make literary gestures of such a nature.) My neighbor ignored the question altogether and resumed his whispered monologue. I should probably have shared his excitement if I had known what heroic deed it was that had prompted Appenzell to give Carl Auer a reward beyond the wildest dreams of a Central European refugee in those years. But it was only when my neighbor started getting his things together to leave the train in Bern that I had the chance to ask what it was that he had done.

For the first time since we had left Zurich he turned to me, his face the epitome of incredulity. "You mean you don't know? You've not heard?" While maneuvering his luggage down from the rack he said something of which it was only the very last word that caused me no problems of interpretation. That word was "castrated." Then my friend from Appenzell squeezed his way out of the compartment and disappeared.

A dozen other questions were clamouring for an answer in my head. One of them was, of course, whether Professor Auer was a skier. I was tempted to get out, there and then, in order to find out more about Carl Auer. But wiser councils prevailed; I had more important worries on my mind.

Reisekoma gesunken. Meine Gedanken kreisten um den Mann im Nebel und sein Gedicht. Um es nun wieder zu lesen, mußte ich mich vorbeugen und das bereits zerknitterte Blatt aus der Zeitschrift beinahe in Augenhöhe halten. Beim vierten oder fünften Mal spürte ich, daß der Herr, der neben mir saß, erwacht war. „A Zuberchünschtler isch der Carl!" sagte er. Es war ein heiseres Flüstern, anscheinend zu sich selbst. Ohne auf eine Bestätigung zu warten, fuhr er in dickem Schweizerdeutsch fort, offensichtlich darauf bedacht, die Schlafenden nicht zu wecken. Kein einziges Mal hob er die Stimme; dennoch verriet er einen Überschwang, wie ich ihn bei den Bewohnern jener Gegend nie zuvor erlebt hatte. Obschon mir die längst entwöhnte Mundart Schwierigkeiten machte, lieferte der Ausbruch dieses Fremden mir Einzelheiten, die ich kaum hätte anderwärts finden können.

Ich erfuhr zunächst, daß der Mitreisende dem Kantonalrat von Appenzell angehörte und daß dieser Kantonalrat soeben beschlossen habe, den Professor Auer zum Ehrenbürger zu machen. - „Wegen seiner schönen Parodien?" fragte ich verblüfft. (Aufgrund meiner helvetischen Jugenderfahrungen fand ich es ziemlich unglaublich, daß der kleinste Kanton der Schweiz sich zu literarischen Gesten bewegt fühlen sollte.) Mein Nachbar nahm meine Äußerung jedoch nicht zur Kenntnis und setzte seinen bewegten Flüstermonolog unbeirrt fort. Seine Erregung hätte mich zweifellos angesteckt, hätte ich gewußt, welcherart die Heldentat war, deretwegen Appenzell dem Carl Auer eine Belohnung gab, die alles überstieg, was ein flüchtiger Mitteleuropäer zu jener Zeit erträumen konnte. Es war jedoch erst, als mein Nachbar sich anschickte, in Bern auszusteigen, daß er eine Pause machte, die es mir ermöglichte, die Frage zu stellen.

Zum ersten Mal drehte er sich zu mir und schaute mich ungläubig an. „Das wisset Sie nüht? Davon hänt Sie nüt ghört?" Während er seine Handtasche aus dem Gepäcknetz manövrierte, sagte er dann etwas, von dem mir nur das letzte Wort keine Interpretationsprobleme machte. Es lautete „chaschtriert". Dann zwängte der Appenzeller sich aus unserem Abteil und verschwand.

Ein Dutzend andere Fragen schwirrten mir durch den Kopf, darunter freilich auch die, ob der Professor wohl auch ein Skialpinist sei. Ich war versucht auszusteigen, um mehr über Carl Auer zu erfahren. Doch ich hielt mich zurück, denn ich hatte in jenen Tagen noch schwerer wiegende Sorgen.

As I continued my journey I did my best to arrive at a clearer understanding of what I had heard and to find some plausible explanation. It appeared that the production of Appenzell's famous cheese had been all but brought to a standstill by the appearance of a hitherto unknown insect. I cannot say whether it was an insect of the winged variety, whether it was of a biting or stinging persuasion, as the only definition they had for it in Appenzell was "devil-mite." The source of the mortal fear that this apocalyptic insect had instilled in them was that it influenced either the cows or the milk or the cheese-making process in such a way that the product had no longer so much as a vestige of the flavor that had made it world-famous. The implications for the economic survival of the area, perhaps even for the whole canton, were of course catastrophic. The crisis had reached its climax when Professor Auer arrived in the neighborhood and rented rooms there. Of course he was soon apprised of the emergency and (this is at least my own possibly too prosaic view) as he probably knew how difficult it was to obtain an unlimited residence permit for Switzerland, the first thing he turned his attention to, when he had set up a small laboratory in his garret, was the Appenzell Cheese Problem.

As so often, Carl Auer was successful. A few weeks later he informed the postmaster (possibly the only native that he had managed to exchange a few words with in the first few months of his stay) that he thought he might be able to help.

My fellow-traveller's narration became so confused at this point that I can venture no more than a vague hypothesis about the nature of the miracle wrought by Carl Auer. Apparently he succeeded in isolating one of those hitherto unknown sex-related substances that the nervous system of certain insects is one hundred percent responsive to, and not only that but also to produce that substance independently. Thereupon - and this is perhaps an even more astonishing achievement - he managed to convince the elders of the community of the plausibility of his plan. It seems as if in the course of that winter vast amounts of that mysterious substance were in fact produced in the giant cheese vats of the dairies. Then - and if I know Carl Auer at all this will have appealed particularly strongly to his predilection for irony - the substance was taken out in the course of those local spring festivities that are a remnant of pre-Christian fertility rites and pasted over the tree-trunks of the entire vicinity by every single member of

Während der Weiterreise versuchte ich, das soeben Gehörte etwas besser zu verstehen und mir eine einigermaßen annehmbare Erklärung zurechtzulegen. Anscheinend war die Herstellung des berühmten Appenzeller Käses durch das Auftauchen eines bisher unbekannten Insekts so gut wie blockiert worden. Ich weiß nicht, ob das Tier flog oder kroch, biß oder stach, denn die Appenzeller hatten von ihm anscheinend nur als „Tüfelsvieh" gesprochen. Was ihnen aber die Todesangst eingejagt hatte, war, daß dieses apokalyptische Insekt die Kühe, die Milch oder das Käsereiverfahren so beeinflußte, daß der Käse nicht mehr den leisesten Hauch seines weltberühmten Aromas aufwies. Für die wirtschaftliche Zukunft des Dorfes, vielleicht sogar des ganzen Kantons, war das eine Katastrophe. Die Krise hatte ihren Höhepunkt erreicht, als der fremde Professor Auer sich in Hintertüpfli eine Wohnung mietete. Natürlich hörte er von der Notlage im Dorf, und da er (das mag freilich meine allzu prosaische Auslegung sein) wahrscheinlich wußte, wie schwer es war, in der Schweiz eine unbegrenzte Aufenthaltsbewilligung zu bekommen, nahm er das Appenzeller Problem als erstes in Angriff, als er sich in seiner Dachkammer ein kleines Laboratorium eingerichtet hatte.

Wie so oft in seinem Leben, war Carl Auer auch in diesem Fall erfolgreich. Nach ein paar Wochen erklärte er dem Postmeister (möglicherweise der einzige Einheimische, mit dem es ihm gelungen war, in den ersten Monaten seines Aufenthalts ein paar Worte zu wechseln), er glaube, er könne helfen.

Die Erzählung meiner Reisebekanntschaft wurde von diesem Punkt an so verwirrt, daß ich in Bezug auf Carl Auers wunderwirkendes Eingreifen nur eine ganz vorläufige Hypothese aufstellen kann. Anscheinend gelang es ihm, eine jener damals unbekannten chemischen Substanzen, denen das Nervensystem bestimmter Insekten hörig ist, nicht nur zu isolieren, sondern auch herzustellen. Alsdann - und das ist vielleicht eine noch bewundernswertere Leistung - gelang es ihm, die Dorfältesten von der Plausibilität seines Plans zu überzeugen. Es scheint, daß im Laufe des Winters die geheime Substanz in den Riesenkesseln der Käsereien tatsächlich in großen Mengen produziert wurde. Dann - und soweit ich Carl Auer kennengelernt habe, dürfte das seine Vorliebe für Ironie besonders ergötzt haben - wurde das Konzentrat im Rahmen der landesüblichen Frühjahrsfeier, die ja ein Überbleibsel vorchristlicher Fruchtbarkeitsriten ist, von der gesamten Dorfbevölkerung an alle Baumstämme der

the local population. No sooner were the odious insects hatched than the males flocked to the irresistible bait, there to squander their entire reproductive potential - or as my informant put it, they were "castrated." (Anyone familiar with our author may be tempted to interpret this episode as the source of Auer's later highly controversial suggestions with regard to the problem of overpopulation.)

Although I am convinced that, in essentials at least, the information given to me by the stranger on the train were not mere invention, my hypothetical interpretation is of course a daring one, and certainly requires further substantiation, particularly as my excitable friend constantly compared Professor Auer to "Doktor Faustus" and also used the terms "witches' broth" and "black magic." On the other hand, what I later read concerning Carl Auer's work in such a wide range of different branches did go some way towards substantiating my version. One of the essential principles postulated by that great scholar is that effective change can only be achieved via approaches that the organism in question is already familiar with. It was thus to be expected that such an unprejudiced and clear-headed thinker as Carl Auer would attack organisms where they are most familiar, i. e. in their sexuality.

In the turmoil of the months that followed, spent largely in search of a place where I would be allowed to stay even though I could not work miracles, I put the whole affair completely out of my mind.

IV

The next indirect encounter was of a different kind, but no less astonishing. About five years after the events in Switzerland, I was in Dublin with my young wife. James Joyce's last work *Finnegan's Wake* had just come out. As great admirers of Joyce we bought the book immediately and tried to read it, both separately and jointly. One morning as I was in the bathroom shaving, my wife called out: "What are . . ." and then an incomprehensible word. I wiped my face, went to the bed and read the passage my wife indicated. The passage was as follows:

Umgebung gestrichen. Kaum waren die odiösen Insekten ausgeschlüpft, schwärmten die Männchen zu dem duftenden Köder und vergeudeten ihr Fortpflanzungspotential, oder wurden - wie mein Informant sich ausdrückte - „kastriert". (Wer unseren Autor weitgehend gelesen hat, mag versucht sein, in dieser Episode den Ursprung der später so heftig diskutierten Auerschen Beiträge zum Übervölkerungsproblem zu sehen.)

Obschon ich überzeugt bin, daß die wesentlichen Anhaltspunkte, die mir der Mann im Zug gab, nicht erfunden waren, ist meine hypothetische Auslegung, wie gesagt, ein gewagte, die weiterer Belege bedürfte. Umsomehr, als der Reisende in seinem erregten Bericht Professor Auer mit dem „Doktor Fauschtus" verglich und von „Hexensuppe" und „Zauberei" sprach. Andererseits ließ meine Auslegung sich im Lichte dessen, was ich später über Carl Auers vielseitige Arbeiten erfuhr, nicht ausschließen, denn einer der Grundsätze, die wir dem großen Forscher verdanken, ist ja wohl der, daß effektive Änderungen stets nur auf Wegen zu erreichen sind, die dem betreffenden Organismus schon vorher geläufig waren. Einem vorurteilslosen und einzigartig klaren Denker wie Carl Auer mußte es darum naheliegen, Organismen an der Stelle anzugreifen, die ihnen am geläufigsten ist, also in ihrem Geschlechtsleben.

Im Trubel der folgenden Monate, die ich fast ununterbrochen auf der Suche nach einem Ort verbrachte, wo ich, der ich keinerlei Wunder wirken konnte, dennoch eine Aufenthaltsbewilligung bekommen könnte, vergaß ich die ganze Geschichte.

IV

Die nächste indirekte Begegnung war zwar anderer Art, aber nicht weniger erstaunlich. Etwa fünf Jahre nach den Schweizer Begebenheiten war ich mit meiner jungen Frau in Dublin, gerade als James Joycens letztes Werk, „Finnegan's Wake", erschien. Als große Joyce-Verehrer hatten wir das Buch gleich gekauft und versuchten nun, es sowohl abwechselnd als auch zusammen zu lesen. Eines Morgens rief meine Frau ins Badezimmer, wo ich mich rasierte: „Was sind ..." und ein unverständliches Wort. Ich wischte mir die Seife ab, ging zum Bett und las die Stelle, wo meine Frau ihren Finger hatte. Hier ist eine ungefähre Übersetzung (insofern man da von Übersetzung sprechen kann):

> In newrotic ages the pterobly dactile carlosaurian engentians earnest machinations on the vicotorious march of skientific progress to the iambatistan rhythm of Himmelayan pistemologies.[3]

The allusion to Giambattista Vico was obvious. A reading of the first page of the book in the company of friends had already brought us up against the Italian philosopher. Nor was Ernst Mach difficult to detect. But I had to reduce the passage to its constituent syllables before I became aware of the presence of Carl Auer. Not, of course, that one could be absolutely sure. The name Carlo is not so rare and there was nothing about the link with the saurians to make certain identification any easier. But "ski" and "gentian" were a patent reference to the mountains.

Suddenly I realized that I had never told my wife of my pre-war encounters with Carl Auer. When I had made good this omission as best I could, she said: "Carl Auer, Carl Auer, I think I once came across an article of his in the library. I remember thinking that the title sounded like Wagner, 'The Ring of Neuro-Linkages' or something like that."

We unearthed the journal in the library and the article was indeed entitled "The Ring of Neuro-Linkages: Inner Formation instead of Information."[4] Condensed in the space of two pages, we found here not only the concept of the closed system but the whole range of unnerving consequences that this idea had for biology as well as cognitive development and epistemology. - To be honest, we understood very little of what he was saying. The neurobiological examples he quoted required specialized knowledge that we were not even remotely possessed of. But there was one passage that I found acutely gratifying. Unfortunately I have since mislaid the article but the message of the passage in question has remained inscribed indelibly on my mind.

In a section with the knee-weakeningly allusive sub-heading "The Biological *Noli Tangere*," Auer set out to demonstrate that in the last resort living beings had only one aim and that was the preservation of their inner harmony. In the course of time what they feel to be constituent of that harmony may change. But if it changes in such a way to make it harder to preserve and to require even greater

> In Neurozeiten unterbreitiert der vielverkanntete Carlosaurier Ernst Machinationen sowie des Neapolitikers Firstwerk in puncto vicoser Skienziane (immer noch neu, oh weh!) und himaleisiger Jambattistemologien.[3]

Die Anspielung auf Giambattista Vico sahen wir schnell, weil wir schon mit Freunden beim Lesen der ersten Seite in *Finnegans Wake* auf den italienischen Philosophen gestoßen waren. Ernst Mach war auch nicht schwer zu finden. Ich mußte die Zeilen aber mehrere Male in Silben zerlegen, bevor mir Carl Auer ins Auge sprang. Freilich konnte man da wieder einmal nicht sicher sein. Der Name Carlo ist ja nicht besonders selten und die Verbindung mit „Saurier" trug nichts zur Identifikation bei. Doch „Ski" und „Enzian" wiesen in die Berge.

Nun war mir aber plötzlich klargeworden, daß ich meiner Frau nie von den Vorkriegsbegegnungen mit Carl Auer erzählt hatte. Als ich das, so gut ich konnte, nachholte, sagte sie: „Carl Auer, Carl Auer, ich glaube, ich hab einen Artikel von dem in einer Zeitschrift in der Bibliothek gesehen. Mir ist der Titel aufgefallen, weil er irgendwie an den Ring der Nibelungen erinnerte, 'The ring of neuro-linkages' oder so was Ähnliches."

Wir fanden die Zeitschrift in der Bibliothek, und der Artikel hieß tatsächlich: „The ring of neuro-linkages: Inner formation instead of information".[4] Auf knapp zwei Seiten war da nicht nur die Idee des geschlossenen Systems, sondern auch eine ganze Reihe ihrer unheimlichen Konsequenzen in der Biologie sowie auf dem Gebiet der kognitiven Entwicklung und der Erkenntnislehre zusammengepreßt. - Ich muß ehrlich sagen, daß wir fast nichts davon verstanden. Die neurobiologischen Beispiele, die da angeführt wurden, verlangten ein Fachwissen, mit dem wir nie in Berührung gekommen waren. Dennoch fand ich ein paar Zeilen ungemein befriedigend. Der Artikel ist mir inzwischen leider abhanden gekommen, doch der Sinn des betreffenden Absatzes ist mir unvergeßlich geblieben.

In einem Abschnitt, der den für mich geradezu überwältigenden Untertitel „Das biologische *Noli Tangere*" hatte, wurde da erklärt, Lebewesen hätten letzten Endes nur ein Ziel und das sei die Bewahrung einer inneren Harmonie. Worin die Harmonie besteht, kann sich mit der Zeit ändern. Wehe, wenn sie sich so verändert, daß sie schwerer zu erhalten wird und immer größere Opfer erfordert. Ist ein

sacrifices, then there is going to be trouble. Once such a risky course has been embarked upon then even a slight shift in environmental conditions can trigger a disaster. The fate of the dinosaurs, whose weight, strength and hence cell proliferation developed at the expense of everything else was, Auer said, a grim warning to avoid any one-sided development. (A footnote referred to a more detailed discussion of this point by the author elsewhere.[5])

This then was the link-up with the "circles" that we must not break, with the dinosaurs, and finally with the manic fear of unambiguity that makes *Finnegans Wake* all but unreadable. There was now no doubt that the man in the fog was Carl Auer, here delineated clearly as an unflinchingly innovative thinker and the founder of a pioneering philosophical approach.

In addition, the article contained a multitude of terms which were extremely unfamiliar in those days, such as "mono-autonomy," "co-phenomenal," "self-concatenation" which must have taken root in my unconscious only to emerge at a later date in my own work. This, of course, must not be taken to mean that I understood them in the sense that Carl Auer was using them, only that (as with so many others) time and my own experience finally made it possible for me to invest them with some kind of sense.

V

Then came World-War II and the postwar years, a long period in which one had little indication to reminisce about past experiences. It must have been when I was working in Milan around 1950 that a colleague of mine showed me the announcement of a lecture by a visiting professor. The Italian title intrigued me: *La problematica delle soluzione*. Preoccupied as I was day and night with translation, I automatically asked myself whether this meant the problem of finding solutions or the problems that solutions bring with them.

It was then that I read the name Carlo Auer. And in my mind's eye I saw an unrecognizable and yet not unfamiliar figure coming towards me out of the fog, like all those years before, on the glacier.

As far as lectures were concerned I had already gathered some considerable experience. Without actually admitting it to myself I tended to divide them up into two groups, those (rare) occasions on which one does one's best to follow what the speaker is saying and all

so riskanter Weg einmal eingeschlagen, so kann auch eine geringe Verschiebung der Umweltverhältnisse zur Katastrophe werden. Das Schicksal der Saurier, bei denen Gewicht, Körperkraft und somit Zellvermehrung die Oberhand gewannen, sei eine eklatante Warnung, alle Arten von Einseitigkeit zu vermeiden. (Eine Fußnote verwies auf Carl Auers breitere Ausführung dieser Idee.[5])

Da war also der Zusammenhang mit den Kreisen, die man nicht stören darf, mit den Sauriern, und schließlich auch mit der manischen Angst vor Eindeutigkeit, die „Finnegans Wake" nahezu unlesbar macht. Der Mann im Nebel war nun unzweifelhaft Carl Auer, klar umrissen als unerschrockener Denker und Begründer einer bahnbrechenden Philosophie.

Zudem enthielt der Artikel eine Menge von damals kaum geläufigen Wörtern, wie etwa „Selbstverkettung", „Monautonomie", „cophänomenal", die mir wohl im Unterbewußtsein hängenblieben, um dann viele Jahre später im Rahmen der eigenen Arbeit wieder aufzutauchen. Das soll freilich nicht heißen, daß ich sie im Sinne Carl Auers verstanden hätte, nur daß ich ihnen (wie bei so manchen anderen Autoren) im Lauf der Zeit aufgrund eigener Erfahrungen schließlich einen Sinn zuschreiben lernte.

V

Dann kamen der Krieg und die Nachkriegsjahre, die einem lange Zeit die Lust vertrieben, früheren Erlebnissen nachzuhängen. Es muß um 1950 gewesen sein, als ich in Mailand arbeitete, daß mir ein Kollege die Anzeige eines Vortrags brachte, dessen Titel meine Neugier erregte. „La problematica delle soluzioni", hieß es da auf Italienisch, und da ich Tag und Nacht mit Übersetzung zu tun hatte, fragte ich mich unwillkürlich, ob man auf Deutsch da „Die Problematik *der* oder *von* Lösungen" sagen würde.

Dann sah ich den Namen Carlo Auer, und wie damals auf dem Gletscher sah ich eine unerkenntliche und nun doch bekannte Gestalt aus dem Nebel meiner Vorstellung auf mich zukommen.

Zu jener Zeit war ich, was Vorträge anbelangt, längst kein Neuling mehr. Ohne es ausdrücklich formuliert zu haben, hatte ich Vorträge in zwei Gruppen eingeteilt: Die seltenen, bei denen man sich bemüht, dem Sprecher gedanklich zu folgen, und all die anderen, bei

those others, where the main problem is to conceal both from one's colleagues and the speaker, that one has lapsed into profound torpor. No sooner had Carl Auer mounted the platform that I knew that this was going to be a different experience altogether.

Of course, it would be absurd to suggest that I recognized him. I had only seen him in snow-goggles and a hood covering the rest of his face. But the very way he scaled the platform immediately marked him out as a mountaineer. He grasped the edge of the lectern with both hands as if he were about to thrust himself downhill on a pair of skis. With head bent and shoulders slightly raised the classic posture, one might say he began his remarks in fluent, indeed excellent Italian and spoke without interval, sometimes more slowly but never faltering. His whole body was attuned to the rhythms of his speech, just as a skillful skier will unconsciously match his every movement to the rises and hollows of the ground he is negotiating. I was fascinated, no less by the physical dynamism of the man than by what he actually had to say.

Other contributors to this *festschrift* are undoubtedly more competent than I to situate the work of Carl Auer in the history of Western thought. I took it to be the central idea of his lecture in Milan that, necessary as it may be to look for the solution to a problem in one direction or another, it invariably has embarassing not to say devastating consequences to indulge in the fond belief that the solution we find is the *right* one and hence the only possible one.

At the end of his lecture, Carl Auer summed up the essence of his philosophy in a play on words that casts far more light on his true nature than I ever could. And it is with this profound pun that I shall close my account of these quasi-encounters with the great man, whom I have not in fact ever seen again.

Even before the applause had ebbed away, people started thronging the platform from all corners of the room. I followed suit, but was unable to get anywhere near the speaker. A group of self-important "colleagues" monopolized him so successfully that the less impertinent questioners finally turned away in disappointment. But then a German voice bellowed from some distance back: "Herr Professor, what is your opinion of Ernst Mach?" - Carl Auer, who thus far had inclined a patient, albeit not tremendously enthusiastic ear to the questions of those beleaguering him, suddenly drew himself up to his

denen das Hauptproblem darin besteht, weder die Kollegen noch den Vortragenden merken zu lassen, daß man eingeschlafen ist. Kaum war jedoch Carl Auer auf das Podium getreten, wußte ich, daß nun ein Erlebnis ganz anderer Art begonnen hatte.

Natürlich wäre es Unsinn, zu sagen, daß ich ihn erkannte. Ich hatte ihn ja nur mit Sturmkapuze und Schneebrille gesehen. Doch schon die Art und Weise, wie er auf das Podium stieg, ließ mich den Bergsteiger erkennen. Mit beiden Händen faßte er den Rand des kleinen Pultes, als bereite er sich vor, zu einer Schußfahrt abzustoßen. Den Kopf vorgebeugt, die breiten Schultern etwas hochgezogen - mit zünftiger Vorlage - könnte man sagen, fing er in fließendem, ausgezeichnetem Italienisch an und sprach pausenlos, manchmal schnell, manchmal langsamer, aber ohne je zu zögern, und sein ganzer Körper folgte dem Rhythmus der Rede, genau wie ein gewiegter Skifahrer sich unbewußt mit jeder Bewegung dem kupierten Gelände anpaßt. Ich war gebannt, nicht minder von der körperlichen Dynamik des Vortragenden als von den Ideen, die er vortrug.

Andere, die zu dieser Festschrift beitragen, sind ohne Zweifel kompetenter als ich, das Werk Carl Auers in die Geschichte des abendländischen Denkens einzureihen. Mir schien der Kernpunkt des Mailänder Vortrags die Einsicht zu sein, daß es wohl zuweilen wichtig ist, ein Problem auf die eine oder andere Weise zu lösen, daß es aber stets peinliche, wenn nicht gar verheerende Folgen hat, wenn man sich in den Glauben verirrt, die gefundene Lösung sei die *richtige* und darum einzig mögliche.

Viel besser aber, als ich es könnte, faßte Carl Auer selbst zum Abschluß des Mailänder Abends sein philosophisches Werk in einem Wortspiel zusammen. Damit will denn auch ich diesen Bericht meiner Quasibegegnungen mit dem großen Mann beenden, denn ich habe ihn seither nie mehr gesehen.

Schon bevor der Applaus im großen Auditorium abgeflaut war, drängten Leute sich von links und rechts an das Podium. Ich folgte, doch es gelang mir nicht, dem Sprecher nahezukommen. Eine Gruppe der üblichen Wichtigtuer hatte ihn so fest umzäunt, daß die weniger aufdringlichen Fragesteller sich schließlich enttäuscht abwandten. Doch dann rief auf einmal eine deutsche Stimme aus einiger Entfernung: „Herr Professor, was halten Sie von Ernst Mach?" - Carl Auer, der sich vorher geduldig, aber ohne Begeisterung zu den Nahestehenden gebeugt hatte, richtete sich zu seiner vollen Größe

full height, cast an irresistibly satirical glance at the earnest, bespectacled gentleman who had asked the question and then gave his answer, not only to the inquirer but to the whole world: "I owe a great deal to Ernst Mach but I think I match Ernst as far as sensational analysis is concerned!" With that he bowed and sailed out of the hall with consummate elegance.

Envoy

How often does a man of words, be he scientist or poet, look down at the sentence he has just written and say: Where did I get that from? Is it really my own idea?

In recent years doubts of this nature have been assailing me more and more frequently. And summoning up these memories of events that I have only inadequately recounted here has all but confirmed my suspicions. As I see it, it is Carl Auer - the only contemporary whom the term "Renaissance Man" really seems to fit - who in fact said more or less everything that I have laboriously fumbled together myself. Presumably that should be a source of mortification to me. But it isn´t. The myriad echoes that I now think I can discern in my work give me a deeper satisfaction. Those insights of Carl Auer's that were most influential for me now appear so important for the salvation of our ailing world that the question of who expressed or repeated them when and where is of small moment. And quite aside from that, Carl Auer is probably the last person who would claim author's rights.

Hence I look forward to this birthday celebration and the first "real" encounter with my inadvertent mentor with an easy conscience and more than pleasurable anticipation.

Notes

[1]Klabund, *Chinesische Gedichte*. Zürich: Phaidon, 1954, p. 14.

[2]*Die gelbe Spinne*, März 1937, Jahrgang 3, Nr. 1, p. 12.

[3] James Joyce, *Finnegan's Wake*. London: Faber & Faber, 1939, p. 19 (passage later deleted by the author).

[4]Carl Auer, "The Ring of Neuro-Linkages: Inner Formation Instead of Information," *Nature*, 1943, 79, pp. 273-275.

[5]Carl Auer, "Die Versponnenheit der Saurier," *Neue Naturwissenschaft*, 1939, 13, p. 79-87.

auf, streifte den seriösen, bebrillten Herrn, der die Frage gestellt hatte, mit einem unwiderstehlich heiteren Blick und antwortete nicht nur ihm, sondern der ganzen Welt: „Ja dem Ernst Mach, dem hab ich eine ganze Menge zu verdanken, aber ich mach Ernst mit der Analyse der Erfindungen!" Dann verbeugte er sich und schwang in elegantem Bogen aus der Vortragshalle.

Schlußbemerkung

Wie oft passiert es einem Wissenschaftler oder Dichter, daß er auf den Satz schaut, den er eben geschrieben hat, und sich plötzlich fragt: Woher hab ich das eigentlich? Ist das wirklich von mir?

In den letzten Jahren sind mir Zweifel dieser Art immer öfter gekommen. Das Heraufbeschwören meiner Erinnerungen an die hier so unvollkommen beschriebenen Ereignisse hat den Verdacht beinahe zur Gewißheit gemacht. Mir will nun scheinen, daß Carl Auer, der einzige Zeitgenosse, auf den meines Erachtens die so oft mißbrauchte Bezeichnung „Renaissancemensch" paßt, so ziemlich alles gesagt hat, was ich mir je zusammengetüftelt habe. Das sollte mir wohl peinlich sein, doch es ist es nicht. Die vielen Echos, die ich nun zu entdecken glaube, geben mir im Gegenteil eine gewisse Befriedigung, denn die Einsichten Carl Auers, die für mich maßgebend gewesen sein mögen, scheinen mir heute so wichtig für unsere sieche Welt, daß es nicht darauf ankommen kann, wo, wann und von wem sie wiederholt oder neu erfunden werden. Zudem ist Carl Auer sicher der letzte, der da irgendwelche Ansprüche auf Urheberrecht erheben würde.

Somit sehe ich der Geburtstagsfeier und der ersten „wirklichen" Begegnung mit meinem unabsichtlichen Mentor mit gutem Gewissen und freudiger Erwartung entgegen.

Anmerkungen

[1]Klabund, *Chinesische Gedichte*. Zürich: Phaidon, 1954, S. 14.

[2]*Die gelbe Spinne*, März 1937, Jahrgang 3, Nr. 1, S. 12.

[3]James Joyce, *Finnegan's Wake*. London: Faber & Faber, 1939, S. 19 (Abschnitt wurde später vom Autor gestrichen).

[4]Carl Auer, „The Ring of Neuro-Linkages: Inner Formation Instead of Information", *Nature*, 1943, 79, S. 273-275.

[5]Carl Auer, Die Versponnenheit der Saurier, *Neue Naturwissenschaft*, 1939, 13, S. 79-87.

You Cannot Cross a River Once

Du kannst keinen Fluß einmal überqueren

Tell Me Carl, Where Do I Exist?

Karl Tomm

The wood was burning feverishly as I threw in another log and quickly closed the door. The stove was hot, really hot! But it needed to be . It was another one of those cold winter nights in the Canadian Rockies - it must have been at least 30 degrees below zero! Maybe even 35! And it was very dark outside.The snow-capped mountains and the frozen lake were barely visible in the twinkling starlight.

Fortunately, the little stove threw a lot of heat. The young salesman said it would, and I was glad that he was right. Despite the cold, it was able to keep the whole cabin warm. He said the stove had been built in New Zealand and was designed for efficiency. It burned not only the wood but also the gases released from the wood before they went up the chimney. The idea was intriguing at the time, but actually seeing it happen was even more so. Through the big glass window at the front of the stove, I could see the flames dancing with the gases right there in front of me. It was an exquisite and fascinating sight!

I leaned back into the large soft cushions on the floor as I watched the fire burn. The sound of the crackling blaze and the smell of hot charred wood added to the warmth and comfort in the cabin as I imagined the contrasting cold outside. It was a wonderful place to relax and reflect. I could spend hours in the cabin simply staring into the hypnotic dance of undulating flames as they were glowing in the dark.

On this particular occasion, I found myself in a deep conversation with a delightful old man. He was the kind of person one often

Sag mir, Carl, wo existiere ich?

Karl Tomm

Das Holz brannte prasselnd, als ich ein weiteres Scheit zulegte und schnell die Tür zumachte. Der Ofen war heiß, richtig heiß! Aber das war auch nötig. Es war wieder eine jener kalten Winternächte in den kanadischen Rockies - es muß mindestens 30 Grad unter Null gewesen sein! Wenn nicht 35! Und draußen war es sehr dunkel. Die schneebedeckten Berge und der zugefrorene See waren im glitzernden Sternenlicht kaum auszumachen.

Zum Glück gab der kleine Ofen eine Menge Wärme ab. Der junge Verkäufer hatte es ja gesagt, und ich war froh, daß er recht hatte. Trotz der Kälte schaffte er es, die ganze Hütte warm zu halten. Er hatte gesagt, der Ofen sei in Neuseeland gebaut worden und sei sehr leistungsfähig. Er verbrannte nicht nur das Holz, sondern auch die vom Holz freigesetzten Gase, bevor sie durch den Kamin abzogen. Damals hat mich dieser Gedanke fasziniert, es aber wirklich vor mir zu sehen, faszinierte mich noch mehr. Durch die dicke Glastür an der Vorderseite des Ofens konnte ich die mit den Gasen tanzenden Flammen direkt vor meiner Nase sehen. Es war ein einmaliger und faszinierender Anblick!

Während ich ins Feuer blickte, lehnte ich mich in das große weiche Kissen auf dem Boden zurück. Das Geräusch des knackenden Feuers und der Geruch heißen, verbrannten Holzes ließen mich die Wärme und die Gemütlichkeit in der Hütte noch mehr spüren, wenn ich an die beißende Kälte draußen dachte. Es war ein wundervoller Platz, um zu entspannen und nachzudenken. Ich konnte Stunden damit verbringen, einfach dem hypnotischen Tanz der sich schlängelnden Flammen zuzuschauen, wie sie in der Dunkelheit leuchteten.

Zu diesem Zeitpunkt war ich mit einem wunderbaren alten Mann in ein Gespräch vertieft. Er war jemand, den man sich als Verfasser

imagines when thinking about the author of a great philosophical work - thoughtful, wise, and dignified. I think his name was Carl von Auer but I can't be sure. It is mainly the conversation itself that I recall. Just how it happened that we came to be together at the cabin that night remains a mystery. Sometimes I even wonder if it didn't all take place in my imagination and if the conversation I had wasn't really with myself! Perhaps I slipped into a trance as I was watching the mesmerizing fire. The dancing flames triggered a personal philosophical question that had been haunting me for some time:

"Carl, how can I know that I, Karl, am anything more than a dynamic swirl of pure process like those flames?"

He was resting casually on the floor about a meter to my left. With his head and shoulders propped up on a large red pillow, he was also gazing into the blazing fire. "What a delightful thought!" he said. "I am very impressed with your empathy and humility today!"

"Now just hang on here! I didn't say there was nothing more to me than a flame! I asked an honest question and you side-stepped it." I thought that he had deliberately misunderstood and admit I felt a tinge of annoyance.

"O.K., O.K.," he said calmly. "It's just that it sounded like such a refreshingly humble way to think of oneself in this age of arrogance."

"Are you implying that it would be arrogant of me to say that as a human being I am more than a dancing flame?"

"No, not necessarily. It depends on the manner and context in which you make the claim."

"Well, I'm thinking of myself as a living organism, and as a human being that *knows* that he is alive. I don't think we can say that of the flame."

"O.K., I could agree with you on that. . . . So what's your question?"

"Well, when I wonder what I am, I look at myself and see a body that I can identify with. I seem to be made up of flesh and bones, of physical matter that I can touch and feel. Yet the physicists are telling us that what we experience as solid matter is only a swirl of atoms and molecules which, in turn, are only swirls of energy with differing

großer philosophischer Arbeiten vorstellt - nachdenklich, weise und würdevoll. Ich meine, er hätte Carl von Auer geheißen, bin mir allerdings nicht sicher. Es ist im wesentlichen das Gespräch selbst, an das ich mich erinnere. Weshalb wir ausgerechnet in jener Nacht zusammen in der Hütte waren, bleibt ein Rätsel. Manchmal frage ich mich sogar, ob ich mir alles nur eingebildet und vielleicht ein Selbstgespräch geführt habe! Womöglich bin ich beim Beobachten des faszinierenden Feuers in Trance gefallen. Die tanzenden Flammen lösten bei mir eine persönliche philosophische Frage aus, die mich seit geraumer Zeit beschäftigte:

„Carl, wie kann ich wissen, daß ich, Karl, mehr bin als ein dynamischer Wirbel eines reinen Prozesses wie diese Flammen?"

Er ruhte etwa einen Meter zu meiner Linken entspannt auf dem Boden. Seinen Kopf und seine Schultern auf ein großes rotes Kissen gebettet, starrte er ebenfalls in das lodernde Feuer. „Was für ein wunderbarer Gedanke!" sagte er. „Ich bin heute sehr beeindruckt von deinem Einfühlungsvermögen und deiner Demut!"

„Jetzt mach' mal halb lang! Ich hab nicht gesagt, ich wäre nichts anderes als eine Flamme! Ich habe eine ehrliche Frage gestellt, und du weichst ihr aus." Ich dachte, er hätte mich absichtlich mißverstanden, und gebe zu, daß ich einen Anflug von Ärger fühlte.

„Schon gut", sagte er ruhig. „Es hörte sich nur überaus erfrischend und bescheiden an, in diesem Zeitalter der Arroganz so über sich selbst zu denken."

„Willst du damit sagen, daß es arrogant von mir wäre, wenn ich sage, daß ich als menschliches Wesen mehr bin als eine tanzende Flamme?"

„Nein, nicht unbedingt. Es hängt von der Art und dem Kontext ab, in dem du diese Behauptung aufstellst."

„Nun, ich halte mich für einen lebenden Organismus und für ein menschliches Wesen, das *weiß*, daß es am Leben ist. Ich glaube, man kann das von der Flamme nicht behaupten."

„Ja, so weit kann ich dir zustimmen . . . Was ist denn nun deine Frage?"

„Wenn ich mich frage, was ich bin, betrachte ich mich und sehe einen Körper, mit dem ich mich identifizieren kann. Ich scheine aus Fleisch und Knochen zu bestehen, aus Materie, die ich berühren und fühlen kann. Dennoch sagen uns die Physiker, daß es sich bei dem, was wir als feste Materie erfahren, nur um einen Wirbel von Atomen

intensities. Is my existence an illusion and my substance a mere swirl of molecular activity?"

"Do you believe the physicists or do you believe your own experience?"

"Are you saying that it's only a matter of belief?" I said incredulously.

"No, no, Karl, it's a matter of giving priority to experience, rather than to scientific theory. It has to do with trusting your own experience, rather than with trusting the molecular theories created and taught to you by others."

I wasn't sure that I entirely understood what he was getting at and fell silent. At least he seemed to be listening more seriously now.... My eye caught a particularly graceful pattern of activity in the swirling flames - a waving yellow and orange fan with a tinge of blue on the edge. The glowing fan danced as the blue played a game of "hide and seek" along the edges ofthe orange core. It was a magnificent sight!

It suddenly struck me that it wouldn't be so bad if all I was, was a beautiful swirl! Perhaps, in his wisdom Carl was right and my original question did reflect a useful insight.... But now he's talking about experience. That's strange. It almost sounds as if he is resorting to claims of objective knowledge.

"Carl, I thought you were a constructivist! What is this talk of giving priority to experience? You're beginning to sound like an empiricist! What ever got into you?! Do you have a fever or something?"

I reached out jokingly to feel his brow. But he pulled away and chuckled.

"Yes, yes, I know. Most of these systemic people think that I'm a constructivist. Furthermore, to distinguish me from some of the earlier constructivists like Piaget, some of them even pinpoint me as a *radical* constructivist like von Glasersfeld. But I think I'm closer to being a bringforthist."

"A *what*?!"

und Molekülen handelt, die wiederum nichts anderes als Energiewirbel von unterschiedlicher Intensität sind. Ist meine Existenz eine Illusion und meine Substanz ein bloßer Wirbel molekularer Aktivität?"

„Glaubst du den Physikern oder deiner eigenen Erfahrung?"

„Willst du damit sagen, es sei alles nur eine Frage des Glaubens?" sagte ich ungläubig.

„Nein, nein, Karl, die Frage ist, ob man der Erfahrung Priorität einräumt oder der wissenschaftlichen Theorie. Es hat etwas zu tun mit dem Vertrauen in deine eigene Erfahrung, anstatt auf molekulare Theorien zu vertrauen, die von anderen geschaffen und gelehrt werden."

Ich war nicht sicher, ob ich völlig verstanden hatte, worauf er hinaus wollte, und schwieg. Zumindest schien er inzwischen ernsthafter zuzuhören ... In mein Blickfeld fiel ein besonders anmutiges Bewegungsmuster der wirbelnden Flammen - ein winkender, gelb und orangefarbener Fächer mit einem Hauch von Blau am Rand. Der glühende Fächer tanzte, während das Blau um den Rand des orangenen Kerns herum Versteck spielte. Es war großartig anzuschauen!

Mir ging plötzlich auf, daß es gar nicht so schlecht wäre, wenn ich so ein schöner Wirbel wäre! In seiner Weisheit hatte Carl vielleicht recht, und meine ursprüngliche Frage spiegelte tatsächlich eine brauchbare Einsicht wider ... Aber jetzt redet er über Erfahrung. Das ist merkwürdig. Es hört sich fast so an, als ob er davon ausgeht, daß es ein objektives Wissen gibt.

„Carl, ich dachte, du wärst Konstruktivist! Was soll dieses Gerede, der Erfahrung Priorität einzuräumen? Du hörst dich allmählich wie ein Empiriker an! Was ist nur in dich gefahren?! Hast du etwa Fieber oder sowas?"

Spaßeshalber streckte ich die Hand aus, um seine Stirn zu befühlen. Er aber wich zurück und lachte in sich hinein.

„Ja, ja, ich weiß. Die meisten dieser Systemiker halten mich für einen Konstruktivisten. Um mich von den frühen Konstruktivisten wie Piaget zu unterscheiden, bezeichnen mich manche von ihnen sogar als einen *radikalen* Konstruktivisten wie von Glasersfeld. Ich meine allerdings, daß ich eher ein Hervorbringer bin."

„Ein *was*?!"

"A bringforthist."

"What on earth is a bringforthist?"

"Actually, I hate being labelled with any such words. Sticking labels like constructivist, empiricist, bringforthist, etc., on people makes me squirm. But it seems to be the only way we can talk about each other and our positions when we get into the abstractions of epistemology and ontology. So I'll accept the description for now, as long as you agree that it's only for the purposes of this conversation."

"O.K. That's fair enough."

"Well, in accepting the description of being a bringforthist, I am trying to set myself apart from the looseness and extravagance of radical constructivism. It troubles me when constructivists get carried away in their solipsistic reveries and talk as if just about anything can be constructed in our distinctions."

"Yes, I know what you mean. I also feel uneasy when some therapists rely too heavily on constructivism. Sometimes they generate alternative descriptions of clinical situations as if they were at liberty to construct anything they wanted. Then they have the gall to claim that their alternative is better, healthier, deeper, more accurate, or more systemic than the client's own description! Such therapy often seems disrespectful and rather wild to me!" I could feel myself getting quite worked up about the issue.

He seemed to sense my frustration. "You see Karl, I am in agreement with Maturana that we cannot honestly construct just anything when we make distinctions. We can only bring forth into our awareness and our descriptions that which is consistent with our lived experience."

"But isn't that what von Glasersfeld calls 'fit'? The construct fits the experience like the key fits the lock?"

"Yes, but von Glasersfeld focuses primarily on the viability of the construct. He doesn't explain how the construct arises in the first place. He simply takes the observer as the generator of constructs as a given."

„Ein Hervorbringer.“

„Was in Gottes Namen ist ein Hervorbringer?“

„Eigentlich hasse ich es, auf diese Weise etikettiert zu werden. In mir dreht sich alles, wenn man Menschen mit solchen Etiketten wie Konstruktivist, Empiriker, Hervorbringer usw. versieht. Es scheint jedoch die einzige Möglichkeit zu sein, übereinander und über unsere Einstellungen zu reden, wenn wir zu den Abstraktionen der Epistemologie und der Ontologie kommen. Also akzeptiere ich die Beschreibung jetzt, vorausgesetzt du bist damit einverstanden, daß sie nur dem Zweck dieses Gesprächs dient.“

„O.k. Das scheint mir fair.“

„Also, indem ich die Bezeichnung Hervorbringer akzeptiere, versuche ich, mich damit von der Ungenauigkeit und Extravaganz des radikalen Konstruktivismus abzusetzen. Es beunruhigt mich, wenn die Konstruktivisten es mit ihren solipsistischen Träumereien übertreiben und so tun, als könne so gut wie alles aus unseren Unterscheidungen konstruiert werden.“

„Ja, ich verstehe, was du meinst. Es beunruhigt mich auch, wenn sich manche Therapeuten zu sehr auf den Konstruktivismus stützen. Manchmal erzeugen sie alternative Beschreibungen klinischer Situationen, als stehe es ihnen frei, alles, was ihnen einfällt, zu konstruieren. Dann haben sie die Unverschämtheit, zu behaupten, ihre Alternative sei besser, gesünder, tiefer, genauer oder systemischer als die Beschreibung des Klienten selber! Eine solche Therapie scheint mir oft ohne den angebrachten Respekt und etwas überzogen!“ Ich merkte, wie ich mich zunehmend über dieses Problem ereiferte.

Er schien meine Frustration zu bemerken. „Siehst du, Karl, ich stimme mit Maturana überein, daß wir ehrlicherweise nicht einfach irgendwas konstruieren können, wenn wir Unterscheidungen treffen. Wir können uns bloß das ins Bewußtsein und in unsere Beschreibungen bringen, was mit unseren erlebten Erfahrungen übereinstimmt.“

„Ist das nicht das, was von Glasersfeld ‘passen’ nennt? Die Konstruktion paßt zu der Erfahrung wie der Schlüssel ins Schlüsselloch?“

„Ja, aber von Glasersfeld konzentriert sich primär auf die Viabilität der Konstruktion. Er erklärt nicht, wie die Konstruktion überhaupt zustande kommt. Er nimmt den Beobachter als Erzeuger von Konstruktionen einfach als gegeben an.“

I had to agree. "Yes, the constructivists' constructs do seem to come from nowhere. . . . By the way, where did you get this idea of being a bringforthist?"

"Maturana is the main originator of bringforthism. He offers a heuristic explanation of the phenomenon of observing and of how the observer arises. He also explains how observations and constructs are brought forth in language and in consciousness."

In my reading of the literature about Maturana, he seemed to be presented as a constructivist - at least this was the case with those who wrote about him. "I thought Maturana *was* a constructivist."

"He claims he is not, and I agree with him. There is much more to bringforthism than simply generating constructs that can be used to 'fit' our experience."

Now I was getting really curious. "Apart from the broader scope of Maturana's theory to include biology and evolution, how does he differ from the constructivists? . . . Could you give me a specific example?"

"Well now, let me see. . . . O. K., von Glasersfeld tends to focus on the construct and its viability while Maturana attends not only to the construct and its domain of existence but also to the viability of both. That is, Maturana assumes a simultaneity in the bringing forth of 'figure and ground' whenever a distinction is made. Any particular distinction or construct cannot stand alone; it needs to have a context or domain of existence if it is to be brought into our experience with any degree of coherence and authenticity. The construct has to experientially fit its medium in a complementary manner before it can come into existence in the first place, and only then can it be applied to fit our ongoing experience. In other words, bringforthism demands a multiple fit in one's experience."

I was a bit puzzled. He seemed to be referring to experience an awfullot. "But doesn't this emphasis on experience begin to get rather close to empiricism?"

Ich mußte zustimmen. „Ja, die Konstruktionen der Konstruktivisten scheinen tatsächlich aus dem Nichts zu entstehen ... Woher hast du übrigens die Idee, ein Hervorbringer zu sein?"

„Maturana ist der eigentliche Erfinder des Hervorbringens. Er bietet eine heuristische Erklärung für das Phänomen des Beobachtens an und dafür, wie der Beobachter entsteht. Er erklärt auch, wie Beobachtungen und Konstruktionen in Sprache, in Gesprächen und im Bewußtsein hervorgerufen werden."

In der Literatur, die ich über Maturana gelesen hatte, schien er als Konstruktivist beschrieben zu werden - zumindest hielten ihn jene, die über ihn schrieben, dafür. „Ich dachte, Maturana *wäre* Konstruktivist."

„Er behauptet, er sei keiner, und ich stimme da mit ihm überein. Es gehört viel mehr zum Hervorbringen als das einfache Erzeugen von Konstruktionen, die benutzt werden können, um zu unseren Erfahrungen zu 'passen'."

Ich wurde allmählich richtig neugierig. „Worin unterscheidet sich Maturana von den Konstruktivisten, abgesehen davon, daß seine umfassendere Theorie die Biologie und Evolution einschließt? . . . Könntest du mir ein konkretes Beispiel geben?"

„Nun ja, laß mich überlege . . . Also, von Glasersfeld hat die Tendenz, sich auf die Konstruktion und ihre Viabilität zu konzentrieren, während Maturana sowohl der Konstruktion und ihrem Existenzbereich Beachtung schenkt als auch der Viabilität beider. Das heißt, Maturana geht von der Gleichzeitigkeit des Hervorbringens von 'Gestalt und Feld' aus, wann immer eine Unterscheidung gemacht wird. Keine bestimmte Unterscheidung oder Konstruktion kann für sich alleine stehen. Sie benötigt einen Kontext oder Existenzbereich, wenn sie einigermaßen zusammenhängend und authentisch in unseren Erfahrungsbereich gebracht werden soll. Zuerst einmal muß die Konstruktion erfahrungsmäßig auf eine komplementäre Art und Weise zu ihrer Umgebung passen, bevor sie überhaupt ins Leben gerufen werden kann, und erst dann kann sie verwandt werden, um mit unseren laufenden Erfahrungen zusammenzupassen. Mit anderen Worten: das Hervorbringen verlangt ein vielfältiges Passen in unserer Erfahrung."

Ich war ein wenig verblüfft. Er schien sich wahnsinnig häufig auf Erfahrung zu beziehen. „Nähert man sich mit dieser Betonung der Erfahrung nicht sehr dem Empirismus?"

"Not in my mind. But I suppose it depends on your understanding of empiricism. As I understood it, the empiricists assume that there is an ontologically separate and real world out there. As a bringforthist I don't make that assumption. Instead, I assume that the world that I distinguish is actively brought forth by my own actions and, hence, that I am always inextricably part of it. The empiricists maintain a separation between the observer and the observed. They claim that as observers we can apprehend the world passively through our sensory perceptions. Furthermore, they assume that this 'real' world can be known with confidence and with certainty."

"Isn't that a rather old and naive version of empiricism?" I asked.

"Yes, but most people live according to that view most of the time."

„That's probably true but you must be familiar with some of the more recent philosophical developments that grew out of classical empiricism and which support modern science, like logical positivism." I felt that Carl was being a little unfair in his critique of empiricism.

"Yes, the logical positivists are more sophisticated. . . . Although they still assume a separate and real world, they acknowledge that it can never be known with certainty. In contrast to the classical empiricists, they only claim that our knowledge *approximates* the real world. But they have a serious problem, too."

"And what is that?"

"In my opinion, they do not realize that embedded in their notion of approximation is the implicit assumption that it is possible to *know* when one description is closer to reality than another description. What is overlooked when one uses this covert assumption is that one must have some kind of prior knowledge of the 'real world' before one can make the judgment, that one of two differing descriptions is, indeed, a closer approximation to reality than the other. As a bringforthist, I am content to relate one experience to other experiences when trying to explain something. I do not resort to any separate objective knowledge of the outside world. I think it is potentially

„Nicht wie ich das sehe. Aber ich nehme an, das hängt davon ab, was man unter Empirismus versteht. So wie ich das verstanden habe, nehmen die Empiriker an, daß es eine ontologisch getrennte und reale Welt gibt. Als Hervorbringer gehe ich nicht von dieser Annahme aus. Stattdessen nehme ich an, daß die von mir unterschiedene Welt durch meine eigenen aktiven Handlungen hervorgebracht wird und daß ich deshalb immer ein von ihr untrennbarer Teil bin. Die Empiriker bestehen auf einer Trennung zwischen dem Beobachter und dem Beobachteten. Sie behaupten, wir könnten als Beobachter die Welt durch unsere sinnliche Wahrnehmung passiv begreifen. Ferner nehmen sie an, daß man diese 'reale' Welt vertrauensvoll und sicher erkennen könne."

„Ist das nicht eine recht alte und naive Form des Empirismus?" fragte ich.

„Ja, aber die meisten Menschen leben die meiste Zeit entsprechend dieser Ansicht."

„Das stimmt wahrscheinlich, aber sicher kennst du einige der jüngeren philosophischen Entwicklungen, die aus dem klassischen Empirismus entstanden sind und auf denen die moderne Wissenschaft aufbaut, wie z.B. den logischen Positivismus." Ich fand, daß Carl in seiner Kritik des Empirismus ein wenig unfair war.

„Ja, die logischen Positivisten sind etwas differenzierter . . . Obwohl sie immer noch von einer getrennten und realen Welt ausgehen, gestehen sie ein, daß sie niemals mit Sicherheit erkannt werden kann. Im Gegensatz zu den klassischen Empirikern nehmen sie nur an, daß sich unser Wissen der realen Welt *annähert*. Sie haben jedoch ebenfalls ein ernsthaftes Problem."

„Und welches?"

„Meiner Meinung nach erkennen sie nicht, daß in ihrem Verständnis von Annäherung implizit die Annahme verankert ist, daß es möglich ist, zu *wissen*, wann eine Beschreibung näher an der Realität ist als eine andere Beschreibung. Was man übersieht, wenn man von dieser versteckten Annahme ausgeht, ist, daß man eine Vorkenntnis der 'realen Welt' haben muß, bevor man urteilen kann, ob eine von zwei unterschiedlichen Beschreibungen tatsächlich eine größere Annäherung an die Realität darstellt als die andere. Als Hervorbringer genügt es mir, eine Erfahrung mit anderen Erfahrungen in Beziehung zu setzen, wenn ich etwas zu erklären versuche. Ich stütze mich nicht

dangerous to assume that we possess such knowledge about the world."

It was fascinating to hear him articulate the inconsistency in the logical positivist position so clearly by disclosing the underlying assumption. "But why is it dangerous?" I asked.

"Because it leads us back to the same objectivity and certainty of the naive empiricists. And, as you know, explicit and/or implicit claims of objective knowledge are used regularly to impose one's will upon another and to justify all kinds of violence in doing so. Hence, I prefer to avoid making truth claims derived from any sort of empiricism that is grounded in objectivity."

I thought he was getting a bit smug in what he was saying and wondered how he could be so sure about his own stance. "But how can you ground yourself in experience and claim *not* to be an empiricist or a positivist? Maybe your bringforthism is just another, more subtle form of empiricism." And before he could answer, I went on to proclaim: "Aha! I can see the headlines already! 'Carl von Auer's bringforthism: A new form of closet positivism'!" To my surprise, my tone seemed a bit sarcastic and confrontational.

There was a loud explosive 'snap' in the stove at that moment. It was followed by a burst of sparks and a dramatic flare of flame. But the fire didn't distract him and he was swift in his response: "Now you are being unfair, Karl.... I thought we agreed that I would only accept the label of 'bringforthist' for the purposes of this conversation."

He then turned away and looked into the stove. I could see from the reflection of the fire in his face that my confrontation had triggered some pain. I began to wonder if our dialogue was at risk. In reviewing what had happened, I realized that I had slipped into objectifying him as a person. I did this by assuming that he was making an objective reality claim about himself as a bringforthist rather than just using that description as a reference point. Thus, his claim about the dangers of objectivity became a case in point at that moment in our conversation. By adopting an 'objective' view of him and his

auf ein unabhängiges, objektives Wissen über die Außenwelt. Ich halte es für potentiell gefährlich, wenn man davon ausgeht, daß wir ein solches Wissen über die Welt haben könnten."

Es war faszinierend, zuzuhören, wie er die Widersprüchlichkeit des positivistischen Standpunktes so deutlich darlegte, indem er die zugrundeliegenden Annahmen enthüllte. „Aber warum ist das gefährlich?" fragte ich.

„Weil es uns zu derselben Objektivität und Gewißheit der naiven Empiriker zurückführt. Und wie du weißt, werden explizite und/oder implizite Behauptungen des objektiven Wissens regelmäßig dazu benutzt, einem anderen seinen Willen aufzuzwingen und dabei alle möglichen Formen der Gewalt zu rechtfertigen. Also ziehe ich es vor, Wahrheitsbehauptungen, die von jedweder sich auf Objektivität gründenden Empirie abgeleitet sind, zu vermeiden."

Ich hatte das Gefühl, seine Bemerkungen seien etwas selbstgefällig, und fragte mich, wie er sich seines eigenen Standpunktes dermaßen sicher sein konnte. „Aber wie kannst du dich auf Erfahrung stützen und gleichzeitig behaupten, du seist *kein* Empiriker oder Positivist? Vielleicht ist dein Hervorbringertum bloß eine andere, subtilere Form der Empirie." Bevor er antworten konnte, fuhr ich fort: „Aha! Ich sehe schon die Schlagzeilen! Das Hervorbringertum des Carl von Auer: 'Eine neue Form verdeckten Positivismus'!" Zu meiner Überraschung schien mein Ton etwas sarkastisch und herausfordernd.

In dem Augenblick gab es im Ofen ein lautes, explosives Knakken, gefolgt von sprühenden Funken und dramatisch aufflackernden Flammen. Das Feuer lenkte ihn jedoch nicht ab, und seine Antwort kam prompt: „Jetzt wirst du aber unfair, Karl . . . Wir hatten doch vereinbart, daß ich das Etikett des 'Hervorbringers' nur für den Zweck dieser Unterhaltung akzeptiert habe."

Dann wandte er sich ab und schaute in den Ofen. Durch die Widerspiegelung des Feuers in seinem Gesicht sah ich, daß meine Konfrontation ihn doch schmerzte. Ich fragte mich, ob unser Dialog in Gefahr sei. Ich überdachte das Geschehen und erkannte, daß ich ihn als Menschen objektiviert hatte. Ich hatte nämlich angenommen, er stelle eine Behauptung der objektiven Realität über sich als 'Hervorbringer' auf, anstatt zu berücksichtigen, daß er diese Beschreibung bloß als Bezugspunkt verwendet hatte. So wurde seine Behauptung über die Gefahren der Objektivität an diesem Punkt

descriptions, even momentarily, I had endangered our discussion.... An apology was in order.

"I'm sorry. You're right, I was being unfair. It just seemed that you were so clear about your 'bringforthist' stance that I began to think that you held it with certainty. Maybe I was confusing clarity with certainty."

He seemed to accept my apology and actually seemed a bit pleased that I could see the difference between clarity and certainty. I was relieved, but still not satisfied. I still couldn't understand that Carl could give experience so much authority without implicitly resorting to some sort of 'real' world out there. I also wasn't quite sure how he saw himself differing from the new radical constructivists.

But never mind. What was of greater concern to me was how I could understand myself. Why did I experience myself as existing as a concrete entity even though the idea of dynamic process appealed to me so much? And if I was constituted by pure process, where did that process exist? Was it reasonable for me to expect Carl to answer my questions? He seemed to be drawing upon Maturana's framework a great deal. In fact, it almost seemed that Carl von Auer and Humberto Maturana were soul brothers! I too was attracted to Maturana's ideas about knowledge and existence.... I began to feel a new set of associations bubbling into my awareness.... "Carl, do you remember a few years ago when I was so excited after I first heard Maturana's explanation of 'mind' as a social phenomenon?"

"Yes! I too was pleased to hear his explanation of how we become observers of the world and of ourselves through language, and how languaging arose in the recursive coordination of actions among us. For a long time I have felt that as human beings we bring the whole of reality, including ourselves, into existence through our conversations. But I could never have explained it as systematically and clearly as Maturana did." Fortunately, he seemed pleased with the change of topic.

"Well, around that time I began to think of my 'self' as an internalized constellation of conversations about 'Karl' which originated in external conversations among others. In other words, I

unserer Unterhaltung beispielhaft verdeutlicht. Indem ich ihn und seine Beschreibungen, wenn auch nur für einen Augenblick, 'objektiv' betrachtete, brachte ich unsere Diskussion in Gefahr . . . Eine Entschuldigung war fällig.

„Tut mir leid. Du hast recht, das war unfair. Mir schien, du brachtest deine 'Hervorbringer'-Einstellung so klar zum Ausdruck, daß ich dachte, du wärest von ihr überzeugt. Vielleicht habe ich Deutlichkeit mit Bestimmtheit verwechselt."

Er schien meine Entschuldigung anzunehmen und schien tatsächlich davon angetan zu sein, daß ich den Unterschied zwischen Deutlichkeit und Bestimmtheit erkennen konnte. Ich war erleichtert, aber noch nicht zufrieden. Ich verstand nicht ganz, wie Carl der Erfahrung so viel Bedeutung beimessen konnte, ohne sich implizit auf irgendeine 'wirkliche' Welt da draußen zu stützen. Ich war mir auch nicht ganz darüber im klaren, inwiefern er sich von den neuen radikalen Konstruktivisten unterschied.

Doch was soll's. Mir war wesentlich wichtiger, wie ich mich selbst verstehen könnte. Warum erfuhr ich mich als konkret existierendes Wesen, obwohl mir die Vorstellung dynamischer Prozesse so sehr zusagte? Und wenn ich aus einem reinen Prozeß bestand, wo existierte dieser Prozeß? War es vernünftig, zu erwarten, daß Carl meine Fragen beantworten könnte? Er schien sich stark auf Maturanas Ideen zu beziehen. Es schien sogar fast so, als seien Carl von Auer und Humberto Maturana seelenverwandt! Auch ich fühlte mich von Maturanas Vorstellungen über Wissen und Existenz angezogen . . . Ich spürte, wie allmählich eine neue Reihe von Assoziationen in mein Bewußtsein quoll . . . „Carl, erinnerst du dich daran, wie ich vor ein paar Jahren so aufgeregt war, nachdem ich zum ersten Mal Maturanas Erklärung des 'Geistes' als soziales Phänomen hörte?"

„Ja! Ich war auch sehr erfreut, seine Erklärung dafür zu hören, wie wir durch Sprache zu Beobachtern der Welt und uns selbst werden, und wie Sprache aus der rekursiven Koordination unserer Handlungen miteinander entstand. Seit langem spürte ich, daß wir als Menschen die gesamte Realität, einschließlich uns selbst, durch unsere Gespräche ins Leben rufen. Doch hätte ich es niemals so systematisch und deutlich erklären können wie Maturana." Zum Glück schien er sich über den Themenwechsel zu freuen.

„Also, etwa zu dieser Zeit fing ich an, mein 'Selbst' als verinnerlichte Konstellation von Gesprächen über 'Karl' zu begreifen, die ihren Ursprung in externen Gesprächen zwischen anderen hatte.

began to think of my 'self' as first existing in the social domain of languaging rather than in my body. By thinking of myself in this way it became possible for me to begin to feel free of the physical boundaries of my body. Sometimes it was like I was outside of my skin!"

Carl laughed as he put his hand on my shoulder: "So you became a disembodied spirit for a while?" . . . The firmness and warmth of his hand felt good to me. It was nice to have some physical contact.

"Yes, the significant 'I', the person that I really experienced myself to be, just didn't exist in a physical sense at all. In fact, in those days I used to say 'I don't exist!' and I felt liberated in doing so. I loved the feeling it gave me."

"So what exactly was your 'I' that was making the claim that you didn't exist?" He smiled and gave my shoulder an encouraging squeeze.

"Well, the 'I' and 'Karl' are linguistic distinctions in a network of conversations that make up my identity as a person. I presume they originated in conversations that initially took place around me as I grew up in my family. With time, the distinctions about 'me' eventually became internalized within me. 'I' became a node in the network and I started making the distinctions about myself."

He smiled approvingly as I continued: "And since the context of these conversations per se were not material, the meaningful 'I' really didn't exist in the physical world at all! I existed in the domain of the conversations that constituted me. Furthermore, thinking about myself in this manner turned out to be a way that I could sort of transcend my physical being."

"It sounds like an exciting realization!" There was a tone of genuine excitement in his voice.

"It was!"

"Did this realization make a difference to your experience of yourself as a person?"

"Oh yes! Having discovered this pathway to what seemed like a kind of personal 'transcendence' I now set myself on it from time to

Mit anderen Worten: ich begann zu denken, daß mein 'Selbst' eher im sozialen Bereich der Sprache (languaging) existierte als in meinem Körper. Indem ich so über mich dachte, war es mir möglich, mich allmählich frei von den physischen Grenzen meines Körpers zu fühlen. Manchmal war es so, als wäre ich außerhalb meiner eigenen Haut!"

Carl lachte, während er die Hand auf meine Schulter legte: „Also wurdest du für eine Weile ein körperloser Geist?" . . . Die Festigkeit und Wärme seiner Hand taten mir gut. Der körperliche Kontakt war schön.

„Ja, das bedeutungsvolle 'Ich', die Person, als die ich mich in Wirklichkeit erfuhr, existierte im physischen Sinn überhaupt nicht. In jenen Tagen sagte ich tatsächlich 'Ich existiere nicht!' und fühlte mich dadurch befreit. Ich mochte das Gefühl, das es mir bereitete, sehr."

„Was war denn genau dieses 'Ich', das behauptete, du existiertest nicht?" Er lächelte und drückte meine Schulter ermutigend.

„Also, das 'Ich' und 'Karl' sind linguistische Unterscheidungen in einem Netz von Gesprächen, die meine Identität als Person ausmachen. Ich nehme an, sie hatten ihren Ursprung in Gesprächen, die anfangs um mich herum stattfanden, als ich in meiner Familie heranwuchs. Mit der Zeit habe ich die Unterscheidungen über 'mich' schließlich verinnerlicht. 'Ich' wurde ein Knoten im Netz und begann, die Unterscheidungen über mich selbst zu machen."

Er lächelte zustimmend, während ich fortfuhr: „Und da der Inhalt dieser Gespräche an sich nicht materiell war, existierte das bedeutungsvolle 'Ich' wirklich überhaupt nicht in der physischen Welt! Ich existierte im Bereich der Gespräche, die mich bildeten. Außerdem stellte sich diese Art des Nachdenkens über mich selbst als Weg heraus, wie ich über mein physisches Leben irgendwie hinausgehen konnte."

„Es hört sich wie eine aufregende Erkenntnis an!" Seine Stimme vermittelte echte Teilnahme.

„Das war es auch!"

„Hat diese Erkenntnis beeinflußt, wie du dich selbst als Person erfährst?"

„Oh ja! Nachdem ich nun diesen Weg zu so einer Art persönlicher 'Transzendenz' entdeckt habe, begehe ich ihn auch von Zeit zu Zeit,

time when I feel constrained or trapped. Doing so seems to open an enormous amount of space for me as a person and adds life to my life!"

"Fantastic!", he exclaimed.

I was delighted that he seemed so thoroughly enthusiastic about the idea. "And besides, during the times that I can enter into such an understanding of myself, I feel very closely connected with other people in the world. For example, I feel inextricably tied to all those persons who have contributed to the specific conversations that have brought forth the distinctions of 'me' as 'Karl' and 'Karl' as 'me' and thus brought me into existence. It really feels great to be so profoundly connected to others in one's most basic and fundamental identity!"

Carl was beaming from ear to ear. "I'd call that having a systemic 'high'!"

"It certainly is! . . . Sometimes I even get so 'high' that I feel like I am floating above my own body!" Indeed, it seemed like the conversation about it was beginning to entice me back into interpersonal space and get me a bit high.

Carl became thoughtful. He looked into the fire for a while and murmured, "Humm . . . an out-of-body experience."

"Perhaps. But such extremes only last for a short time. I can only reach such heights when my thinking is crystal clear and my emotions are free. But whenever some physical necessity arises, such as the need to walk home, to eat, to wash, or to get dressed, my physical body immediately re-emerges as the primary locus of my experience."

Carl smiled: "It almost sounds as if there are two separate Karls!"

I felt a slight pang of pain somewhere in my being. "Yes, that is exactly what is so confusing for me. There do seem to be two of me: one located in the social domain of conversations, the other in the physical domain of mass and energy. The one has a familial and cultural history, the other has a biological and phylogenetic history."

"Are you struggling with some sort of mind-body split?"

"I really don't know. I don't experience myself as being split, even when I'm feeling 'high' and almost out of my body. In my ongoing

wenn ich mich eingezwängt fühle oder mir gefangen vorkomme. Das scheint mir als Person ungeheuer viel Raum zu schaffen und belebt mein Leben!"

„Fantastisch!" rief er aus.

Ich freute mich darüber, daß er sich so sehr für diese Vorstellung begeisterte. „Außerdem fühle ich mich mit anderen Menschen auf der Welt sehr eng verbunden in den Zeiten, in denen ich zu einem solchen Verständnis von mir selbst finden kann. Zum Beispiel fühle ich mich all jenen eng verbunden, die sich an den spezifischen Gesprächen beteiligt haben, die die Unterscheidungen von 'mir' als 'Karl' und 'Karl' als 'mir' hervorgebracht und mich somit ins Leben gerufen haben. Es ist ein großartiges Gefühl, in seiner grundlegendsten und fundamentalsten Identität anderen so tief verbunden zu sein!"

Carl strahlte über das ganze Gesicht: „Das würde ich ein systemisches 'high' nennen!"

„Ganz sicher! . . . Manchmal bin ich sogar so 'high', daß es mir vorkommt, als schwebe ich über meinem eigenen Körper!" Tatsächlich schien mich das Gespräch darüber in einen interpersonellen Raum zu locken und mich ein wenig 'high' zu machen.

Carl wurde nachdenklich. Er schaute eine Zeitlang ins Feuer und murmelte: „Hm, . . . eine Erfahrung des Astralleibes."

„Vielleicht. Doch dauern solche Extreme nicht lange an. Ich kann solche Höhen nur dann erreichen, wenn ich völlig klar denke, und wenn meine Emotionen frei sind. Sobald jedoch ein physisches Bedürfnis auftritt, wie das Bedürfnis, nach Hause zu gehen, zu essen, mich zu waschen oder mich anzuziehen, tritt mein physischer Körper sofort als Hauptort meiner Erfahrung wieder hervor."

Carl lächelte: „Es hört sich fast so an, als gäbe es zwei verschiedene Karls!"

Ich spürte einen leichten Schmerz irgendwo in meinem Wesen. „Ja, das ist es ja, was mich so verwirrt. Es scheint wirklich zwei von mir zu geben: einen, der im sozialen Bereich der Unterhaltungen lokalisiert ist, und einen anderen, der im physischen Bereich der Masse und der Energie zu Hause ist. Der eine hat eine Familien- und Kulturgeschichte, der andere eine biologische und phylogenetische Geschichte."

„Hast du mit irgendeiner Art Geist-Körper-Spaltung zu kämpfen?"

„Ich weiß es nicht so recht. Ich erfahre mich nicht als gespalten, auch dann nicht, wenn ich 'high' bin und fast außerhalb meines

lived experience there is only *one* of me. But in my reflections there seem to be two."

"Perhaps the split lies in the dual explanations you give yourself about the physical and psychological aspects of yourself."

"Yes, that's it! Differing explanations! But how do I get them together? How does one connect a swirl of molecules and energy, with a swirl of conversations? Or do I exist in different domains simultaneously? And where does the single integrated experiential 'me' exist?" My voice had become plaintive, almost pleading. I finished my series of questions as if I was imploring him to provide me with a comprehensive answer that would tie it all together.

Carl slowly turned towards me and leaned forward. The light from the fire was quite faint by now. The earlier blaze had died down and only the red embers were still glowing. Yet I could still see well enough to notice the corner of his left eye begin to swell with a big tear. "But Karl, an explanation never replaces the phenomenon being explained anyway. An explanation of your 'self' may add to your understanding of 'self', but it can never become a substitute for your 'self'. Furthermore, your efforts to search for closer connection with your experiential 'self' through a logical explanation might only serve to distance you even further from the desired experience."

Suddenly, everything in my mind stopped. It was like I had been arrested in mid-flight! The futility of my demand for an explanatory answer became painfully apparent: my intellectual question served to preclude the experiential answer I sought! The insight moved me emotionally and I became tearful. Carl moved closer and gently put his arm around my shoulder.

He spoke comfortingly: "I once experienced a similar struggle and gained some measure of relief when I gave up striving to understand more than what was possible for me."

What came over me just then is not clear but I began to weep. Tears began streaming down my cheeks as if a water tap had been turned on. It wasn't sadness or despair. It seemed much deeper than that. Carl seemed to have tuned-in to me at quite another level and I was

Körpers. In meiner bisherigen gelebten Erfahrung gibt es mich nur *einmal*. Doch in meinen Überlegungen scheint es mich zweimal zu geben."

„Vielleicht liegt die Spaltung in den zwei Erklärungen, die du dir selbst für deine physischen und psychologischen Aspekte gibst."

„Ja, das wird's sein! Unterschiedliche Erklärungen! Aber wie füge ich sie zusammen? Wie verbindet man einen Wirbel von Molekülen und Energie mit einem Wirbel von Gesprächen? Oder existiere ich in verschiedenen Bereichen gleichzeitig? Und wo existiert das einzelne, integrierte, auf Erfahrung beruhende 'Ich'?" Meine Stimme war wehleidig, fast flehend geworden. Ich beendete meine Fragerei, als wollte ich ihn beschwören, mir eine zusammenfassende Antwort zu geben, die alles erklären würde.

Carl wandte sich mir langsam zu und beugte sich vor. Inzwischen war der Schein des Feuers recht schwach geworden. Die Flamme war erloschen, und nur die rote Glut war noch übrig. Doch konnte ich immer noch genug sehen, um zu erkennen, wie sich sein linker Augenwinkel mit einer großen Träne zu füllen begann. „Aber Karl, eine Erklärung ersetzt nie das Phänomen, das wegerklärt wurde. Eine Erklärung deines 'Selbst' kann dein Verständnis des 'Selbst' vergrößern, kann aber nicht dein 'Selbst' ersetzen. Außerdem könnten deine Bemühungen, durch eine logische Erklärung eine engere Verbindung mit deinem auf Erfahrung beruhenden 'Selbst' zu finden, nur dazu führen, dich immer weiter von der erwünschten Erfahrung zu distanzieren."

Plötzlich stand mein Geist still. Es war, als wäre ich mitten im Flug angehalten worden! Die Sinnlosigkeit meines Drängens nach einer erklärenden Antwort wurde mir schmerzlich bewußt: meine intellektuelle Frage diente dazu, die auf Erfahrung beruhende Antwort, die ich suchte, auszuschließen! Diese Einsicht bewegte mich emotional, und mir kamen die Tränen. Carl kam etwas näher und legte den Arm um meine Schulter.

Er sprach tröstend: „Ich erlebte einmal einen ähnlichen Kampf und erlangte erst dann eine gewisse Erleichterung, als ich aufhörte, mehr verstehen zu wollen, als mir möglich war."

Ich weiß nicht, was dann über mich kam, aber ich fing zu weinen an. Die Tränen strömten mir über die Wangen, als hätte jemand den Wasserhahn aufgedreht. Es war weder Traurigkeit noch Verzweiflung. Es lag tiefer. Carl schien auf einer anderen Ebene auf mich

able to tune-in to him. It was as if our experiences began resonating. I felt totally immersed in love. I put my arms around him and we embraced one another.

It was a long and speechless moment. My original struggle simply dissolved. The experience of my being was solidly grounded in his; and being in the experience felt very good.

A few minutes later when I stood up to open the stove door and throw in another log, I felt integrated and whole - as if Carl was simply part of me and my mind and body were floating together! . . . There wasn't much more to say just then. So we both sat and watched as a new flame took hold and another undulating dance began.

eingegangen zu sein, und ich konnte mich auch auf ihn einstimmen. Es schien, als fingen unsere gegenseitigen Erfahrungen an, einen Resonanzkreis zu bilden. Ich war völlig in Liebe versunken. Ich legte meine Arme um ihn, und wir umarmten einander.

Dieser Augenblick war lang und ohne Worte. Mein ursprünglicher Kampf löste sich einfach auf. Die Erfahrung meines Seins war in dem seinen fest verwurzelt; in dieser Erfahrung zu sein, fühlte sich gut an.

Einige Minuten später, als ich aufstand, um den Ofen zu öffnen, um noch ein Scheit aufzulegen, fühlte ich mich integriert und ganz - als wäre Carl einfach ein Teil von mir, als würden mein Geist und mein Körper zusammen schweben!... Es gab dann nicht mehr viel zu sagen. Wir saßen beide da und schauten zu, während eine neue Flamme aufflackerte und ein weiterer wogender Tanz begann.

Carl Auer (C. A.) and the Temptation of Objectivity

Josef Duss-von Werdt

C. A. was the very incarnation of self-referentiality. Self-referential subjects are world-centers. To realize themselves as such, they have two alternatives, that of the subjective or relative - I am the center of my world or that of the objective, the dis-sociated, the absolute - I am the center of the world in general. C. A. chose the first, the ascetic alternative, and this is why he was so quickly forgotten and we have so much trouble rediscovering his traces. During his lifetime he was already considered not to be objective and thus could only become notorious rather than famous. He was laughed at, spied upon, not taken seriously, particularly in his capacitiy as a scientist, where after all he ought to have been the epitome of objectivity. But he could not de-mean himself so far as to mean only those things that would be accepted by the common mean of his fellows.

The second alternative is the more comfortable one; whoever embarks on that avenue can be sure of the back-handed, double-tongued applause of the multitude, which finds secondary narcistic satisfaction in being totally - not to say in a totalitarian manner - colonized by the objectivity of others coming from the center of the world.

Some fragments of C. A. have come down to us in which he reflects critically on Descartes. Unlike the latter he was not gulled into confusing epistemology with ontology. Thought for him was not proof of his existence but its very precondition. One of his really rather banal principles was: "Everything I think is thought by me." Flying in the face of the Cartesian axiom he wrote down the following: "Cogitata cogitans cogito cogitantem," or "Thinking that which has been thought, I think the thinker." He loved to take words literally and to explore their original meaning. Cogitare is reflexive, derived

Carl Auer (C. A.) und die Versuchung der Objektivität

Josef Duss von Werdt

C. A. war die Selbstrückbezüglichkeit in Person. Selbstrückbezügliche Objekte sind Weltzentren. Um sich als solche zu verwirklichen, stehen ihnen zwei Wege offen: der Weg des Subjektiven, bzw. des Relativen: Ich bin das Zentrum meiner Welt. Oder der Weg des Objektiven, des Losgelösten, des Ab-soluten: Ich bin das Zentrum der Welt schlechthin. C. A. ging den ersten, den asketischen Weg, was der Grund dafür ist, daß er rasch in Vergessenheit geriet und wir nun mühsam seine Spuren wiederfinden müssen. Schon zu Lebzeiten galt er als nicht objektiv und konnte deswegen nur negativ bekannt werden: Er wurde verlacht, bespitzelt, galt als unseriös, besonders in seiner Funktion als Wissenschaftler, als welcher er doch die Objektivität in Person hätte sein sollen. Aber er konnte und wollte sich die All-Gemeinheit nicht leisten, allen gemein zu sein, nur um dazuzugehören.

Der zweite Weg ist breiter und wird mit Händen, Mündern und doppelten Zungen vom großen Publikum beklatscht, welches sekundärnarzißtische Befriedigung darin findet, vom Mittelpunkt der Welt aus total bis totalitär durch die Objektivität anderer kolonisiert zu werden.

Es sind einige Fragmente von C. A. erhalten, in denen er kritisch vordenkend über Descartes nachdachte. Er saß dabei nicht wie dieser der Verwechslung von Epistemologie und Ontologie auf. Sein Denken mußte nicht seine Existenz begründen, sondern setzte diese voraus. Einer seiner eigentlich ganz banalen Grundsätze lautete: „Alles was ich *denke*, denke ich." In offensichtlicher Ablehnung des kartesianischen Axioms notierte er folgendes: „Cogitata cogitans cogito cogitantem." Zu deutsch: Das Gedachte denkend, denke ich den Denkenden. Er liebte es, die Worte beim Wort zu nehmen und

from co-agitare secum, carrying something around with one, turning inside oneself, reflecting, pondering, also meditating. Another version of that same axiom was: "Observata observans observo observantem," or "Observing the observed I observe the observer." Observare has to do with observantia, with obedience, obeisance, observance, fidelity, confidentiality, safe-keeping.

Thinking and observing are mimetic processes. They hug the wall, they do not leap over it. Mimesis judges that which is ergonomic.

Thus C. A. was of course making ethical demands of himself that bordered on the superhuman. If in all thinking and observation, I bethink and observe myself, then I am both subject and object at one and the same time. Without this kind of objectivity vis-à-vis myself, without the duality of subject and object, I can never attain selfhood, i. e. awareness of my own self. I have to put myself in a metaposition with regard to myself in order to say of myself that I am a subject.

Furthermore, there can only be objects for subjects making up together the oneness of awareness. Consciousness becomes self-consciousness, being becomes conscious being, selfhood becomes conscious selfhood. Being as such is not existent in its own right, it is the product of consciousness. A subject turning object to itself goes dual, puts distance between itself and its self. The fashionable term for this is "meta-position," a position which we normally only expect others to assume. Kant and later Husserl were talking about the same thing when they postulated a "transcendental self" which observed the "empiric self" in its dealings with itself, other selves and other things. From its position as a second remove it concerns itself with the relation between the observing observer and the observed object. Thus the transcendental ego is peering at the little egoist egging itself on to fabricate its own world. It is its own Big Brother, the authority responsible for everything that goes on between the empirical self and its objects. I am answerable for everything that I think, find, invent, do or do not do, even if I call this science and am subjecting myself to its rules. The insight that the reality of art, science, money or politics is invariably nothing other than the reality discerned, discovered or invented by the artist, scientist, economist or politician, transforms all

ging ihrer ursprünglichen Bedeutung nach. Cogitare ist reflexiv, denn es kommt von co-agitare secum, mit sich herumtragen, in sich selber drehen, überlegen, hin- und herwenden, auch meditieren. Er wandelte sein Axiom auch so ab: „Observata observans observo observantem": Das Beobachtete beobachtend, beobachte ich den Beobachtenden. Observare hat etwas mit observantia, mit Gehorsam, hörsam, hinhorchen, offen- und treusein, hüten, nicht verraten zu tun.

Denken und Beobachten sind mimetische Vorgänge. Sie gehen entlang und nicht darüber hinweg. Die Mimesis richtet das Ergonome.

Damit stellte C. A. natürlich hohe ethische Anforderungen an sich selbst, welche an die Grenzen des Menschenmöglichen führen. Wenn ich in allem Denken und Beobachten mich selber bedenke und beobachte, bin ich als Subjekt gleichzeitig auch Objekt. Ohne diese Art von Gegen-Stand zu mir selber, ohne die Zweiung von Subjekt und Objekt komme ich nicht zu mir selber, d. h. zum Bewußtsein meiner selbst. Ich muß mir gegenüber „metaponieren", um sagen zu können, ich sei ein Subjekt.

Zudem gibt es Objekte überhaupt nur für Subjekte, welche zusammen die Einheit des Bewußt-Seins ausmachen. Bewußtheit wird zu Selbstbewußtheit, Sein zu Bewußt-Sein, Selbst-Sein zu Selbstbewußtsein. Das Sein *ist* nicht, es wird bewußt. Das Subjekt, welches sich selber zum Objekt wird, verdoppelt sich und geht zu sich auf Distanz. Heute nennt man das eine Metaposition, die man meistens nur von den anderen erwartet. Bei Kant und später bei Husserl handelte es sich um das gleiche Thema beim sogenannten „transzendentalen Ich", welches dem „empirischen Ich" zuschaut, wie es mit sich, mit anderen und anderem umgeht. Aus seiner dritten Position heraus befaßt es sich mit der Beziehung des beobachtenden Beobachters zum beobachteten Gegenstand. Das transzendentale Ego beäugt also den kleinen Egoisten, der sich abstrampelt und seine Welt zusammenbastelt. Es ist sein innerer „Big Brother", also jene Instanz, die für alles, was zwischen dem empirischen Ego und seinen Objekten passiert, verantwortlich ist. Für alles, was ich denke, finde, erfinde, tue und lasse, muß ich geradestehen, auch wenn ich es Wissenschaft nenne und nach ihren Regeln dazu gekommen bin. Wer einmal eingesehen hat, daß die Wirklichkeit der Kunst, der Wissenschaft, des Geldes, der Politik immer nur die vom Künstler, Wissenschaftler, Wirtschafter, Politiker erkannte, ge- und erfundene ist,

objectivity into subjective fabrication, for which everyone of us is personally liable. Thus I cannot hide behind "science" as if such a thing actually existed in its own right, a convenient replica for reality.

For C. A. the causality between being and thinking went in the opposite direction to Descartes. What he saw to be the Cartesian error was the vision of the thinker instituting himself into being by dint of his thinking, in other words epistemology degenerating into ontology. Not "cogito, ergo sum," but "esse est; ergo sum; ergo cogito." Being does not become being through thinking. It is, however, invariably, "being for us," thought being, and thinking becomes the accomplishment of being, its co-agitation, a coming-to-self without ergo. Being is actio, accomplishment, perceived and perceiving reality, which is not to say that it is what it is by dint of perception, or that it originates ex nihilo from perception.

Of course it would be convenient if we were not only the creators of our world of knowledge and actions but if this would represent the sole reality outside of ourselves. And indeed we usually act as if this were in fact the case, by positing objectivity as such. Then there would be no hunger, no hardships, no prisons, no A-bombs, no pollution. It would all depend on how we looked at things. There are, of course, those objective people for whom everything depends on the point of view and on their personal needs. Because this view is free of any kind of valuation, positive or negative, nothing is objectively evil or reprehensible to them. On the contrary. We are doing fine, objectively. We are not only at the center of the world, we are the center of the world.

Without realizing it, C. A. did in fact work out a General Theory of Relativity with reference to what human knowledge is capable of knowing. Whether Einstein knew of this is impossible to say. At all events, he never admitted as much, although it would certainly have done nothing to detract from his undeniable originality, particularly as C. A. was never bothered about such things anyway.

Although a self-referential person through and through, C. A. was no solipsist imprisoning himself in his world. He was responsible for himself alone. He identified with what he said; indeed, in terms of his objectivity, i. e. with reference to himself, he had no other choice; after all he was the one saying it.

für den wird alle Objektivität zu einem subjektiven Gemächte, für das jeder persönlich haftet. Ich kann mich z. B. nicht hinter „die" Wissenschaft verschanzen, als ob es sie „an sich" gäbe und sie ein Wechsel auf das Sein und überhaupt ein solches wäre.

Zwischen Sein und Denken bestand für C. A. in der Descartes entgegengesetzten Richtung ein kausaler Zusammenhang. Den kartesianischen Irrtum sah er darin, daß der Denkende sich selber ins Sein setzt, also Epistemologie zur Ontologie verkommt. Nicht „cogito, ergo sum", sondern „esse est, ergo sum, ergo cogito". Sein wird nicht Sein durch das Denken. Es ist immer aber „Sein für uns", gedachtes Sein, und Denken wird zum Vollzug des Seins, ist seine co-agitatio, ein Zu-sich-kommen ohne ergo. Sein ist actio, Vollzug, wahrgenommene und wahrnehmende Wirklichkeit, was jedoch nicht heißt, daß es durch die Wahrnehmung erst sei, ex nihilo aus der Wahrnehmung hervorgehe.

Wie schön wäre es zwar, wenn wir nicht nur Schöpfer unserer Erkenntniswelt und Tatwelt wären, sondern diese auch unabhängig von uns die alleinige Wirklichkeit darstellte. Wir tun zwar meistens so, als ob sie dies täte, nämlich indem wir Objektivität an sich beanspruchen. Dann gäbe es keinen Hunger, kein Elend, keine Gefängnisse, keine A-Bomben, keine Luft- und Wasserverschmutzung. Alles wäre nur Ansichtssache. Allerdings gibt es die objektiven Leute, für welche das alles je nach Bedarf Ansichtssache ist. Objektiv gesehen ist für sie überhaupt nichts schlimm, weil diese Sicht wert- und unwertfrei ist. Im Gegenteil. Es geht uns ja gut, objektiv gut. Wir befinden uns ja nicht nur im Zentrum der Welt, wir sind es schließlich auch.

C. A. hat, ohne sich dessen bewußt zu sein, eine allgemeine Relativitätstheorie der geistigen Erkenntniswelt des Menschen ausgearbeitet. Ob Einstein davon gewußt hat, läßt sich nicht nachweisen. Auf jeden Fall hat dieser es nie zugegeben, obwohl es seiner unbestrittenen Originalität keinen Abbruch getan hätte, zumal C. A. nie auf eine solche aus war.

Als konsequent selbstrückbezüglicher Mensch wurde er trotzdem kein Solipsist, der sich in seiner Welt inhaftierte. Er haftete nur für seine eigene Person. Er stand zu dem, was er sagte, und es blieb ihm nach seiner Objektivität, also bezogen auf sich selber, keine andere Wahl, denn *er* sagte es ja.

This gave many of his contemporaries sufficient grounds to doubt his sanity. Surely this was not "normal." Only objectivity is normal, regardless of C. A. Normality is in the last resorts a question of statistical majorities and self-imprisoned constraints. Catanoic, however, i. e. according to his understanding, C. A. proceeded on the assumption that man can only possess understanding of things within the framework of his own subjective referential system (and the scientific reference system is only one of many). But as soon as he attempts to understand something without taking himself into account, he becomes paranoid. "Objects of thought dissociated from the thinker are the essence of madness," we read in another fragment.

One essential criterion affirming that he understood himself as the center of his world and not of the world is to be found in his remarks on the understanding of others, the "Thou" problem. One of his fragments reads as follows:

> "You are a subject"is an ontological statement under epistemological restriction. The ontological side consists in the fact of my necessarily conceding to you an existence dissociated from me with the same claims and requirements as I have for myself. The epistemological restriction lies in the fact that 'you' become an object when I become aware of you. You become an object in me, the observer, the thinker, the artist, the therapist, the doctor. . . . I do not create you, I perceive you. You are, of course, independently of my perception, but for me you are the person I perceive. What you are for yourself I cannot know. Even if you tell me, I still cannot perceive you independently of myself. It will always be I hearing what you say. And even if I repeat what you say it is I myself doing so and it then takes on my meaning and my significance.

Here we have that decisive warning not to confuse objectivity with neutrality, not to neutralize, indeed neuterize, objects, not to treat them like so many articles and handle them as if we knew who and what they are.

Objects in C. A.'s understanding are not solid bodies, not value- and meaning-free facts but visible, symbolically, audible, with the senses perceivable *moments of encounter* with oneself as well. When I encounter you, I encounter "you in me," not myself alone and yet myself as well, not you alone, and yet you as well. Thus objects do not

Viele seiner Zeitgenossen ließ das an seiner geistigen Gesundheit zweifeln, denn das war wirklich nicht „normal". Nur die Objektivität ist normal, C. A. hin oder her. Normal ist letztlich eine Sache der statistischen Mehrheiten und der selbstgebauten Sachzwänge. C. A. jedoch ging katanoisch, also verstandesgemäß, davon aus, daß der Mensch nur im Rahmen des eigenen subjektiven Referenzsystems (und auch das wissenschaftliche ist nur eines unter vielen) Sachverstand habe. Will er jedoch ohne sich selber irgend etwas verstehen und bedenkt sich dabei nicht selber mit, ist er paranoid. „Das vom Denker losgelöste Gedachte, das ist der Inbegriff des Wahnsinns", heißt es in einem andern Fragment.

Ein entscheidendes Kriterium dafür, daß er sich als Zentrum seiner und nicht der Welt verstand, bilden seine Ausführungen über die Fremderkenntnis, über das Du. Auf einem Fragment lesen wir folgendes:

> „Du bist ein Subjekt" ist eine ontologische Aussage unter epistemologischer Beschränkung. Das Ontologische besteht darin, daß ich dir eine von mir losgelöste Existenz mit den gleichen Ansprüchen zuerkennen muß, wie ich sie für mich habe. Die epistemologische Beschränkung besteht darin, daß 'du' zum Objekt wirst, wenn ich deiner inne werde. Du wirst zum Objekt in mir, dem Beobachter, dem Denker, dem Künstler, dem Therapeuten, dem Arzt . . . Ich schaffe dich nicht, sondern nehme dich wahr. Du bist zwar ohne meine Wahrnehmung, aber für mich bist du der oder die, wie ich dich wahrnehme. Wie du hingegen für dich bist, weiß ich nicht. Selbst wenn du es mir sagst, nehme ich dich nicht unabhängig von mir wahr. Was du sagst, höre *ich*. Auch wenn ich es nachsage, tue ich es und es bekommt meinen Sinn und meine Bedeutung.

Darin liegt die entscheidende Weichenstellung, Objektivität nicht zu versachlichen, die Objekte nicht zu versächlichen, wie Waren zu behandeln, und mit ihnen umzugehen, als ob man wüßte, was und wer sie sind.

Objekte im Sinne von C. A. werden nicht zu Festkörpern, oder zu wert- und bedeutungsfreien Tatsachen, sondern sind sichtbare, symbolische, hörbare, sinnlich wahrnehmbare, *Momente von Begegnung* immer auch mit mir selber: Dir begegne ich „dir in mir", nicht einfach nur mir, aber mir auch, nicht einfach nur dir, aber dir auch.

become a-historical, they have their temporality too. They take place, are in a state of flux, come and go in time. They are not just there, they are infinitely multiple, different for each and everyone of us. Either they are internal materializations in the subject or they are nothing. Objectivity is thus a concretely structured subjectivity. When it is taken for the truth, in a dissociated, absolute, dis-embodied sense, then this happens at the dictates of one or more subjects claiming absoluteness for themselves by the same token. Instead of something being whatever it is for me, it then becomes something of itself. This kind of objectivity is the basis of all fundamentalisms and the primal form of violence. Then science does away with religion, for example, and religion denies the validity of reality as postulated by science because it represents a danger to its own version, etc. The fact that objectivity can also be a form of intellectual indolence, or indeed arrogance, comes to the same thing. Objectivity as we know it is of course very reassuring once everyone has got accustomed to it. Politicians, for example, are very highly dependent on habit becoming the objectivity of as many individuals as possible. Only he who in no way disrupts the habits of the indolent has any chance of success. And only the successful can be in the right, i. e. objective.

Effects were made to get C. A. into politics and for a time he felt not only an external impulsion but also something akin to an internal compulsion. Inwardly he felt drawn towards political activity by the respect he had for the "subjectivity" of every individual and the commitment to ensuring that it be given due heed. Many of those who encouraged him felt that here at last was someone who would fight for politics with a human countenance. He however was subjective enough to realize that such people only had their own interests at heart, that this was an attempt to monopolize the idea of "humanity." Again and again he was brought face to face with the fact that it is all but impossible to be both a consistent relativist and at the same time to relativize the absolute necessity of being precisely that. Thus he finally decided - and this again was an outsider's decision - to remain faithful to science. For him scientia was synonymous with con-scientia, that form of cognizance that transforms science into conscience. The question of whether this kind of con-science was compatible with politics he left open. He had enough trouble with his con-scientious colleagues, most of all with those for whom scientia was largely indistinguishable from pecunia. Pecunia non olet, money does not stink, in other words it too is value-free.

Objekte werden damit nicht ahistorisch, sondern haben ihre Zeit. Sie ereignen sich, fließen, kommen und gehen in der Zeit. Es gibt sie nicht einfach, sondern unendlich vielfach, für jede und jeden anders. Sie sind innere Gebilde im Subjekt oder sie sind nicht. Objektivität ist daher eine gegenständlich strukturierte Subjektivität. Wenn sie davon losgelöst, ab-solut, zum Ding an sich, zur Wahrheit wird, geschieht dies nur unter dem Diktat eines oder mehrerer Subjekte, die sich damit selber absolut setzen. Statt an und für mich wird etwas dann an und für sich. Diese Art Objektivität ist die Basis aller Fundamentalismen und die Grundform der Gewalt. Wissenschaft schafft dann z. B. die Religion ab, die Religion leugnet das wissenschaftliche Wirklichkeitskonstrukt, weil es das ihre gefährdet, usw. Daß Objektivität auch Trägheit des Geistes und seiner Hybris sein kann, kommt auf dasselbe heraus. Landläufige Objektivität beruhigt natürlich sehr, wenn sich nur erst einmal alle daran gewöhnt haben. Gewiegte Politiker z. B. sind darauf angewiesen, daß die Gewohnheit zur Objektivität möglichst aller wird. Nur wer die Gewohnheiten der Trägen nicht stört, hat Erfolgschancen. Und nur wer Erfolg hat, hat recht, d. h. ist objektiv.

Man wollte auch C. A. in die Politik bringen, und er wurde äußerlich und fühlte sich eine Zeit sogar innerlich dazu gedrängt. Innerlich aus Hochachtung vor der „Subjektivität" jedes Menschen, für deren Beachtung er gekämpft hatte. Von außen her glaubten viele, in ihm würde sich endlich jemand für eine humane Politik einsetzen. Er war aber subjektiv genug, um zu merken, daß sie damit nur ihre eigenen Interessen im Sinn hatten und das Humane monopolisieren wollten. Er erlebte es immer wieder, daß es eine schiere Unmöglichkeit ist, konsequent Relativist zu bleiben und diesen Absolutheitsanspruch gleichzeitig zu relativieren. So entschied er sich schließlich, obwohl auch da ein Außenseiter, der Wissenschaft treu zu bleiben. Scientia war ihm gleichbedeutend mit con-scientia, mit jener Mitwisserschaft, welche das Wissen zum Gewissen werden läßt. Die Frage, ob diese „Gewissenschaft" mit Politik zu vereinen sei, ließ er offen. Er hatte genug Sorgen mit seinen mitwissenden Kollegen, vorab mit jenen, denen scientia soviel wie pecunia war. Pecunia non olet, Geld stinkt nicht und ist also ebenfalls wertfrei.

Nobody really knows what became of C. A. This habit of his of reducing himself to his initials may lead us to suppose that he did not set any great store by his own person. Nor do we have any indication whether he ever toyed with the idea of embarking on a course of psychotherapy. It seems at all events highly probable that he was urgently advised to do so, for the approach was still a very novel one in his times. But all the same, objectively speaking, who else could possibly have been more in need of it than people like C. A.?! On the other hand with his personality make-up he would probably have had difficulty in finding an analyst. He was constantly forgetting himself and thus lacked that essential instrument of analysis, the ability to recall, to retrieve those deep-frozen products, those objective "facts" and things of his own little history.

If we look around in world history in search of like-minded scholars and philosophers, three major figures immediately spring to mind Laotze in China, Heraclitus a century later and another century later Kratylos, in Greece and Asia Minor. All three have something in common. They left us a legacy of wisdom, left it in the truest sense of leaving it behind them while they moved on into unknown realms, into regions where nobody would follow. It is said of Laotze and Heraklitus that they, as it were, took themselves out of circulation; they simply disappeared. Kratylos relativized Heraklitus' own relativity ("You cannot get into the same river twice") by insisting that "you cannot even get into the same river once." Thereafter he withdrew into himself, made signs with his little finger if there was anything he urgently needed but aside from that never opened his mouth to speak again. All of these resisted the temptation of objectivity; their legacy is the annoyance they caused. The way they were constituted represented a certain kind of ethics that made spoilsports out of them. For in this sporting life it is objectivity that is the great gambler, putting everything at stakes, life, mankind, air, genetic structure, spirit, mind, the Earth. To all this objectivity does violence.

If our sources are correct those three pre-Christian philosophers did not look upon themselves as specialists in a particular subject. Laotze in fact would probably have said that a "subject" can only emerge when there's nothing left of substance to talk about. C. A. was so supremely ethical that he was not even self-righteous. It is for this reason that he remains like a thorn in the flesh of our thinking - come to think of it, a pretty successful "survival strategy" for someone outwardly so unsuccessful!

Niemand weiß so recht, was aus C. A. geworden ist. Wenn er sich immer mit den Initialen C. A. abkürzte, läßt das darauf schließen, daß er nicht allzuviel auf sich hielt. Es ist auch nicht bekannt, ob er sich jemals mit dem Gedanken trug, sich einer Psychoanalyse zu unterziehen, obwohl es wahrscheinlich ist, daß ihm dringend dazu geraten wurde. Denn schließlich war die Sache zu seiner Zeit noch neu. Aber ganz davon abgesehen, objektiv betrachtet, wer hätte sie schon damals mehr gebraucht, als Leute wie C. A.?! Doch bei seinen Voraussetzungen hätte er wahrscheinlich Mühe gehabt, einen Analytiker zu finden. Er vergaß sich einfach immer wieder und besaß ein wesentliches Instrument der Analyse nicht, das Erinnerungsvermögen an tiefgekühlte Produkte, an die objektiven „Tatsachen" und Dinge seiner kleinen Geschichte.

Wer sich in der großen Geschichte nach Geistesverwandten umsieht, stößt auf drei hervorragende Gestalten: Lao tse in China, Heraklit ein Jahrhundert später und Kratylos nochmals hundert Jahre danach in Griechenland und Kleinasien. Alle drei haben etwas gemeinsam. Sie hinterließen Weisheiten, welche sie hinter sich ließen, von denen sie auszogen ins Unbekannte, wo niemand die Weisen selber mehr fand. Von Lao tse und Heraklit wird berichtet, sie hätten sich gleichsam selber aus dem Verkehr gezogen und seien einfach verschwunden. Kratylos relativierte den relativierenden Satz von Heraklit („Man kann nicht zweimal in den gleichen Fluß steigen") mit dem andern: „Man kann nicht einmal *einmal* in den gleichen Fluß steigen". Sprach's, zog sich zurück, gab nur noch Mitteilungen mit dem kleinen Finger, wenn er dringend etwas benötigte, und sagte sonst kein einziges Wort mehr. Alle widerstanden sie der Versuchung zur Objektivität, und was von ihnen geblieben ist, ist das Ärgernis. Sie repräsentierten ein bestimmtes Ethos durch ihr Sosein und wurden dadurch zu Spielverderbern. Denn Objektivität setzt ja schließlich alles aufs Spiel, das Leben, den Menschen, die Luft, die Gene, die Seele, den Geist, die Erde. Allem tut sie Gewalt an.

Die drei Antiken verstanden sich unseren Quellen gemäß nicht als Fachethiker. Lao tse würde sinngemäß dazu gesagt haben, daß ein Fach erst dann entstehe, wenn es die Sache nicht mehr gäbe. C. A. hatte ein so hohes Ethos, daß er nicht einmal selbstgerecht war. Darum bleibt er uns ein Stachel im Geist. Eigentlich eine ganz erfolgreiche „Überlebensstrategie" eines Erfolglosen!

Auer as Smuggler[1]

Carlos E. Sluzki

I never knew whether to believe him or not. I still don't. Perhaps that is an effect intended by him . . . if there is any intent of effect at all! Perhaps that is an effect regardless of intent, a moral of the story conveyed by the great scheme of things. Well, all this convoluted prologue is my feeble attempt to delay my wish to share a startling revelation - if revelation at all - and an incredible story that Carl Auer poured over me during my recent visit to his cottage. First of all, it was April, and you know how Aprils are, neither here nor there. Secondly, he might have been a bit tipsy when he mentioned it to me (one never knew whether that sturdy mug filled with tea-mit-Schnapps which accompanies him whenever he is at home retains miraculously its fluid - theory #1: Carl is a closet teetotaller. Ridiculous! - or is consumed and re-filled again and again throughout his endless evenings - theory #2: Carl is a closet alcoholic. Nonsense!). I don't even know whether his revelations were to be kept secret, a tender confidence that I am shamelessly betraying by writing this, or perhaps general knowledge that only I came by tardily. And thirdly, perhaps I misunderstood the whole tirade: the conversation took place too late at night - too late for me, a morning dove, but not for Carl, definitely a night owl. You see, I am at my best at 6 a.m. and tend to decline progressively throughout the day, becoming a mumbling idiot at 6 p.m. and a total zombie after dark, body present and soul in suspended animation - while Carl is just the opposite: he barely manages to struggle to the kitchen in pyjama and robe, grab his double, nay, triple expresso swiftly prepared and handed to him by whatever tender guardian angel - that is how he calls them - around him (and how does this rather conservative-looking old man manage to secure those silent, attractive, almost etherial guardian angels around him. This seems to me to be another act of magic!), drags himself to the bathtub,

Auer als Schmuggler[1]

Carlos E. Sluzki

Ich wußte nie, ob ich ihm glauben sollte oder nicht. Ich weiß es immer noch nicht. Vielleicht hat er diese Wirkung beabsichtigt... wenn eine Absicht überhaupt eine Wirkung haben kann! Vielleicht ist das eine Wirkung, die unabhängig von der Absicht die Moral von der Geschichte ist, wie sie durch den großen Plan vermittelt wird. Nun, dieser gewundene Prolog ist nichts anderes als der klägliche Versuch, meinen Wunsch aufzuschieben, eine aufregende Enthüllung mitzuteilen - wenn man überhaupt von Enthüllung sprechen kann - und eine unglaubliche Geschichte zu erzählen, die sich Carl Auer bei meinem kürzlichen Besuch in seinem Häuschen von der Seele geredet hat. Erstens war es April! Sie wissen ja, wie Aprilwetter ist: weder Fisch noch Fleisch. Zweitens war er womöglich etwas beschwipst, als er sie mir erzählte (man wußte nie, ob dieser derbe, mit Tee und Schnaps gefüllte Becher, der ihn immer begleitete, wenn er zu Hause war, wunderbarerweise nie leer wurde - Theorie Nr. 1: Carl ist Antialkoholiker. Lächerlich! - oder im Verlauf seiner endlosen Abende geleert und immer wieder gefüllt wurde - Theorie Nr. 2: Carl ist Alkoholiker. Unsinn!). Ich weiß nicht einmal, ob er mir seine Enthüllungen im Vertrauen erzählt hat, ein naives Vertrauen, das ich jetzt mit dieser Veröffentlichung schamlos mißbrauche; oder ob es sich dabei um Allgemeingut handelte, von dem ich nur später als alle anderen erfahren habe. Drittens habe ich vielleicht die gesamte Tirade falsch verstanden: Die Unterhaltung fand zu spät in der Nacht statt - zu spät für mich Morgentaube, aber nicht zu spät für Carl, der zweifellos eine Nachteule ist. Sie müssen sehen, daß ich um sechs Uhr morgens am besten drauf bin und danach kontinuierlich abbaue. Bis um sechs Uhr abends bin ich dann ein stotternder Idiot und nach Anbruch der Dunkelheit ein völliger Zombi, der Körper ist anwesend und die Seele in einem Zustand vorübergehender Leblosigkeit. Carl

unable to mutter even an appreciation, only to reappear an hour later looking refreshed but still as if drawn with *mezzatinta* and *sfumatura*, and becomes progressively alive as the day goes by, to bloom at night in a blinding display of intellectual pyrotechnics, frequently witnessed only by his cat (and whatever female guardian angel may be floating around), sometimes solely by the somber presence of whatever remained of Bertha after the well-known mishap, and, alas, sometimes just by him and his old battered Olympia, much to everybody's delayed benefit.

Well, the whole thing started during one of those nights by the fireplace, just the two of us, when Carl told me, in the middle of a conversation, almost mumbling to himself while looking sleepily at his filled mug: "You know, Carlos, I never ever read a book in my life."

I managed to shake myself from catalepsy and answered, following a social mandate that recommends that when one utterly doesn't understand something, one has to transform it into something understandable, regardless of how banal: "I cannot believe that you didn't like *any* book in your whole life!"

"I liked *many* books! What I said is that I never *read* one."

"In what language?" I insisted, trivializing in order to make sense of it.

"In what language what? In what language didn't I read any book? In all kinds of languages! That is, I didn't read any book only in those seven languages that I know. Needless to say, I haven't even *tried* not to read books in languages that are unknown to me."

He is pulling my leg, I decided, he is teasing me benevolently, perhaps because he notices that I am half asleep and wants to flip me

ist das genaue Gegenteil: Im Pyjama und Morgenmantel schafft er es kaum bis zur Küche, um sich an seinen doppelten, was sag ich, dreifachen Espresso zu klammern, der ihm rasch von dem gerade anwesenden Schutzengel - so nennt er sie - gekocht und gereicht wird (wie dieser doch recht konservativ ausschauende alte Mannes es schafft, diese stillen, attraktiven, fast ätherischen Schutzengel zu verpflichten, ist für mich eine weiteres Rätsel!). Unfähig auch nur zu einem Worte des Dankes, schleppt er sich dann in die Badewanne, erscheint eine Stunde später wieder und schaut erfrischt aus, aber immer noch, als ob er mit *mezzatinta* und *sfumatura* gezeichnet wäre. Er wird im Lauf des Tages zunehmend lebendiger, und erblüht nachts in den blendenden Farben eines intellektuellen Feuerwerks, das häufig nur von seiner Katze (und von dem ihn gerade umschwebenden weiblichen Schutzengel) wahrgenommen wird; manchmal auch nur von der düsteren Anwesenheit dessen, was von Bertha nach dem bekannten Unglück übrig blieb, und hin und wieder leider nur von ihm und seiner alten ramponierten Olympia, zum verspäteten Nutzen aller.

Die Sache begann in einer dieser Nächte, die wir beide vor dem Kamin verbrachten. Er sprach fast zu sich selbst und schaute seinen gefüllten Becher schläfrig an: „Weißt du, Carlos, ich habe noch nie in meinem Leben ein Buch gelesen."

Es gelang mir, mich aus meiner Erstarrung zu lösen und ich antwortete, indem ich einer gesellschaftlichen Gepflogenheit folgte, nach der man etwas völlig Unverständliches in etwas umwandeln muß, das man versteht, auch wenn es noch so banal ist: „Ich kann nicht glauben, daß dir in deinem ganzen Leben nicht einmal *ein* Buch gefallen hat!"

„Mir haben *viele* Bücher gefallen. Ich sagte, daß ich niemals eins *gelesen* habe."

„In welcher Sprache?" beharrte ich trivial, um den Sinn verstehen zu können.

„Was in welcher Sprache? In welcher Sprache ich kein Buch gelesen habe? In allen möglichen Sprachen! Das heißt ich habe nur in den sieben Sprachen, die ich kenne, kein Buch gelesen. Es versteht sich von selbst, daß ich in Sprachen, die ich nicht kenne, nicht einmal *versucht* habe, kein Buch zu lesen."

Er macht sich über mich lustig, dachte ich, er mokiert sich vielleicht auf seine gutmütige Art, vielleicht weil er merkt, daß ich halb einge-

into an altered state, as he has been known to do now and then. I remember drawing at that moment a flash comparison between Carl and Gregory Bateson. Well, there's a difference if ever I've seen one, I thought. If Gregory saw you meandering, and even if not, he wouldn't pull your leg, he would simply fly higher with the effect of making you feel like a wingless insect, he would mutter something abstruse to assure that you would be lost, no pebbles to follow him through the clouds, his flying coordinates hopelessly above and beyond your reach. And don't come to me with any positively connoting metaphor about the Buddhist master and the transcendental nature of the incomprehensible: Bateson didn't mind being cruel. But not Auer. He may occasionally be a teaser - I told myself, and still believe - but his mischievousness is always tinted by the warm colors of his kind soul. I managed to shake off my sleepiness and attempted to probe in which direction he was meandering: "And what about all you have written?"

"But, Carlos," he threw his arms up in (mock?) despair, "we are not talking about my writings! It's nothing to do with my writings, really, I just follow the blessed advice that André Gide offered me once. It happened, let's see . . . it was Paris . . . yes, I remember, in 1949. I was lamenting to him the pangs of inhabiting the body of a person for whom creativity is a core value and therefore is condemned to expect daily of himself what occurs only by miracle - as you see, a variation of the 'be spontaneous' paradox. Gide stabbed me in the chest with his bony index finger, then shook it in front of me as if to prove that it was still intact, and admonished me with his high pitched *falsetto*: "*Mein freund*" - that was the extent of his German! - "everything has already been written and said before! But since nobody listens or remembers, we have to keep going back and beginning again. We don't write, we only re-write! And that is what I do, Carlos, I re-write. Only as nobody remembers what the other have written, I am called 'original'!"

schlafen bin, und will mich in einen anderen Zustand versetzen, wie man das gelegentlich von ihm kennt. Ich erinnere mich, daß sich mir damals plötzlich ein Vergleich zwischen Carl und Gregory Bateson aufdrängte. Wenn ich je einen Unterschied feststellte, war es der, dachte ich: Wenn Gregory bemerkte, daß man abschweifte, und selbst wenn er es nicht bemerkte, machte er sich nicht lustig, sondern wäre einfach höher gestiegen und hätte damit bewirkt, daß man sich wie ein flügelloses Insekt fühlte. Er murmelte etwas Abstruses, um sicherzustellen, daß man nicht mehr mitkam. Da waren keine Wegweiser, die einem helfen würden, ihm durch die Wolken zu folgen. Seine fliegenden Koordinaten hoffnungslos über dir und außer Reichweite. Und komm' mir nicht mit positiv konnotierenden Metaphern über den buddhistischen Meister und die transzendentale Natur des Unverständlichen: Bateson hatte nichts dagegen, grausam zu sein. Anders Auer. Er macht sich vielleicht gelegentlich lustig - sagte ich mir, und das meine ich immer noch - aber seine Verschmitztheit ist immer geprägt von den warmen Farben seiner gütigen Seele. Ich schaffte es, meine Schläfrigkeit abzuschütteln und versuchte zu sondieren, in welche Richtung er abgeschweift war: „Und was ist mit all dem, was du geschrieben hast?"

„Aber Carlos", er schlug in (gespielter?) Verzweiflung die Hände über dem Kopf zusammen, „wir sprechen nicht über das, was ich geschrieben habe. Damit hat das nichts zu tun. Ich befolge eigentlich nur den gesegneten Rat, den mir André Gide einst gab. Es war, laß mich nachdenken . . . es war in Paris, ja ich erinnere mich, 1949. Ich jammerte ihm etwas über die Qual vor, in dem Körper einer Person zu stecken, für die Kreativität von zentraler Bedeutung ist und die deshalb dazu verdammt ist, täglich das von sich zu erwarten, was nur durch ein Wunder geschieht. Wie du siehst handelt es sich hier um eine Variation des 'Sei spontan'-Paradoxes. Gide stieß mir seinen knochigen Zeigefinger gegen die Brust, schüttelte ihn dann vor mir, als wolle er beweisen, daß er noch ganz war, und ermahnte mich mit seiner hohen Fistelstimme: *„Mein Freund"* - mehr Deutsch sprach er nicht! - „es ist alles schon einmal geschrieben und gesagt worden! Da niemand zuhört und niemand sich erinnert, müssen wir immer wieder zurückgehen und wieder neu beginnen. Wir schreiben nicht, wir schreiben nur um!" Und genau das tue ich, Carlos, ich schreibe um. Nur weil sich niemand daran erinnert, was andere geschrieben haben, spricht man meinen Werken 'Orginalität' zu."

A mantle of sadness enveloped us and tinted the silence that followed. God, was I awake! And ready to cry, at what I wasn't sure. And Carl seemed equally moved, a genius condemned by his own wisdom to re-writing, even when the most original pieces were pouring from the seemingly bottomless well of his creative mind. "Well, Carlos," he seemed to extract himself from the quagmire by pulling himself up by his own bootstraps, *à la* Munchhausen, "after all, true sculptors only chisel away the excess granite in order to discover the finished piece that lies hidden in the rock."

The lifting effect of that idea was instantaneous: to define Michelangelo as a discoverer rather than as a creator, or perhaps as a chamber-boy that meticulously dusted away with his chisel whatever pieces were hiding a pre-existing, already formed *Pieta* seemed so ludicrous that my somber mood faded away as quickly as it had come. Stubbornly, I returned to my track: "Carl, I distinctly remember your quoting almost verbatim, not too long ago, in one of your Heidelberg lectures, some passages of the *Tractatus Logico-Philosophicus*. Where did you get that quote from, if you didn't read it?"

"*Wovon man nicht sprechen kann, darüber muß man schweigen*. But, why not, it was so long ago . . . Do you want to know how I quote it? Let me tell you, Carlos," he mumbled, his eyes closed, while rolling up his sleeve to show me his left forearm, which was decorated by a rather ugly flat remnant of an old wound, one of those pinkish, melted-cheese-looking, scar-over-scar-over-scar things, the size and shape of a fossil giant trilobite. "Do you know where I got this tattoo? It comes from the very last days of The War To End All Wars (he pronounced each capital letter distinctly), where I volunteered - for the wrong side, of course, meaning by that, I guess, 'for the side that lost it' - when I was fresh from *Gymnasium*, too young to know any better. Anyhow, in October 1918 I ended up with a piece of shrapnel in my arm and was taken prisoner by the Italians - and don't ask me which side the Italians were on: I still don't know, and they probably didn't know either. I was sent, wound and all, to a prison camp near Monte Cassino. And there a miracle occurred: prisoners were distributed in cells not according to rank, nor to age, nor by alphabetic order, but according to still another equally silly bureaucratic

Eine traurige Stimmung hüllte uns in einen Mantel des Schweigens. Mein Gott, wie wach ich war! Mir war zum Heulen. Worüber, war mir nicht klar. Carl schien gleichermaßen bewegt; ein Genie, von der eigenen Weisheit zum Umschreiben verdammt, auch wenn Stükke von größter Orginalität aus der scheinbar unerschöpflichen Quelle seines kreativen Geistes flossen. „Nun, Carlos", er schien sich *à la* Münchhausen an den eigenen Haaren aus dem Sumpf zu ziehen, „schließlich meißeln die wahren Bildhauer nur den überflüssigen Granit weg, um das fertige Stück zu entdecken, das im Felsen versteckt liegt."

Die erhebende Wirkung dieses Gedankens war unmittelbar spürbar: Michelangelo als Entdecker zu definieren, anstatt als Schöpfer, oder vielleicht als Zimmerjungen, der mit seinem Meißel sorgfältig all jene Stücke entfernte, die eine bereits existierende und schon vorgeformte *Pietà* verbargen, schien so grotesk, daß meine düstere Stimmung so schnell verschwand, wie sie gekommen war. Hartnäckig nahm ich meine Spur wieder auf: „Carl, ich erinnere mich genau, daß du vor nicht allzu langer Zeit in einer deiner Heidelberger Vorlesungen fast wörtlich einige Passagen aus dem „Tractatus Logico-Philosophicus" zitiert hast. Woher hast du das Zitat, wenn du es nicht gelesen hast?"

„Wovon man nicht sprechen kann, darüber muß man schweigen. Aber warum nicht darüber sprechen, es ist alles schon so lange her. Willst du wissen, warum ich das zitieren kann? Also, ich werde es dir erzählen, Carlos", murmelte er mit geschlossenen Augen, während er sich den linken Hemdärmel hochkrempelte, um mir seinen Unterarm zu zeigen. Er war mit einer häßlichen flachen Narbe dekoriert, die von einer alten Verwundung stammen mußte, eine jener rosafarbenen, wie geschmolzener Käse aussehenden, furchenreichen Vernarbungen in der Form eines Riesenurweltkrebses. „Weißt du, wo ich mir diese Tätowierung eingefangen habe? Es ist ein Andenken an die letzten Tage des Krieges, der Alle Kriege Beenden Sollte (deutlich betonte er jeden Anfangsbuchstaben seiner Worte). Ich war Freiwilliger auf der falschen Seite, falsch insofern, als ich auf der Seite derer stand, die den Krieg verloren haben. Ich kam frisch vom Gymnasium und war noch zu jung, um es besser zu wissen. Wie auch immer, im Oktober 1918 hat mich ein Granatsplitter am Arm erwischt, und ich wurde von den Italienern gefangengenommen - und frag' mich nicht, auf welcher Seite die Italiener standen: Ich weiß es

parameter - could you believe it - place of birth! And I ended up sharing a cell with a total stranger, a fellow prisoner in that camp. It was, Carlos, of all the people in the world, Ludwig Wittgenstein. I must confess that I had never heard of him - I recognised his family name, of course, as his father was a well-known industrialist in Austria. He was many years my senior, 30 years old, while I was . . . well, still a toddler. Can you believe it, Carlos, Ludwig, bursting with ideas, carrying in his jacket at all times the only copy of the manuscript of his *Tractatus*, re-working it daily, making it tighter, clearer, cleaner, but in a desparate need of a dialogue with peers, stuck in a cell with this *ignoramus*. However, God bless him! rather than cursing the gods - or worse, cursing me! - for his fate, he made from the start what could be defined as the most desperate or the most genial move in that terribly constrained situation: he carried me conceptually, he taught me meticulously from the very basics to the very frontier of his own thoughts - imagine, Carlos, Wittgenstein by Wittgenstein! - in the hope of making of me somebody he could learn from. In turn, I, being as I was almost *a tabula rasa*, and totally unaware that his was an impossible task, immersed myself into this work with devotion. And this irritable, hyper-sensitive man, prone to mood swings and at times unable to exorcise the dark clouds that followed him, was consistently warm and endlessly patient with me. I, in turn, was stubbornly receptive. We would converse incessantly, from dawn to dusk, in the cell and in the yard, alone or surrounded by fellow prisoners. The guards were probably convinced that they were dealing with a pair of lunatics and treated us accordingly: they left us in peace. He would explain his propositions again and again - '*Die Logik muß für sich selber sorgen,*' he would mutter stubbornly - and I would also argue again and again until I understood, and then continue arguing until we both understood that I understood. In fact, in those four months of endless conversations, many parts of his manuscript were re-written and re-written anew. Mind you, it is not that I was such a genius, it was simply that here and there I seemed to ask the right questions to force some revisions, and was able to provide here and there the right alternatives that allowed for new propositions to be formulated.

nicht und sie wußten es wahrscheinlich selbst nicht. Ich wurde verwundet in einem Gefangenenlager in der Nähe von Monte Cassino eingelocht. Dort geschah ein Wunder. Die Gefangenen wurden nicht nach Rang, Alter oder Alphabet auf die Zellen verteilt, sondern nach einem ähnlich schwachsinnigen, bürokratischen Parameter - ob du's glaubst oder nicht - nach dem Geburtsort. Ich mußte mir mit einem völlig Fremden die Zelle teilen. Und das, Carlos, war ausgerechnet Ludwig Wittgenstein. Ich muß gestehen, daß ich nie zuvor von ihm gehört hatte. Natürlich kannte ich den Namen, da sein Vater ja ein bekannter österreichischer Industrieller war. Er war viel älter als ich, 30 Jahre alt, während ich . . . nun ja, noch fast ein Baby war. Du kannst es dir nicht vorstellen, Carlos, Ludwig platzte vor Ideen und trug die ganze Zeit in seiner Jacke die einzige Kopie des Manuskripts seines 'Tractatus' mit sich 'rum. Täglich überarbeitete er das Manuskript, verdichtete es und beseitigte Unklarheiten. In dem verzweifelten Bedürfnis nach einem gleichwertigen Geprächspartner fand er sich nun in der Zelle mit mir Ignoranten wieder. Anstatt jedoch, Gott segne ihn, die Götter zu verfluchen, bzw. noch schlimmer, mich für sein Schicksal zu verfluchen, machte er von Anfang an etwas, was man als sehr genialen oder auch sehr verzweifelten Schritt in dieser Zwangslage ansehen kann. Er lehrte mich seinen Entwurf zu verstehen, lehrte mich akribisch alles, vom Grundlegendsten bis hin zu den weitesten Horizonten seiner Gedanken. Stell' dir vor, Carlos, Wittgenstein von Wittgenstein - alles in der Hoffnung, mich so weit zu fördern, daß er von mir lernen könnte. Als Gegenleistung stürzte ich mich hingebungsvoll in diese Arbeit. Ich war ja am Anfang wirklich fast eine *Tabula rasa* und mir war überhaupt nicht klar, was er sich für eine unmögliche Aufgabe vorgenommen hatte. Und dieser leicht irritierbare, hochsensible Mann, seinen seelischen Schwankungen hilflos ausgeliefert und zeitweilig unfähig, die dunklen Wolken, die ihn verfolgten, zu vertreiben, unterrichtete mich nun mit steter Zuneigung und unendlicher Geduld. Ich, meinerseits, nahm beharrlich alles auf, was er mir beibrachte. Wir sprachen ununterbrochen, vom Morgengrauen bis spät in die Nacht, gleich, ob in der Zelle oder auf dem Hof, ob unter uns oder in Gegenwart anderer. Die Aufseher waren wohl überzeugt, es mit zwei Verrückten zu tun zu haben und behandelten uns dementsprechend: Sie ließen uns in Frieden. Er erklärte seine Thesen immer wieder. *'Die Logik muß für sich selber sorgen'*, brummte er verbohrt vor sich hin, und ich diskutierte solange

Ludwig ended up referring to it, bless his soul, as 'our' manuscript. My! for me it was a daily miracle. Those months have been, Carlos, by far the paramount intellectual *fest* of my life. Ridiculous as it may sound, the most cherished period of my whole existence took place in that cold, rotten, prison camp. But, as in all stories, suddenly, one morning the unexpected occurred (and it occurred on a Wednesday, which is a good day to expect the unexpected): during early roll call, one of the prison's wardens appeared, medals and all, and informed us, in broken German, with the unavoidable seasoning of Italian epithets, that he was carrying good news, 'even though you, *rompescatole*, always complaining of cold and hunger, don't deserve any': all prisoners who were 18 years old or less were going to be pardoned and released immediately. The screams of joy were deafening - there were many adolescents, caught by the war machinery as 'dead meat of last resource' that managed to land in the camp. Ludwig and I looked at each other's eyes for a seemingly endless lapse, flabberghasted, tears cascading freely down our cheeks. We then hugged each other in what felt like a lovers' soul-tearing departing embrace - I am sure that many fellow prisoners in fact thought that there *had to* be some suspicious hanky-panky between us. Then, with an urgency I had never heard in his voice, Wittgenstein whispered anxiously in my ear: 'This is our chance, Carl. You have to take this risk for me.' I didn't know what he was talking about. He went on: 'You *have* to smuggle our manuscript out of Monte Cassino. You have to take it to the British Embassy and urge them to send it to my teacher, to Bertrand Russell, - I believe he is now at the University of Peking. I *need* his feedback. I have gone as far as I can go and even further thanks to you, my beloved friend. But I need Russell, I need to hear from him. I may not get out of this camp ever!' His sobbing made his words almost unintelligible. 'Tell me that you will do it, tell me, Carl, please!' His distress was overwhelming: it was no longer us, dear

mit ihm, bis ich es verstanden hatte, und dann diskutierten wir weiter, bis wir beide verstanden, daß ich es verstanden hatte. In der Tat, in diesen vier Monaten endloser Gespräche wurden viele Teile seines Manuskripts umgeschrieben und immer wieder verändert. Nicht, daß du glaubst, ich wäre ein solches Genie, es war einfach so, daß ich hier und da die richtigen Fragen stellte, um bestimmte Veränderungen zu bewirken, und hier und da Alternativen vorschlug, die zur Formulierung neuer Thesen beitrugen.

Ludwig, Gott segne ihn, fing schließlich damit an, von 'unserem' Manuskript zu reden. Also wirklich, für mich war es ein tägliches Wunder. Carlos, diese Monate waren mit Abstand das größte intellektuelle Fest meines Lebens. So lächerlich es klingen mag, die schönste Zeit meines ganzen Lebens verbrachte ich in diesem kalten, elenden Gefangenenlager. Aber wie in allen Geschichten passierte eines Morgens das Unerwartete (es passierte an einem Mittwoch, ein guter Tag, um das Unerwartete zu erwarten). Im Laufe des Morgenappells erschien ein Offizier der Wachmannschaft mit Orden und allem Drum und Dran. Er informierte uns in gebrochenem Deutsch und mit den unvermeidlichen italienischen Beiwörtern garniert, daß er gute Nachrichten für uns habe: 'Obwohl ihr *rompescatole,* die ihr euch ständig über Hunger und Kälte beklagt habt, sie nicht verdient habt.' Alle Gefangenen, die 18 oder jünger waren, wurden auf der Stelle begnadigt und entlassen. Das Freudengeheul war ohrenbetäubend - es gab viele Jugendliche, die von der Kriegsmaschinerie als 'totes Fleisch der letzten Reserven' erfaßt worden waren und die es schafften, in dem Lager zu landen. Ludwig und ich sahen uns für einen schier endlos anmutenden Augenblick in die Augen und dann rannen uns die Tränen hemmungslos über die Wangen. Wir umarmten uns dann in herzzerreißender Weise, wie zwei Liebende, die voneinander Abschied nehmen müssen. In der Tat müssen die Mitgefangenen wunders was gedacht haben, welches rosarote Techtelmechtel wir miteinander haben. Dann flüsterte mir Ludwig mit einer Eindringlichkeit, die ich nie zuvor in seiner Stimme gehört hatte, voller Angst ins Ohr: 'Das ist unsere Chance, Carl. Du *mußt* dieses Risiko für mich auf dich nehmen.' Ich hatte keine Ahnung, was er meinte. 'Du *mußt* unser Manuskript hier aus Monte Cassino rausschmuggeln und in die Britische Botschaft bringen und sie drängen, es an meinen Lehrer Bertrand Russell weiterzuleiten - derzeit ist er, soweit ich weiß, als Gastprofessor an der Universität in Peking. Ich

friends, master-disciple, saying good-bye, it was a desperate father pleading for me to save his baby from certain death, an artist urging me to rescue his masterpiece from a sinking ship.

All along I had been soothing him - and I meant it, mind you - 'Of course, Ludwig, of course,' but he seemed to need to finish his tirade. It took me a while to realize that, while talking, right there, in the middle of the noisy crowd on the prison's chilly yard, surrounded by cheering youngsters and somber adults, in what seemed an awkwardly extended embrace, he was pulling out surreptitiously his - our! - manuscript from his jacket - where he carried it constantly, priceless treasure as it was - and pushing it with despair into the inner pocket of my jacket. In fact, I realized later, that maneuver had to be done there and then, in that moment of confusion: we, the youngsters, were *ipso facto* bathed, shaven, given clean clothes, and ushered to the train.

Anyhow, I managed to smuggle it away. After fencing off countless secretaries and attachés, I was able to deliver it in person to the new British Consul in Vienna. The manuscript reached Bertrand in Peking as planned, he was in turn able to write to Ludwig at Monte Cassino, courtesy of the Red Cross, Ludwig then wrote to me, I wrote to Bertrand, and so on and so forth. The rest you probably know. So, summarizing, how come I have been able to quasi quote the *Tractatus* without reading it? Because I participated in some minor fashion in *writing* it, that's how, and because I discussed it inside out with its (main) author! So stop asking."

So stop asking! On my behalf this man was displaying incredible archeological artifacts from his own history - from the collective history of our culture, in fact - and then dismissing them as obvious with a flippant "So stop asking." I brushed aside his comment, my mind in turmoil and awe. I remember that at that moment the enigmatic dedication of the first edition of Wittgenstein's last book, *Philosophische Untersuchungen*, crossed my mind: "To C. A., student,

muß wissen, was er davon hält, denn vielleicht komme ich hier nie wieder raus', schluchzte er mit tränenerstickter Stimme. 'Versprich mir bitte, daß du es tun wirst, Carl, bitte, versprich es.' Sein Schmerz war überwältigend: Es war nicht länger der Abschied guter Freunde oder von Lehrer und Schüler, es war der Abschied eines verzweifelten Vaters, der mich beschwor, sein Kind dem sicheren Tode zu entreißen, ein Künstler, der mich bekniete, sein Meisterwerk von einem sinkenden Schiff zu retten.

Die ganze Zeit über hatte ich ihn besänftigt - und meinte es auch so - 'Natürlich, Ludwig, natürlich', aber er schien seinen Wortschwall beenden zu müssen. Ich brauchte eine Weile, um zu merken, daß er, während er redete, mitten in der lauten Menge des kalten Gefängnishofes, umgeben von jubelnden Jugendlichen und ernsten Erwachsenen, sich verzweifelt mühte unter dem Schutz einer peinlich ausgedehnten Umarmung, sein (unser!) Manuskript aus seiner Jacke zu ziehen - wo er es ständig trug, unbezahlbarer Schatz der es war - und es voller Verzweiflung in die Innentasche meiner Jacke zu stecken. Später wurde mir klar, daß dieses Manöver genau in diesem Durcheinander hatte ausgeführt werden müssen. Wir Jugendlichen wurden *ipso facto* gebadet, rasiert, man gab uns saubere Kleidung und geleitet uns zum Zug.

Jedenfalls schaffte ich es, es herauszuschmuggeln. Nachdem ich zahllose Sekretärinnen und Attachés abgewehrt hatte, gelang es mir, es dem neuen Britischen Konsul in Wien zu übergeben. Wie gewünscht erhielt Bertrand das Manuskript in Peking. Ihm wiederum gelang es dank des Roten Kreuzes, Ludwig nach Monte Cassino zu schreiben. Ludwig unterrichtete mich davon, ich schrieb an Bertrand u.s.w. Den Rest kennst du wahrscheinlich. Um es zusammenzufassen, weshalb ich den „Tractatus" quasi zitieren konnte, ohne ihn gelesen zu haben: weil ich geringfügig daran beteiligt war, ihn zu *schreiben*, deshalb, und weil ich ihn von vorn bis hinten mit seinem (Haupt-) Autor diskutierte! Hör also auf zu fragen."

Hör also auf zu fragen! Dieser Mann zeigte ausgerechnet mir unglaubliche archäologische Artefakte seiner eigenen Geschichte - aus der kollektiven Geschichte unserer Kultur - und tat sie dann mit einem dahingeworfenen: „Hör also auf zu fragen" ab, als läge das auf der Hand. Ich wischte seine Bemerkung völlig verwirrt und voller Ehrfurcht beiseite. Ich erinnere mich, daß mir just in dem Moment die rätselhafte Widmung der ersten Ausgabe von Wittgensteins letztem

mentor and smuggler." 'The first time I saw that inscription I already suspected that "C. A." had to be Carl Auer. But why "smuggler"? I had my question answered.

The dance of the flames in the fireplace suddenly came into focus at the end of that story. I allowed myself to sink into the warmth of the fire and of the moment, mesmerized by the vibrant silence that followed, like an aftermath, that privileged incursion through a time warp. After a while, still in trance, I asked Carl: "And have you ever returned to Monte Cassino?"

"To Monte Cassino? No! In fact, I couldn't, even if I had wanted to: one can never go to any place twice, as there isn't such a thing as places that stay while time and oneself, the visitor, evolve. In fact," he interrupted me just when I was starting to cry mercy, "not long ago I heard Ludwig's nephew Heinz[2] presenting a variation of what I told him once, which I will repeat for your benefit: one can never visit a place *once* - Heinz transformed it into 'one cannot cross a river once,' but that's because he doesn't want to get wet, hein? It's late, Carlos, I'll go to bed now, if I may. Thank you for accompanying me in my story. Make yourself at home, you know where the bar and the bathroom and the guest bedroom are if you wish to stay - it's rather chilly outside. One way or another, to be continued."

Once again, there I was, dizzy from the effects of another punch into my mental plexus. "Just one quick question, just a 'yes' or 'no', Carl. Does your 'never having read a book' and your 'being unable to go to a place once,' or twice, or whatever, belong to the same gender?"

Auer looked at me, faintly smiling, his head slightly tilted. "It's late, Carlos, don't torture me," he pleaded.

Sucker for human rights as I am, I dropped the issue and bid him good night.

[1] Chapter 7 of Carlos E. Sluzki: *The Re-drawing of the Jigsaw Puzzle: Fireside Conversations with Carl Auer*. New York and Heidelberg, Neueman Verlag, 1990 (in press, bilingual edition). Reproduced here with permission of the author and the publisher.
[2]Heinz von Foerster (the editors).

Buch „Philosophische Untersuchungen": „Für C.A., Schüler, Mentor und Schmuggler", in den Sinn kam. Als ich diese Widmung das erste Mal gesehen hatte vermutete ich schon, daß C.A. Carl Auer sein mußte. Aber weshalb „ Schmuggler"? Meine Frage war beantwortet.

Der Tanz der Flammen in der Feuerstelle hielt am Ende der Geschichte plötzlich meine Blicke gefangen. Ich erlaubte mir, in die Wärme des Feuers und des Augenblicks zu versinken, gefesselt von der vibrierenden Stille, die diesem privilegierten Eindringen durch einen Zeitsprung wie ein Nachbeben folgte. Nach einer Weile, noch immer in Trance, fragte ich Carl: „Und bist du jemals nach Monte Cassino zurückgekehrt?"

„Nach Monte Cassino? Nein, Das könnte ich nicht, selbst wenn ich es wollte. Man kann zu keinem Ort zweimal gehen, da es so etwas wie Orte, die bleiben, während die Zeit und man selbst, der Besucher, vergehen, nicht gibt. Tatsächlich", er unterbrach mich als ich gerade um Verzeihung bitten wollte, „hörte ich vor nicht allzu langer Zeit, wie Ludwigs Neffe Heinz[2] eine Variation von dem, was ich ihm einst gesagt hatte, präsentierte. Dir zuliebe wiederhole ich sie: man kann keinen Ort *einmal* besuchen - Heinz verwandelte es in 'man kann keinen Fluß *einmal* überqueren', aber das liegt wohl daran, daß er nicht naß werden will, oder? Es ist spät, Carlos, ich geh' jetzt ins Bett, wenn du nichts dagegen hast. Vielen Dank für deine Begleitung durch meine Geschichte. Mach' dir's bequem, du weißt wo Bar, Bad und Gästezimmer sind, falls du bleiben willst - draußen ist es ziemlich kühl. Jedenfalls, Fortsetzung folgt."

Wiederum war mir schwindlig von einem weiteren Schlag auf meinen geistigen Plexus. „Nur eine kurze Frage, antworte einfach mit 'ja' oder 'nein', Carl. Gehören dein 'ich habe noch nie ein Buch gelesen' und dein 'man kann zu keinem Ort einmal gehen' oder zweimal oder was weiß ich, zum selben Geschlecht?"

Auer schaute mich an, lächelte leicht mit zur Seite geneigtem Kopf. „Es ist spät, Carlos, quäle mich nicht", bat er.

Da ich nun mal so ein Heini bin, der sich für die Menschenrechte einsetzt, ließ ich das Thema fallen und wünschte ihm gute Nacht.

[1]Das 7. Kapitel aus Carlos E. Sluzki: *Die Nachzeichnung des Puzzles: Kamingespräche mit Carl Auer.* New York und Heidelberg, Neueman Verlag, 1990 (in Druck, zweisprachige Ausgabe). Hier abgedruckt mit Genehmigung des Autors und des Verlags.
[2]Heinz von Foerster (Anm. der Redaktion).

Proofs

Beweise

Carl Auer and the Ethics of the Pythagoreans

Heinz von Foerster

I am, of course, delighted that Carl Auer, this extraordinary, strange and extremely creative man, is at last being commemorated by this Festschrift. I am particularly grateful to the editors of this Festschrift for giving me the opportunity to present Carl Auer with my thanks for the strong influence he had on me in his early youth. Let me tell you how I met and got to know Carl Auer.

In my youth the Austrian school system was organized in such a way that all children started primary school ("Volksschule") at the age of five or six and stayed there for five years. After finishing primary school they moved up to the secondary school ("Mittelschule") for a further eight years, after which they could attend college, either university or technical college. I started primary school at about five years of age and spent the first four years at a state school. I was one of the worst pupils. To be more precise, I was not only *one of* the worst pupils. I was maybe even *the* worst pupil. I well remember having to sit at the very last desk. In front of me, at the last desk but one, sat two of the many orphans who came from an institution in Vienna where orphans were interned. Every morning a few minutes before eight they came marching along in their striped - horizontally striped - prison clothes. Their heads were shaved so that not even a few lice could stray onto or into their heads. Dieter Medwed, one of these pupils, sat in front of me, and he really didn't know the answer to one question. Yet I still had to sit behind him, for sometimes I knew an answer, but it was generally considered to be "impudent". On these occasions the teacher, Mr. Holzinger, would come towards me smiling kindly. He would twist the hair growing behind and in front

Carl Auer und die Ethik der Pythagoräer

Heinz von Foerster

Ich bin natürlich entzückt, daß schließlich und endlich diesem außerordentlichen, diesem seltsamen und äußerst kreativen Menschen, Carl Auer, durch diese Festschrift ein Denkmal gesetzt wird. Ich bin auch den Herausgebern dieser Festschrift besonders dankbar, daß sie es mir erlauben, meinen Dank an Carl Auer für seinen großen Einfluß, den er auf mich in seiner frühen Jugend gehabt hat, abzustatten. Lassen Sie mich kurz erzählen, in welcher Weise ich Carl Auer getroffen und kennengelernt habe.

In meiner Jugend war das österreichische Schulsystem so organisiert, daß alle Kinder so mit etwa fünf oder sechs Jahren in die Volksschule kamen, dort fünf Jahre lernten, nach Absolvieren der Volksschule dann in die Mittelschule übergeführt wurden, dort acht Jahre weiterlernten, bis sie dann, nach Beenden der Schule, auf die Hochschule gehen konnten, und zwar entweder auf die Universität oder auf die Technische Hochschule. Ich trat mit etwa fünf Jahren in die öffentliche Volksschule ein und verbrachte dort meine ersten vier Jahre. Ich war einer der schlechtesten Schüler. Genau gesagt, ich war nicht *einer* der schlechtesten Schüler, ich war vielleicht sogar *der* schlechteste Schüler. Ich erinnere mich noch sehr gut, wie ich in der allerletzten Bank sitzen mußte; vor mir in der vorletzten Bank saßen zwei der vielen Waisenkinder, die damals von einem Institut in Wien interniert worden waren. Die Kinder kamen an jedem Morgen ein paar Minuten vor acht in ihren gestreiften - quergestreiften - Sträflingsanzügen und mit ihren kahlgeschorenen Köpfen, damit nun ja nur nicht ein paar Läuse sich auf diese Köpfe verirren könnten, anmarschiert. Dieter Medwed, einer von diesen Schülern, saß vor mir. Er wußte wirklich auf keine Frage eine Antwort. Ich mußte aber hinter ihm sitzen, denn manchmal wußte ich zwar eine Antwort, die wurde aber gewöhnlich als 'frech' beurteilt. Und so kam dann der

of my ear together and pull me up by this hair, so that I had to climb onto the bench and then onto the desk to make me understand my impudence.

I didn't feel very happy in this school, so my parents decided to transfer me from primary school to secondary school a little earlier than normal. This was possible, but one had to take an examination if one wished to go to secondary school after just four years in primary school. The problem was, however, how could I, such a bad pupil, survive or pass this exam, the centerpiece of which was in mathematics.As I wasn't really that bad at math, my parents thought a few hours extra tuition would enable me to cope with the curriculum required for the exam. Thus it was suggested that a young man come to us as private tutor. His name was Carl Auer. He was recommended to my family as he was said to have been a very bad pupil too. He had failed several times and had had to repeat a year or two, but he was known to be very good in mathematics and physics. So it was that Carl Auer came to our house and began to prepare me for secondary school.

I had a lot of fun with this young man who not only knew a lot, but was also very interested in what interested me. I remember well that I was particularly interested in a certain mathematical step: the idea of proof. Carl was particularly skillful in introducing me to the "proof." We began with my having to prove the Pythagorean theorem. Carl introduced me to this proof by demonstrating the proof Socrates showed Menon. As you may remember, Pythagoras' theorem consists in proving that in a right triangle the sum of the squares above the two legs, a, b, namely $a^2 + b^2$, is equal in area to the square which can be drawn above the hypotenuse: c^2. This results in Pythagoras' theorem: $a^2 + b^2 = c^2$.

Lehrer Holzinger auf mich zu, freundlich lächelnd, drehte die Haare, die hinter meinem Ohr und vor meinem Ohr wuchsen, zusammen und zog mich an diesen Haaren langsam hoch, so daß ich zuerst die Bank und dann den Schreibtisch hinaufklettern mußte, um meine Frechheit zu verstehen.

Ich fühlte mich nicht sehr wohl in dieser Schule und so beschlossen meine Eltern, mich schon etwas früher aus der Volksschule in das Gymnasium überwechseln zu lassen. Das war möglich, aber man mußte eine Offenbarungsprüfung machen, wenn man nur vier Jahre in der Volksschule zugebracht hatte und dann schon ins Gymnasium gehen wollte. Das Problem war aber, wie ich, dieser schlechte Schüler, diese Offenbarungsprüfung überstehen oder bestehen konnte, deren Hauptteil eine Mathematikprüfung war. So dachten meine Eltern, da ich ja gar nicht so schlecht in Mathematik war, mir ein paar Nachhilfestunden geben zu lassen, so daß ich das Pensum, welches von mir verlangt wurde, tatsächlich bei dieser Offenbarungsprüfung bewältigen konnte. Mein Vater hatte gute Beziehungen zur Industrie, auch zur chemischen Industrie. Und so wurde vorgeschlagen, mir einen jungen Mann als einen Hauslehrer zukommen zu lassen: sein Name war Carl Auer. Er wurde deshalb unserer Familie empfohlen, weil er auch ein sehr schlechter Schüler gewesen sein soll. Er war in mehreren Fällen durchgefallen, hatte eine oder zwei Klassen wiederholen müssen, aber war bekannt dafür, in Mathematik und in Physik gut zu sein. So kam Carl Auer in unser Haus und begann, mich auf das Gymnasium vorzubereiten.

Ich hatte großen Spaß mit diesem jungen Menschen, der wirklich sehr viel wußte und sich sehr für meine Neigungen interessierte. Ich kann mich noch sehr gut erinnern, daß mich ein bestimmter Schritt in der Mathematik ausgesprochen interessierte: nämlich der „Beweis". Carl hatte eine besonders geschickte Weise, mich in diese Beweisidee einzuführen. Und zwar haben wir damit angefangen, daß ich den Pythagoräischen Lehrsatz beweisen sollte. Natürlich er hat mich in diese Beweistheorie damit eingeführt, daß er mir den Sokratischen Beweis, den Sokrates mit Menon auch durchgeführt hat, vorführte. Wie Sie sich erinnern, besteht dieser Pythagoräische Lehrsatz darin, daß man beweist, daß in einem rechtwinkligen Dreieck die Summe der Quadrate über den beiden Katheten, nämlich $a^2 + b^2$, flächengleich ist mit dem Quadrat über der Hypothenuse, c^2. Das gibt den berühmten Pythagoräischen Lehrsatz: $a^2 + b^2 = c^2$.

Socrates' proof consists in drawing squares above the hypotenuse and over the two legs in an isosceles right triangle (see Fig. 1), and showing that the area of the two small squares (each consisting of two isosceles right triangles) corresponds exactly to the area of the large square over the hypothenuse (consisting of four isosceles right triangles). I was so fascinated by this illustrative proof because I understood what it means when one 'sees' something: the idea of insight. One suddenly says: Aha, now I see how these relations come about. When you have understood this proof of Pythagoras' theorem for an isosceles right-triangle it is no longer difficult to understand this method of proof or a similar one for right triangles in general.

Fig. 1

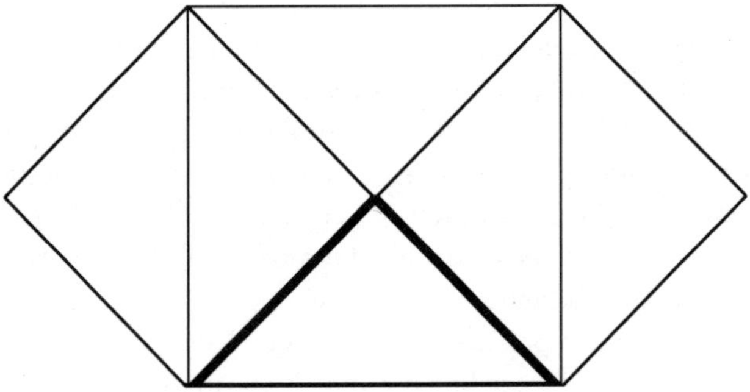

Carl Auer soon realized that this young boy had easy access to graphic and geometrical problems and that this shouldn't be exploited too far, but he should rather be given insight into algebraic relations. And so he taught me that, apart from these fascinating geometrical relations between a^2 and b^2 and c^2, there are also interesting algebraic relations. That, for example, there are whole numbers such as 3, 4 and 5 that have Pythagorean relations, namely: $3^2 + 4^2 = 5^2$. And that this relation not only exists for 3, 4 and 5, but for many other triples, such as 5, 12 and 13 or 7, 24 and 25, which all have in common that the sum of the square of the first two numbers equals the square of the third.

Der Sokratische Beweis besteht darin, daß man Quadrate über der Hypothenuse und den beiden Katheten eines gleichschenkligen und rechtwinkligen Dreiecks (siehe Abb. 1) zeichnet und damit aufzeigt, daß die Fläche der zwei kleinen Quadrate (jedes bestehend aus zwei gleichschenkligen und rechtwinkligen Dreiecken) exakt mit der Fläche des großen Quadrats über der Hypothenuse (bestehend aus vier gleichschenkligen und rechtwinkligen Dreiecken) korrespondiert. Mich hat dieser anschauliche Beweis so fasziniert, weil ich verstanden habe, was es bedeutet, wenn man etwas einsieht: die Idee der Einsicht. Man sagt plötzlich: Aha, jetzt sehe ich, wie es zu diesen Relationen kommt. Natürlich ist es dann auch gar nicht schwer, wenn man diese Einsicht des Pythagoräischen Lehrsatzes für ein rechtwinkliges Dreieck gesehen hat, daß man dann diese oder eine verwandte Beweismethode für allgemeine Dreiecke auch einsehen kann.

Abb. 1

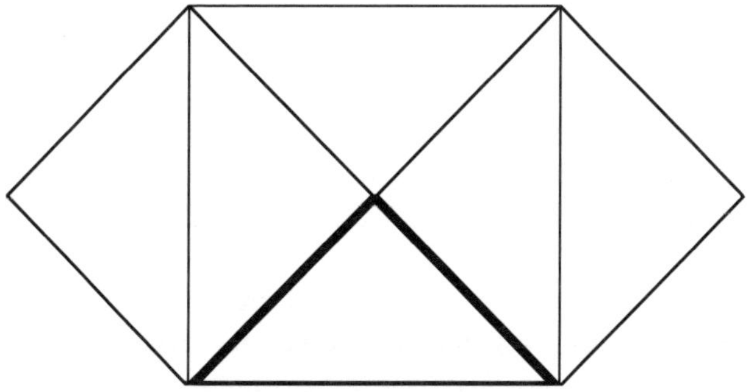

Bald hat Carl Auer gesehen, daß dieser kleine Bub, der ich war, einen leichten Zugang zu anschaulichen und geometrischen Problemen hat. Er wollte mir nun auch Einsicht in die algebraischen Relationen beibringen. So hat er mir sehr bald beigebracht, daß es neben diesen geometrisch faszinierenden Relationen zwischen a^2, b^2 und c^2 auch algebraisch interessante Relationen gibt. Er hat mir erklärt, daß es ganze Zahlen, wie z. B. 3, 4 und 5 gibt, die die Pythagoräische Relation haben, nämlich $3^2 + 4^2 = 5^2$, und daß es diese Beziehung außerdem auch zwischen vielen anderen, wie z. B. 5, 12 und 13 oder 7, 24 und 25 gibt. Für alle diese Dreiergruppen gilt, daß die Summe der Quadrate der ersten beiden, dem Quadrat der dritten Zahl gleich ist.

These mathematical somersaults were great fun. And when the time came for the examination I passed with no difficulty at all.

A few weeks later I was admitted to the secondary school. As was the custom at that time, each new pupil was introduced to the headmaster of the school. So I went in too, and the headmaster said: "You passed the math exam very nicely. We are happy to have you here. Who taught you math?" Proudly I replied: "Mr. Carl Auer." At that the headmaster immediately slapped me. He grabbed me by the ear, lead me out of the room and showed me the school's large yard. From there one could see that almost everywhere streaks of black ink had been smeared over the stone walls of the building from the windows of the third floor. And he hinted that these ink spots had been made by Carl Auer when he was a pupil of this school many years ago. He remarked: "Should you have learned characteristics other than those of a mathematician from your Carl Auer, I would advise you to get rid of them as soon as possible."

In spite of the headmaster's warning I continued my relationship with Carl Auer and went to see him evenings, or he came to us. We spoke about mathematical proofs of other problems.

One day I asked him: "Tell me, Carl, you introduced me to Pythagorean numbers, where you square two natural numbers and the sum of these two corresponds to the square of a third number. Are there higher powers, so that, for example, not only a^2 plus b^2 equals c^2, but maybe a^3 plus b^3 equals c^3. Are there any numbers, a, b, c, which fulfill this condition?"

He became very serious after I had asked this question. He kept absolutely quiet, then after a few minutes he said: "You have touched on a big problem that a great mathematician postulated 200 years ago. His name was Fermat. Fermat gave this problem a lot of thought and finally came to the conclusion that there are no such numbers. He reported the fact that he had come to this conclusion in the margin of a book in which this problem was posed. It must have been a text book on the theory of numbers in which Fermat wrote in the margin: "I can prove that for no exponents, n, larger than two are there three

Ich hatte großen Spaß bei diesen mathematischen Purzelbäumen. Und wie es nun schließlich zur Prüfung kam, habe ich sie ohne Schwierigkeiten bestanden.

Ein paar Wochen später wurde ich daher zum akademischen Gymnasium zugelassen. Und wie es damals üblich war, wurde jeder neue Ankömmling dem Direktor vom Gymnasium vorgestellt. So kam auch ich herein, und der Direktor hat gesagt: „Du hast sehr nett diese Mathematikprüfung bestanden. Wir freuen uns, dich hier zu haben. Wer hat dir denn die Mathematik beigebracht?" Stolz sagte ich: „Das war ein Herr Carl Auer." Worauf ich sofort eine Ohrfeige vom Direktor bekam. Er packte mich am Ohr, führte mich aus dem Zimmer heraus und zeigte mir den großen Hof des Gymnasiums. Dort konnte man sehen, daß von den Fenstern des dritten Stocks aus fast überall schwarze Tintenstriche über die Steinmauern des Gebäudes geschmiert waren. Und er deutete an, daß diese schwarzen Tintenflecke von Carl Auer gemacht wurden, als er vor vielen Jahren ein Schüler in dieser Schule war. Er bemerkte: „Solltest du andere Eigenschaften als die eines Mathematikers von deinem Carl Auer gelernt haben, dann würde ich sehr empfehlen, diese Eigenschaften so schnell als möglich abzulegen."

Trotz der Warnung des Direktors habe ich mein Verhältnis mit Carl Auer noch weiter fortgesetzt und ging abends zu ihm oder er kam zu uns. Dann haben wir uns über mathematische Beweise anderer Probleme unterhalten.

Eines schönen Tages fragte ich ihn: „Sag einmal, Carl, du hast mir diese Pythagoräischen Zahlen beigebracht, bei denen die Summe der Quadrate zwei natürlicher Zahlen dem Quadrat einer dritten Zahl entspricht. Gibt es höhere Potenzen, wie z. B. $a^3 + b^3 = c^3$, bei denen drei natürliche Zahlen, a, b, c, diese Bedingung erfüllen?"

Er wurde ganz ernst, nachdem ich ihn diese Frage gefragt hatte. Er war sogar ganz still und nach einigen Minuten sagte er: „Du hast ein ganz großes Problem berührt, das ein großer Mathematiker vor 200 Jahren schon einmal postuliert hat. Das war Fermat. Fermat hat sich über dieses Problem lange den Kopf zerbrochen und ist schließlich zu dem Schluß gekommen, daß es keine solchen Zahlen gibt. Und zwar hat er den Bericht, daß er zu diesem Schluß gekommen ist, am Rand eines Buches hingeschrieben, in dem dieses Problem aufgeworfen wurde. Das muß wohl ein Lehrbuch der Zahlentheorie gewe-

numbers $a^n + b^n = c^n$ so that this relation is valid for whole numbers. Unfortunately though the width of this margin is too narrow for me to set out the whole proof on this page."

During the 200 years since Fermat touched on this problem - it is generally referred to as "Fermat's Last Theorem" - ever more mathematicians have tried to work out this proof for themselves, but no one has ever succeeded. Such unsuccessful efforts of proof are, of course, a fascinating stimulus. And I asked myself straight away: How can Fermat's theorem be proved? And I asked Carl too:

"Now tell me, have you ever tried to prove this theorem?" For a long time he said nothing. Then he nodded and said: "Yes, I have tried." - "And, have you proved it?" - "Yes," he said, "I've proved it." - "Then why don't you publish it, for heaven's sake? Then all the mathematicians who have tried so hard to prove this theorem would be relieved at last!" - "Yes, I've thought about it a lot," Carl answered, "but I have decided not to publish it." - "But why not?" - "The proof could be written in the narrow margin of this paper." - "But that's . . . - Why don't you publish that too?" - "Fermat knew that too, of course," Carl replied, "and if he didn't want to write this proof in the margin of that page, then he must have known why this proof should not be written down. Who am I, Carl Auer, to write this proof down when Fermat decided not to?"

This ethical attitude of Carl Auer's impressed me deeply. Not until much later did I realize that it in fact corresponds to that of the Pythagoreans, who did not wish to impart their deeper insights to others unless they were sure they could not lead to social abuse. One not only finds this ethical position implicit in constructivism, but also in Ludwig Wittgenstein's *Tractatus Logico-Philosophicus*. Proposition 6.421 reads: "It is clear that ethics cannot be articulated" ("Es ist klar, daß sich Ethik nicht aussprechen läßt") That is, that at the very moment when one starts to talk "ethics", one begins to moralize. Then one always says how the *other* should behave: "*Thou* shalt" or "*Thou* shalt not!" But ethics is concerned with one's own behaviour, one can

sen sein. Dort schrieb Fermat auf den Rand: 'Ich kann zeigen, daß es für keinen Exponenten, der größer ist als zwei, drei natürliche Zahlen gibt, die die Beziehung $a^n + b^n = c^n$ erfüllen. Leider aber ist die Breite des Papierrandes hier zu schmal, daß ich den vollen Beweis auf dieser Seite ausführen könnte."

In den 200 Jahren, seitdem Fermat dieses Problem berührte - es wird gewöhnlich als Fermats letztes Theorem bezeichnet - haben Mathematiker und Mathematiker sich bemüht, diesen Beweis für sich selbst zu entwickeln, aber es ist niemandem gelungen. Solche ungeglückten Beweisversuche sind natürlich faszinierende Stimuli. Und ich habe mich natürlich sofort gefragt: Wie kann man diesen Fermatschen Satz beweisen. So hab ich Carl gefragt:

„Na, sag einmal, hast du dich schon einmal bemüht, diesen Satz zu beweisen?" Da ist er lange stumm geblieben, dann hat er genickt und gesagt: „Ja, ich habe mich bemüht." - „Na und, hast du ihn bewiesen?" - „Ja", sagte er, „ich habe ihn bewiesen." - „Ja, um Himmelswillen, warum publizierst du das nicht, dann würden doch diese vielen Mathematiker, die sich so bemühen, diesen Satz zu beweisen, endlich erlöst werden?" - „Ja, ich habe mir das sehr überlegt", antwortete Carl, „aber ich hab mich entschlossen, das nicht zu publizieren." - „Ja, warum denn?" - „Ja, der Beweis läßt sich auf den Rand, auf den schmalen Rand dieses Papieres schreiben." - „Ja, das ist doch, warum veröffentlichst du das nicht auch?" - „Ja, aber Fermat hat das natürlich auch gewußt, und wenn er diesen Beweis nicht auf den Rand des Papieres schreiben wollte, dann hat er wohl sehr gut gewußt, warum dieser Beweis nicht geschrieben werden soll. Woher soll ich, Carl Auer, dann diesen Beweis schreiben, wenn Fermat sich entschlossen hat, ihn nicht zu schreiben?"

Diese ethische Haltung Carl Auers hat mich tief beeindruckt. Und viel später habe ich dann gesehen, daß sie eigentlich der der Pythagoräer entspricht, die ja auch nicht ihre tieferen Einsichten anderen mitteilen wollten, nämlich anderen, von denen sie nicht sicher waren, ob sie diese Einsichten, nicht zu einem Mißbrauch (auch einem sozialen Mißbrauch) verwenden würden. Diese ethische Haltung ist implizit nicht nur im Konstruktivismus zu finden, sondern auch in Ludwig Wittgensteins „Tractatus Logico-Philosophicus". Satz 6.421: „Es ist klar, daß sich die Ethik nicht aussprechen läßt". Das heißt, im Moment, wo man über Ethik sprechen will, beginnt man ja schon zu moralisieren. Dann spricht man immer, wie sich *der andere* zu ver-

apply it only to oneself, i.e., you say to yourself: "I should" or "I should not!" That cannot be said to anyone else, you can only say it to yourself. Just as one can prove Fermat's theory for oneself, just as one can have many insights for oneself. The only thing one can do as a constructivist is to give others the opportunity to construct their own world. I think I owe these insights to Carl Auer's understanding, comprehensible and mild way of talking to me when I was a small boy about mathematics and its insights.

halten hat: *Du* sollst oder *du* sollst nicht. Aber die Ethik bezieht sich ja auf das eigene Verhalten, d. h. man sagt zu sich selbst: Ich soll oder ich soll nicht. Das kann nicht zu anderen gesagt werden, das kann man nur zu sich selbst sagen. So, wie man das Fermatsche Prinzip für sich selber beweisen kann, so wie man für sich selber viele andere Einsichten haben kann. Das einzige, was man machen kann als ein Konstruktivist, ist anderen die Gelegenheit zu geben, ihre eigene Welt zu konstruieren. Diese Einsichten verdanke ich, glaube ich, Carl Auers verständnisvoller, einsichtsvoller und milder Art, mit mir als kleinem Buben über die Mathematik und ihre Einsichten zu sprechen.

Carl/a Auer: An Invention

Donald A. Bloch

My recollection of Auer as you will see is ambiguous. But it may help to knit up the strands of others' memories.

Students of this fascinating life have assembled such varied remembrances that one might, the historical evidence notwithstanding, believe that Carl/a Auer is a fiction, a dream figure in our collective dream. It is hard to think of anyone who would be more amused by this than Auer and at the same time who would take it more seriously. Auer might well say that if we think we have dreamed him, perhaps we should think again, maybe he has dreamed us. Or, more soberly, dreamed himself.

My life intersected with his in 1948. Just back from a year of internship I was a new, very young and very eager resident at the Chestnut Lodge Sanitarium, a psychoanalytic hospital set in the lovely rolling countryside of Maryland, just outside of Washington D.C. The Lodge had rapidly evolved in those post-war years into a flourishing intellectual nursery. I have often wondered why, since Chestnut Lodge (or The Lodge as we all called it) was an unlikely site for this flowering and Dexter Means Bullard an unlikely leader.

In any case, the Lodge had existed in its previous incarnation as a drying out spa for alcoholic Congressmen and other illustrious residents of Washington D.C. Following the close of World War II the city was in the early stages of a transformation from a sleepy post-Civil War small town into the glamorous world capitol and suburban sprawl it would become in the next decades. Dexter Bullard, who had

Carl/a Auer: Eine Erfindung

Donald A. Bloch

Wie Sie sehen werden, habe ich keine eindeutigen Erinnerungen an Auer. Aber vielleicht helfen sie, die Erinnerungen anderer aufzufrischen.

Von den Menschen, die dieses faszinierende Leben studiert haben, wurden so unterschiedliche Erinnerungen zusammengetragen, daß man trotz der historischen Zeugnisse glauben könnte, Carl/a Auer sei eine Fiktion, eine Traumfigur in unserem kollektiven Traum. Man kann sich kaum vorstellen, daß sich jemand mehr darüber amüsieren und es gleichzeitig ernster nehmen würde als Auer. Auer könnte z.B. sagen, daß wir, falls wir ihn für eine Traumfigur halten, besser nochmals darüber nachdenken sollten, denn es könnte sein, daß er uns erträumt habe, oder - nüchterner - sich selbst erträumt habe.

Unsere Lebenswege kreuzten sich 1948. Ich hatte gerade, direkt im Anschluß an mein Medizinalpraktikum, als neuer, sehr junger und sehr eifriger Assistenzarzt am Chestnut Lodge Sanatorium angefangen, einem psychoanalytischen Krankenhaus, das in der wunderschönen, sanften Hügellandschaft Marylands außerhalb von Washington D.C. lag. Die „Lodge" hatte sich in jenen Nachkriegsjahren rasch zu einem blühenden intellektuellen Garten entwickelt. Ich habe mich oft gefragt wieso, da Chestnut Lodge (oder die „Lodge", wie wir sie alle nannten) kein passender Ort für dieses Blühen war und Dexter Means Bullard kein passender Leiter.

Jedenfalls hatte die „Lodge" in ihrer früheren Inkarnation als Kurort zur Trockenlegung alkoholabhängiger Kongressabgeordneter und anderer illustrer Einwohner von Washington D.C. gedient. Nach dem Ende des zweiten Weltkriegs fing die Stadt gerade an, sich von der verschlafenen Kleinstadt aus den Zeiten nach dem Bürgerkrieg in die glamouröse Weltstadt mit wildwuchernden Vororten zu

inherited the Sanitarium from his father, chose to change its character as well and make the hospital into a world capital of psychoanalytic treatment for schizophrenics and other seriously disordered folks. He infused the hospital with the bizarre notion that one could treat such patients with intensive psychotherapy or psychoanalysis. Bullard was guided in this by the quirky American genius Harry Stack Sullivan and by the brilliant European psychoanalysts and philosophers he had imported before, during and immediately after World War II.

Frieda Fromm-Reichman was the most illustrious of this group. I believe she introduced Bullard to Auer, whom she had known as a brilliant colleague before her flight from Germany, but I may be wrong about that.

Rumor had it that Auer had worked on some kind of wartime cryptoanalysis device. Perhaps he had been a collaborator of Turing on the Enigma machine. We were never to know although certainly the term Enigma was appropriate for him. The notion of breaking obscure codes appealed to us as we tried to understand the language of madness.

As young psychiatrists in training we were possessed, drawn into the phantasmagoric fields where our lives and the lives of our patients intersected. This was particularly true at the "Lodge" since the notion of the interpersonal field was a given. Psychometabolic rates were unimaginably high. Most of us suffered from the *furor interpretandis*; all of us were driven to be therapeutically successful, as therapists and as patients, since we all were being psychoanalyzed at the same time. I recall Don Jackson and Harold Searles, who had the same training analyst, in a dry debate as to who had been *best* and who had been *most* analyzed. And (unlike now?) we believed in our current myths: the vaginal orgasm reigned supreme, the clitoris was a rudimentary organ of infantile female sexuality, homosexuality was a disease, and the dual career family laudable but unworkable. We believed in reality, even though it was the reality of Sullivan's consensual validation.

verwandeln, die sie in den nächsten Jahrzehnten werden sollte. Dexter Bullard, der das Sanatorium von seinem Vater geerbt hatte, entschloß sich, dessen Charakter zu ändern und aus dem Sanatorium ein Weltzentrum der psychoanalytischen Behandlung Schizophrener und anderer schwer gestörter Menschen zu machen. Er vermittelte dem Krankenhaus die seltsame Vorstellung, daß man solche Patienten mit intensiver Psychotherapie oder Psychoanalyse behandeln könnte. Dabei wiesen ihm das schrullige amerikanische Genie, Harry Stack Sullivan, und die brillanten europäischen Psychoanalytiker und Philosophen, die er während und unmittelbar nach dem zweiten Weltkrieg importiert hatte, den Weg.

Frieda Fromm-Reichman war wohl die Berühmteste in dieser Gruppe. Ich meine, daß sie es war, die Bullard mit Auer, den sie vor ihrer Flucht aus Deutschland als brillanten Kollegen gekannt hatte, bekannt machte; ich kann mich aber auch irren.

Es gab das Gerücht, daß Auer an militärischen Entschlüsselungscodes gearbeitet hätte. Vielleicht war er ein Mitarbeiter Turings an der Enigma-Maschine. Wir sollten es nie erfahren, obwohl der Begriff Enigma auf ihn sicherlich zutraf. Uns gefiel die Vorstellung, obskure Kodes zu entschlüsseln, während wir versuchten, die Sprache des Wahnsinns zu verstehen.

Als junge Psychiater in der Ausbildung wurden wir von den phantasmagorischen Feldern, in denen sich unsere Lebenslinien mit den Lebenslinien unserer Patienten schnitten, unweigerlich angezogen. Dies war besonders in der „Lodge" der Fall, da die Idee des zwischenmenschlichen Feldes vorausgesetzt wurde. Die psychometabolischen Werte waren unvorstellbar hoch. Die meisten von uns litten an *furor interpretandis*; wir wollten alle unbedingt therapeutisch erfolgreich sein, als Therapeuten und als Patienten, da wir alle zur gleichen Zeit analysiert wurden. Ich erinnere mich, wie Don Jackson und Harold Searles, die denselben Ausbildungsanalytiker hatten, in einer trockenen Debatte darüber stritten, wer denn *am besten* und wer *am meisten* analysiert worden sei. Wir glaubten (im Gegensatz zu heute?) an unsere jeweiligen Mythen: Der vaginale Orgasmus herrschte unumstritten, die Klitoris war ein rudimentäres Organ der infantilen weiblichen Sexualität. Homosexualität war eine Krankheit und die Idee von der Familie, in der beide Partner berufstätig sind, war zwar lobenswert, aber nicht zu verwirklichen. Wir glaubten an die Realität, selbst wenn es sich um die Realität von Sullivans konsensueller Validierung handelte.

Into this steamy and overwrought atmosphere (I have not mentioned our stressed marriages, personal ambitions, and economically precarious situations nor our involvement in the psychoanalytic training wars of those days) Auer materialized. A few months after I arrived, I shall never forget that, Auer materialized. First he wasn't there and then slowly he was. Much in the same fashion less than a year later he dematerialized, on his way to Berkeley it was said.

I would say that Auer made a great impression on me and on the rest of us. He was cool and we were fevered. We were smart enough but he was, how shall I put it, cerebral. His clothing was distinctive; he favored suits that were a bit large on him and that had an unusual European cut. While an aroma of dark deeds, espionage, and double agentry clung to him, he seemed to be a totally gentle person. In some funny way he seemed to always be in soft focus; it was hard to see him but hard to know why that was so. For example, his wartime history was never spoken about and now I cannot recall how that became part of our image of him.

During the early months of his short tenure at the Lodge I tried not to notice him. His coolness contrasted unfavorably with my agitated intensity and I always found myself feeling inadequate in his presence. Towards the end, by contrast, I found myself seeking him out, as if somehow I could learn a great lesson about myself through him.

His role, if such it can be called, was to be a Scholar in Residence. Bullard was a marvel at identifying interesting talents and then letting them sort themselves out. Auer fitted into this scheme well since nothing more was required of him than to be present. It soon became clear that what interested him at the hospital was definitely not therapy. He set about conducting an inquiry into the nature of sanity.

The inquiry was finely grained, carried out by what he called "little conversations." When present Auer was always quietly speaking with one other person, occasionally a staff member but much more commonly a patient. I can still see him, elbows on folded knees,

In dieser erhitzten und überdrehten Atmosphäre (ich habe weder unsere schwierigen Ehen, persönlichen Ambitionen und finanziell prekären Situationen noch unsere Beteiligung an den psychoanalytischen Ausbildungskriegen jener Tage erwähnt) tauchte Auer auf. Einige Monate nachdem ich angekommen war, ich werde das nie vergessen, materialisierte Auer. Zuerst war er nicht da, und dann war er langsam da. Es heißt, daß er ein knappes Jahr später auf seinem Weg nach Berkeley auf eine sehr ähnliche Art und Weise wieder dematerialisierte.

Auer machte auf mich und die anderen großen Eindruck. Er war cool und wir waren im Fieber. Wir waren recht kluge Köpfe, aber er, wie soll ich das sagen, er war durchgeistigt. Er kleidete sich unverwechselbar. Er bevorzugte Anzüge, die ihm ein wenig zu groß waren, mit einem ungewöhnlichen europäischen Schnitt. Obwohl er von der Aura dunkler Taten, der Spionage und des Doppelagententums umgeben war, war er ein völlig sanfter Mensch. Er schien immer irgendwie in einer weichen Wirklichkeit zu leben. Man konnte ihn nur schlecht sehen und wußte nicht so recht, weshalb das so war. So wurde beispielsweise niemals über seine Kriegserlebnisse gesprochen, und ich kann mich jetzt nicht mehr erinnern, wie diese zu einem Teil unseres Bildes von ihm wurden.

Während der ersten Monate seiner kurzen Anstellung in der „Lodge" versuchte ich, ihn zu übersehen. Seine Distanziertheit stellte meine aufgeregte Intensität in ein schlechtes Licht, und ich fühlte mich in seiner Gegenwart immer inadäquat. Gegen Ende suchte ich jedoch seine Nähe, als ob ich durch ihn eine Menge über mich selbst lernen könnte.

Seine Rolle, wenn man das so nennen kann, war die eines „Scholars in Residence". Bullard war ein Genie im Aufspüren interessanter Talente, denen er Zeit ließ, mit sich zurechtzukommen. Auer paßte sehr gut in dieses Schema, denn es wurde nichts von ihm verlangt, als anwesend zu sein. Es wurde bald deutlich, daß es ganz bestimmt nicht die Therapie war, die ihn im Krankenhaus interessierte. Er führte eine Untersuchung über das Wesen der geistigen Gesundheit durch.

Die Untersuchung war fein abgestimmt und wurde, wie er es nannte, durch „kleine Unterhaltungen" durchgeführt. Wenn er da war, unterhielt sich Auer immer ruhig mit irgend jemandem, gelegentlich mit jemandem vom Personal, meistens aber mit einem

thin body, somehow swimming in his habitually oversized grey suits, intently leaning towards his "conversational companion." He would use this latter phrase to politely introduce you to whomever he happened to be speaking with, usually forgetting that you knew them. He had the ability to create a quiet private island even in a hallway streaming with staff and patient psychosis.

In those days severely disturbed patients were commonly quieted down by barbiturates, chloral hydrate and cold wet sheet packs, the wonderful discoveries of latter-day psychopharmacology having not yet been made. Auer would have his "little conversations" anywhere, in seclusion rooms or under a tree on the lawn. And at any hour. They would last for a few minutes or in one instance with a patient of mine for 26 hours. My patient was also a European, a frighteningly paranoid young man, large, blond and fierce, who barely tolerated me.

The 26-hour-"little conversation" began before dawn as the nurses informed me when I arrived at the usual time. Frederick, my patient, had been "dangerously upset" and had been wrestled into a cold wet sheet pack where he promptly became mute. When I arrived on the ward several hours later he and Auer were sitting up still in the seclusion room. (Fear seemed somehow irrelevant to Auer, although he did not seem particularly incautious.) I gather the talk had continued all the while the nurses were unwinding the sheets as if they were not there.

In each of his "little conversations" he was always the student being instructed by the patient, or even me, about something and always quietly pleased when he would "get it." Thus the next day he said to me, "Prince Frederick, (Did I know that he was a prince?) uses large primes to make code breaking difficult." Large primes, code breaking? I had an idea that Auer was a mathematician and cryptographer. (Did I know that about my patient?) Auer went on "and about the blood lines of several royal houses that I have never been able to decipher." Then silence, and "funny how codes seemed to get into it all the time." Frederick left the Lodge shortly thereafter. I do not remember if he improved, or if his family ran out of funds, or both.

Patienten. Ich sehe ihn noch vor mir, den Ellbogen auf die übereinandergeschlagenen Knie gestützt, sein magerer Körper in seinen immer zu großen grauen Anzügen fast ertrinkend, gespannt zu seinem „Gesprächspartner“ hinübergebeugt. Er benutzte diesen Ausdruck, um denjenigen höflich vorzustellen, mit dem er sich gerade unterhielt, und vergaß gewöhnlich, daß man ihn ja ohnehin kannte. Er hatte die Fähigkeit, selbst in einem Flur, der von Mitarbeiter- und Patientenpsychosen wimmelte, eine ruhige, private Insel zu schaffen.

In jenen Tagen wurden schwer gestörte Patienten gewöhnlich mit Barbituraten, Chloralhydrat und feuchten, kalten Umschlägen mit Leintüchern ruhig gestellt, da die wunderbaren Entdeckungen moderner Psychopharmakologie noch nicht gemacht worden waren. Auer führte seine „kleinen Unterhaltungen“ überall, in der Isolierzelle oder auf dem Rasen unter einem Baum. Und zu jeder Zeit. Manchmal dauerten sie nur einige Minuten oder aber, wie mit einem meiner Patienten, 26 Stunden. Mein Patient war ebenfalls Europäer, ein furchterregend paranoider junger Mann, groß, blond und wild, der mich nur gerade eben tolerierte.

Die 26 Stunden dauernde „kleine Unterhaltung“ begann vor Sonnenaufgang, wie ich aus der Notiz der Schwester erfuhr, als ich zur üblichen Zeit kam. Frederick, mein Patient, hatte sich „gefährlich erregt“ und war in einen feuchten, kalten Umschlag gezwungen worden, wo er sofort zahm wurde. Als ich einige Stunden später auf die Station kam, saßen er und Auer immer noch ruhig zusammen in der Isolierzelle (Furcht schien Auer überhaupt nicht zu kennen, obwohl er auch keinen übermäßig unvorsichtigen Eindruck erweckte). Ich vermute, daß sich die beiden weiter unterhielten, während die Schwestern ihn aus den Laken wickelten - so als ob es sie nicht gäbe.

In jeder „kleinen Unterhaltung“ war er der Student, der vom Patienten oder sogar von mir über etwas belehrt wurde, und er zeigte sich immer auf seine leise Art erfreut, wenn er „kapierte“, worum es ging. So sagte er mir am nächsten Tag: „Prinz Frederick (ob ich wüßte, daß er ein Prinz sei?) verwendet hohe Primzahlen, um das Entschlüsseln der Kodes zu erschweren.“ Hohe Primzahlen, Entschlüsseln von Kodes? Mir war wohl vage bekannt, daß Auer Mathematiker und Ver- bzw. Entschlüsseler war. (Ob ich das von meinem Patienten wüßte?) Auer fuhr fort: „ . . . und über die Blutsverwandtschaften verschiedener Königshäuser, die ich nie entschlüsseln konnte.“ Dann schwieg er und sagte schließlich: „Seltsam, wie man immer wieder

Now here is the story I have been meaning to get to. It took place within a few weeks of Auer's scheduled departure from the Lodge. I was a young man in an off-again, on-again marriage, working very hard, almost always sleep-deprived and a bit giddy when the rare social invitation came along. Most entertaining in Washington then went on in private homes. This evening there was a large formal party at a diplomat's residence and I was among the social supernumeraries, invited largely because my father had been a Foreign Service Officer.

Towards the end of a long evening when I was slightly drunk, more exhausted than words can describe, but still game for an adventure if one could be had, I realized that for a time I had been aware of a woman who, through the dense crowd and the haze of cigarette smoke, kept swinging in and out of focus in the middle distance across the room. I felt erotic interest; I tried to focus. And then a totally unwanted and alien thought erected itself in my mind. I became intensely uncomfortable: the insistent thought was that the woman was Carl Auer. Such a strange thought, but I did not seem to be able to stop thinking it. Nor could I stop thinking the other thought; was this what madness was like?

I swam towards her through the crowd feeling more foolish and awkward as I came closer. But the sense that I knew her persisted. She was his height and body build. Could the mass of dark hair be a wig? What nonsense! Her manner was as unlike Auer's as could be, agitated, flirtatious, with rapid small movements, turning from one to another of the group who surrounded her, telling jokes, I guess, because I remember laughter. I edged closer. Her name? Carla, I thought I heard. Then my rising panic swept me away.

auf Kodes stößt." Kurz darauf verließ Frederick die „Lodge". Ich kann mich nicht erinnern, ob es ihm besser ging oder ob seiner Familie die Mittel ausgegangen waren oder beides.

Hier ist jetzt die Geschichte, die ich eigentlich erzählen wollte. Sie ereignete sich einige Wochen vor Auers geplanter Abreise von der „Lodge". Ich war ein junger Mann, dessen Ehe sehr wechselhaft verlief, der hart arbeitete, fast immer zu wenig Schlaf hatte und den es immer ein wenig schwindelte, wenn er eine der seltenen gesellschaftlichen Einladungen erhielt. Die meisten Gesellschaften wurden damals in Washington in Privathäusern gegeben. An diesem Abend gab es einen großen Empfang im Haus eines Diplomaten, und ich war unter den zahllosen gesellschaftlichen Namenlosen, lediglich deshalb eingeladen, weil mein Vater Beamter des Auswärtigen Dienstes gewesen war.

Gegen Ende eines langen Abends, als ich leicht angetrunken war, unbeschreiblich erschöpft, aber immer noch für ein Abenteuer zu haben, wenn es sich ergeben sollte, wurde mir klar, daß ich seit einer Weile eine Frau bemerkt hatte, die durch die dichte Menge und den Dunstschleier des Zigarettenrauchs in mittlerer Entfernung im Zimmer gegenüber immer wieder in mein Blickfeld rückte und wieder daraus verschwand. Ich fühlte mich erotisch angezogen. Ich versuchte klar zu sehen. Und dann richtete sich ein völlig ungewollter und fremder Gedanke in meinem Kopf auf. Ich begann mich extrem unwohl zu fühlen: Der hartnäckige Gedanke war, daß die Frau Carl Auer war. Welch ein seltsamer Gedanke, aber ich schien ihn nicht unterdrücken zu können. Noch konnte ich einen anderen Gedanken unterdrücken: Sah so der Wahnsinn aus?

Ich zwängte mich durch die Menge zu ihr hin, wobei ich mich immer dümmer und verlegener fühlte, je näher ich kam. Aber das Gefühl, daß ich sie kannte, ließ mich nicht los. Sie war so groß wie er und hatte seine Figur. Konnte es sich bei der Masse dunklen Haares um eine Perücke handeln? Welch ein Unsinn! Ihre Art sich zu bewegen hätte sich nicht stärker von der Auers unterscheiden können, aufgeregt, flirtend, mit raschen, kurzen Bewegungen, sich in der Gruppe, die sie umgab, von einem zum anderen wendend, Witze erzählend, nehme ich an, denn ich kann mich an Gelächter erinnern. Ich drängte mich näher. Ihr Name? Carla, vermeinte ich zu hören. Dann riß mich meine aufsteigende Panik fort.

Auer as a drag queen? The idea was weird and abhorrent. Not Auer? Why did the thought persist? What was happening to me? Perhaps he was still an espionage agent; the prodromal signs of that mania could already be seen in Washington. I left, of course, but for days off and on I felt adrift, as if I had slipped my moorings. My analyst was of no help: after a longer than usual silence she mumbled something about "ambivalence" and "projection" as I remember it.

Something needed to be done, if possible. As I recall Auer was leaving shortly for Berkeley. A few days before his departure when an opportune moment presented itself, we had our last little conversation. I asked Auer if he had a sister. "No," he replied. Why was that wash of sadness in his voice. And then he absolutely startled me by adding after a brief silence, "no longer."

Confusion again, this time with an overwhelming tenderness as well, for somehow he evoked that. "Goodbye Carla," I said and gasped. There was a long silence and then he said, "You know, Don, if you are going to invent your life it is necessary not only to think it." Then he paused and smiled his Gioconda smile and asked gently, "don't you think?"

I have never stopped wondering: Had Carl invented Carla or perhaps Carla Carl? Or, had I invented both. Perhaps other contributors to this memorial can help.

Auer als Tunte? Die Vorstellung war verrückt und abstoßend. Nicht Auer? Weshalb wurde ich den Gedanken nicht los? Was geschah mit mir? Vielleicht war er immer noch ein Spion. Die prodromalen Zeichen dieses Wahns konnte man in Washington schon sehen. Ich ging natürlich, aber noch Tage später fühlte ich mich ziellos, als ob ich von meinem Ankerplatz losgerissen worden wäre. Meine Analytikerin konnte mir nicht helfen: Nach einem Schweigen, das länger gedauert hatte als gewöhnlich, murmelte sie etwas von „Ambivalenz“ und „Projektion“, wenn ich mich recht erinnere.

Es mußte etwas geschehen. Soviel ich wußte, sollte Auer in Kürze nach Berkeley gehen. Einige Tage vor seiner Abreise, als sich eine günstige Gelegenheit ergab, hatten wir unsere letzte kleine Unterhaltung. Ich fragte Auer, ob er eine Schwester habe. „Nein“, antwortete er. Weshalb war dieser Anflug von Traurigkeit in seiner Stimme? Und dann erschreckte er mich vollkommen, indem er nach einer kurzen Pause hinzufügte, „nicht mehr.“

Wieder war ich völlig verwirrt, dieses Mal vermischt mit einer überwältigenden Zärtlichkeit. Irgendwie rief er dieses Gefühl hervor. „Auf Wiedersehen, Carla“, sagte ich und hielt den Atem an. Es war eine Weile still und dann sagte er: „Weißt du, Don, wenn man sein Leben erfindet, dann ist es notwendig, es nicht nur zu denken.“ Dann hielt er inne und lächelte sein Gioconda-Lächeln und fragte sanft: „Meinst du nicht?“

Ich habe mich immer gefragt: Hatte Carl Carla erfunden oder vielleicht Carla Carl? Oder hatte ich beide erfunden. Vielleicht können andere, die zu dieser Denkschrift beitragen, helfen.

Voices

David Epston

4/8/89

Dear Michael,[1]

I received your letter today with a copy of Gunthard Weber's request for our reminiscences of Carl Auer. I guess it's not really a surprise as Auer is a hard person to forget. Like so many people say about their encounters with Milton Erickson, his thoughts 'go with you,' seemingly poised to burst to life by the appropriate circumstances. Don't worry; such was the strange spell he cast over me that I did save our correspondence from 1985 and I didn't have to dig down too deep in my filing cabinet before I dug them up.

And what do you think of this? Coincidence? Or paranormal? Today, I met for the second time a 35-year-old man, oppressed by an obligation life-style. He told me he had been a "little less under the obligation of his obligation life-style" since we last met. He hears "voices" which persuade him that he has an unpaid debt to a friend or has left the door of a friend's refrigerator ajar. At times, the "voices" add insults such as "dummy", "cheat", "rip-off artist", "irresponsible", "careless". As he put it, "they have ways to bring me around to their way of thinking." I 'collapsed time' with him and he said that if he was convinced by his "voices" more, his own sphere of influence would contract so that in the end he wouldn't be able to escape from his bed and his "voices" would totally prevail over him. But, in reflecting on this dismal prospect, he recalled a "unique outcome." And was it unique! Keep reading!

Stimmen

David Epston

4.8.1989

Lieber Michael,[1]

ich habe heute Deinen Brief mit einer Kopie von Gunthard Webers Bitte um unsere Erinnerungen an Carl Auer erhalten. Eigentlich ist das gar nicht so sehr überraschend, da Auer jemand ist, den man nicht so leicht vergißt. Wie soviele Menschen über ihre Begegnungen mit Milton Erickson berichten, „begleiten dich seine Gedanken", offensichtlich bereit, im richtigen Moment hervorzusprießen. Keine Angst, er hat mich so mit seinem seltsamen Zauber gefangen genommen, daß ich tatsächlich unsere Korrespondenz aus dem Jahre 1985 aufbewahrt habe und ich mußte nicht einmal so tief unten in meinem Aktenschrank graben, um sie hervorzukramen.

Und was hältst Du davon? Zufall? Oder paranormal? Ich habe heute zum zweitenmal einen 35 Jahre alten Mann gesehen, der sich von zwanghaften Verpflichtungsgefühlen bedrängt sah. Er sagte mir, daß er „diesem Lebensstil, der ihm viele Verpflichtungen auferlegte" seit unserem letzten Zusammentreffen „etwas weniger verpflichtet" sei. Er hört „Stimmen", die ihn davon überzeugen, daß er einem Freund gegenüber eine unbeglichene Schuld habe, oder daß er die Tür des Kühlschrankes eines Freundes habe offen stehen lassen. Gelegentlich fügen die „Stimmen" auch Beleidigungen, wie „Doofmann", „Betrüger", „Halsabschneider", „verantwortungslos", „nachlässig" hinzu. Wie er sagt, haben sie gewisse Mittel, ihn so herumzukriegen, daß er denke wie sie. Ich übersprang in Gedanken einige Jahrzehnte mit ihm, und er sagte, je mehr er von seinen „Stimmen" überzeugt sei, um so mehr schrumpfe sein eigener Einflußbereich zusammen, so daß er schließlich nicht mehr in der Lage sei, seinem Bett zu entfliehen, und seine „Stimmen" ihn ganz und gar beherrschten. Während er über diese trüben Aussichten nachdachte,

He recalled travelling in Europe last year: "When I was troubled by my voices nagging me about things, I reached the conclusion that I should start challenging the reality of the voices - their allegations against me. When I started putting up a counter-case, I could sometimes break away from their grip." I asked my usual question: "How did you discover this? How did you make this discovery?"

He told me he had been hiking near Heidelberg and was resting at a *gasthaus*, perched overlooking the Neckar river. As usual, when he had paid for his *schnapps*, his 'voices' started harrassing him about whether he had paid up or not and he persisted in asking the waiter if he had done so. He could not be reassured. He had been travelling for so long now that he had got into the habit of talking aloud without being aware of it. An elderly man in *lederhosen* leaning on a stout walking stick was sitting nearby and finally turned to him and - in a reasonable version of New Zealand English - said: "Gidday, mate! Your 'voices' are not a matter for psychiatry. They are a matter for rhetoric - the art of persuasion." My client was taken aback on a number of counts, least of all this man's appearance. The description should have given him away but it didn't.

I was dumbstruck myself as his story unfolded. After a brief discussion (or was it a consultation), he suggested my client do the following: that he should invite them (the "voices") to attend a recording session, pointing to my client's tape recorder. When my client queried their willingness to accept his invitation, the man advised him to incite them by acting like a "bad boy." He said that my client might consider that the "voices" had something of importance to tell him. He proposed my client then record them into what he called "your little machine" and then submit them to close scrutiny, especially their rhetorical aspects. My client had little knowledge of rhetoric so the old man, thanks to a classical education, assisted him at some length. He then advised him to tape his own "voice," a voice that presents "your counter-case," as he called it. These are my words

fiel ihm jedoch ein „einzigartiges Ergebnis" ein. Es war wahrhaftig einzigartig. Lies weiter:

Er erinnerte sich an seine Europareise im letzten Jahr: „Wenn ich von meinen Stimmen, die an mir herumnörgelten, belästigt wurde, entschied ich mich, die Realität der Stimmen in Zweifel zu ziehen, bzw. ihre Behauptungen mir gegenüber. Als ich dann Gegenargumente startete, konnte ich mich manchmal aus ihrem Bann befreien". Ich stellte die Frage, die ich immer stelle: „Wie haben Sie das herausgefunden? Wie haben Sie diese Entdeckung gemacht?"

Er erzählte mir, er hätte im Odenwald in der Nähe von Heidelberg eine Wanderung unternommen und in einem Gasthaus mit Neckarblick Rast gemacht. Nachdem er seinen Schnaps bezahlt hätte, hätten ihn seine „Stimmen" schikaniert, ob er denn schon bezahlt habe oder nicht und er hätte den Ober immer wieder fragen müssen, ob er bezahlt habe. Man habe ihn nicht beruhigen können. Er sei zu dieser Zeit schon so lange auf Reisen gewesen, daß er sich ohne es zu merken angewöhnt habe, laut mit sich selbst zu sprechen. Ein älterer Mann in Lederhosen hätte, auf einen kräftigen Spazierstock gestützt, in der Nähe gesessen und sich schließlich mit einem recht brauchbaren neuseeländischen Englisch an ihn gewandt: „Wie geht's, mein Freund? Ihre Stimmen sind keine Sache für die Psychiatrie, sondern eine Angelegenheit der Rhetorik . . . der Überredungskunst." Mein Klient war aus verschiedenen Gründen verblüfft, wobei ihn die äußere Erscheinung dieses alten Mannes noch am wenigsten wunderte. Die Beschreibung hätte ihn verraten müssen, das war aber nicht der Fall.

Selbst mir verschlug der Fortgang der Geschichte die Sprache. Nach einer kurzen Diskussion (oder war es eine Konsultation) habe er meinem Klienten folgendes zu tun empfohlen: Er sollte sie (die „Stimmen") zu einer Tonbandaufnahme einladen. Dabei deutete er auf den Kassettenrekorder meines Klienten. Als mein Klient deren Bereitschaft, dieser Einladung zu folgen, in Frage stellte, hätte der Mann empfohlen, sie dadurch aufzuwiegeln, daß er sich wie ein „böser Junge" aufführe. Er sagte, mein Klient dürfe annehmen, daß ihm die „Stimmen" etwas Wichtiges mitzuteilen hätten. Er schlug vor, mein Klient solle sie dann mit dem, was er seine „kleine Maschine" nannte, aufnehmen und sie einer genauen Prüfung unterziehen, vor allem in Hinblick auf ihre rhetorischen Aspekte. Mein Klient hatte nur geringe Kenntnisse von Rhetorik, deshalb unterstützte ihn der

but the old man said something to the effect that he imagined his "voice" would argue again his further submitting to obligation and its side-effects. He said: "Give voice to your advocate's voice and tape it likewise." He then proposed that he study his "case" for a free life, free from the impoverishment of obligation and always measuring up to others' expectations.

I don't know why I am going into such detail because the important thing was that this was so close to the conversation I had with Auer on my way from Christchurch to Auckland in 1985. Remember, you flew directly to Adelaide and we parted company in the airport. It just had to be old Auer and when I checked some details, sure enough it was. What do you think of all this? What do you think of Auer's "therapy"? You know what they say about Auer that "once met, never forgotten." Auer's life is like a Dickens novel in its dependence upon coincidence. Flabberghasting, is it not?

Yours Auer-ly,

PS: Find enclosed my letter from Oct. 9, 1985.

alte Mann dank seiner humanistischen Bildung dabei. Er habe ihm dann geraten, seine eigene „Stimme“ aufzunehmen, eine Stimme, die „Ihre Gegenargumente vertritt“, wie er das nannte. Dieses sind jetzt meine Worte, aber der Alte habe sinngemäß gesagt, daß er vermute, seine „Stimme“ würde dagegen argumentieren, daß er sich weiterhin seinem strengen Pflichtgefühl und ihren Nebenwirkungen unterwerfen sollte. Er habe gesagt: „Bringen Sie die Stimme Ihres Anwalts zum Ausdruck und nehmen Sie sie gleichermaßen auf.“ Dann habe er vorgeschlagen, daß er die Argumente für ein freies Leben studieren sollte, frei von der Verkümmerung durch Verpflichtungen und der steten Erfüllung der Erwartungen anderer.

Ich weiß nicht, weshalb ich darüber so detailliert berichte, denn das Wichtigste war eigentlich, daß das Ganze sehr viel Ähnlichkeit mit der Unterhaltung hatte, die ich 1985 mit Auer auf meinem Flug von Christchurch nach Auckland hatte. Du bist, wie Du Dich sicher erinnern kannst, direkt nach Adelaide geflogen. Wir verabschiedeten uns im Flughafen. Es muß sich um den alten Auer gehandelt haben und nachdem ich einige Details überprüft habe, bin ich mir sicher. Was hältst Du von alledem? Was hältst du von Auers „Therapie“? Du weißt ja, daß es über Auer heißt, „einmal getroffen, nie vergessen“. Auers Leben ist in seiner Abhängigkeit vom Zufall wie ein Roman von Dickens. Unglaublich, nicht wahr?

Mit auerlichen Grüßen

PS: Anbei findest Du meinen Brief vom 9. Oktober 1985.

Oct. 9, 1985

Dear Michael:
A remarkable thing that happened on my flight to Auckland. I was pretty weary after the workshop as I imagine you were.

As is my custom, I had planned to bury myself inside some headphones and rock-and-roll myself home. I had an aisle seat. An elderly, 'foreign' man excused himself and pressed past me. I had no interest in making contact with anyone after the workshop but there was something about him that attracted me. He looked old but acted young. His eyes were vivacious and when I couldn't suppress my curiosity, I guessed by his leather satchel full of weighty books that he was on Oxford don here on sabbatical. I started sneaking glances at him which wasn't hard to do as he seemed quite in a world of his own. A DC-10 was just another university carrel to him. He vigorously slashed his way through a manuscript with a fountain pen. I remember thinking that I hadn't seen such an antiquated pen in use before.

He seemed to satisfy himself in regard to his editing, sat back and pulled out, of all things, Bateson's *Mind and Nature*. I couldn't contain myself any longer and thought I might start up a conversation with him. I did the usual opening airplane gambit. "Have you enjoyed your stay in New Zealand?" His reply baffled me on two counts: first, he spoke with quite a reasonable New Zealand accent and second, he said: "As an anti-positivist, it has had a special significance to me. But it was nothing like arriving here in 1942 with my late friend, Karl Popper. We both had secured Junior Lectureships at Canterbury University where we weathered the storms of the war years." He then enquired if I knew who Karl Popper was. I indicated I did and that was all it took for him to commence lecturing, much like I am told Wittgenstein used to at Cambridge. More or less, I became a witness to him having out loud a conversation with himself. Aphorisms were followed by oracular riddles, several of which he attempted to solve, much to his own amusement. I didn't quite know what to make of all this, so I remained attentive. I thought to myself that this wasn't rock-and-roll but my mind felt like it was getting a dry-cleaning. Abruptly,

9. Oktober 1985

Lieber Michael,
auf dem Flug nach Auckland ist mir etwas Sonderbares passiert. Nach dem Workshop war ich, wie Du wahrscheinlich auch, ziemlich K.O.

Wie gewöhnlich nahm ich mir vor, in einen Kopfhörer zu kriechen und mich heimwärts zu rock-n-rollen. Ich hatte einen Sitz am Gang. Ein älterer „ausländischer" Herr bat um Entschuldigung und drückte sich an mir vorbei. Nach dem Workshop hatte ich keinerlei Interesse daran, mit jemandem Kontakt aufzunehmen. Er hatte jedoch etwas an sich, was mich anzog. Er sah alt aus, verhielt sich jedoch wie ein Junger. Seine Augen waren sehr lebendig und als ich meine Neugier nicht mehr unterdrücken konnte, schloß ich aus seiner Ledertasche voll schwerer Bücher, daß er ein Professor aus Oxford sei, der hier Forschungsurlaub machte. Ich fing an, ihm verstohlene Blicke zuzuwerfen, was nicht schwerfiel, da er in seine eigene Welt vertieft schien. Für ihn war eine DC-10 so etwas wie jede andere Universitätsarbeitsnische. Mit einem Füller arbeitete er sich energisch durch ein Manuskript. Ich weiß noch, daß ich daran dachte, daß ich noch nie jemanden einen so antiquierten Füller habe benützen sehen.

Er schien mit seinem Redigieren zufrieden zu sein, lehnte sich zurück und zog ausgerechnet Batesons „Geist und Natur" hervor. Ich konnte nicht länger an mich halten und entschloß mich, ein Gespräch mit ihm anzuknüpfen. Ich fing mit der üblichen Flugzeugsunterhaltung an: „Hat es Ihnen in Neuseeland gefallen?" Seine Antwort verblüffte mich aus zwei Gründen: Erstens sprach er mit einem einigermaßen guten neuseeländischen Akzent und zweitens sagte er: „Als Anti-Positivist hatte es für mich eine besondere Bedeutung. Jedoch war es nicht zu vergleichen mit meiner Ankunft im Jahre 1942 zusammen mit meinem früheren Freund Karl Popper. Wir hatten uns beide an der Universität Canterbury einen Lehrauftrag gesichert, wo wir die Stürme der Kriegsjahre überstanden." Er fragte dann, ob ich wüßte, wer Karl Popper sei. Ich bejahte, wonach ihn nichts mehr davon abhalten konnte, mir einen Vortrag zu halten, der, wie mir gesagt wurde, denen ähnlich war, die Wittgenstein in Cambridge hielt. Ich wurde mehr oder weniger Zeuge eines Selbstgesprächs. Auf Aphorismen folgten orakelhafte Rätsel, von denen er einige zu lösen versuchte, was ihn allerdings selbst sehr amüsierte. Ich wußte n

he discontinued his discourse and said: "Tell me the story of your life, young man - or would it be better put, 'story' your life's story." Without any opportunity to try a reply, he broadened his question by further musing, chaining together a number of unanswered questions:

"How does one render events or episodes out of the flow of lived experience? How are those events construed as a story? How is storied experience warranted? Does one tell one's story or is it told? What would become of a person whose story was "untellable"? What if people's lives were considered to be 'texts' and how would it be different to be a 'reader' or an 'author'?" One question seemed to breed another. It didn't seem important to him to stop and try to find an answer. I am not at all sure I understood a word of this although it was pleasing to consider how this man's mind was working. All of a sudden he snapped out of his intellectual reverie, fixed me with intense interest and asked me what I did for a living. I was caught napping and said: "Family therapy." Assuming this would make no sense to him, coming from Europe, I qualified my remarks with ... "something like psychiatry." He laughed: "Voices," he said, "they worry when people hear voices. Their question is badly put - 'Do you hear voices?' A preferable question would be - 'Which of many voices is most attractive to you?' Psychiatry is like my long-lost friend, Karl Popper. Don't you think psychiatry would be better served by scrutinizing its rhetoric? Psychiatry has selected base rhetoric. Why not noble rhetoric?"

With a flourish, he placed *Mind and Nature* in my lap and insisted I should explore its contents. Well, for the first time I felt I could contribute. "Professor," I said, "I want you to know that I am a student of the selfsame book and that Bateson has had a particular influence

recht, was ich von alldem halten sollte, also hörte ich weiterhin aufmerksam zu. Bei mir dachte ich, daß es nicht gerade Rock'n'Roll war, obwohl sich mein Kopf anfühlte, als ob er chemisch gereinigt würde. Völlig abrupt beendete er seinen Vortrag und sagte: „Erzählen Sie mir Ihre Lebensgeschichte, junger Mann, oder müßte man besser sagen, erzählen Sie eine Geschichte Ihrer Lebensgeschichte." Ohne mir die Gelegenheit zu einer Antwort zu geben, erweiterte er nachgrübelnd seine Frage, eine Anzahl offener Fragen aneinanderreihend:

„Wie gibt man Ereignisse oder Vorfälle aus dem Fluß erlebter Erfahrungen wieder? Wie gliedert man diese Ereignisse in einer Geschichte? Wie kann man die Echtheit einer zur Geschichte gemachten Erfahrung beweisen? Erzählt man seine Geschichte oder wird sie erzählt? Was würde aus einem Menschen werden, dessen Geschichte nicht erzählt werden könnte? Angenommen, man betrachtete das Leben der Menschen als 'Texte', was würde einen 'Leser' von einem 'Autor' unterscheiden?" Eine Frage schien die nächste hervorzubringen. Anscheinend war es ihm nicht wichtig, innezuhalten und eine Antwort zu versuchen. Ich bin mir keineswegs sicher, überhaupt etwas verstanden zu haben. Dennoch war es anregend, darüber nachzusinnen, wie der Geist dieses Mannes funktionierte. Urplötzlich riß er sich aus seinen intellektuellen Träumereien, sah mich äußerst interessiert an und fragte, wie ich meinen Lebensunterhalt verdiene. Ich war gerade fast eingeschlafen und sagte: „Familientherapie." Da ich annahm, daß das für einen Europäer keinen Sinn ergeben würde, erläuterte ich ihm meine Aussage folgendermaßen: „So etwas wie Psychiatrie." Er lachte: „Stimmen", sagte er. „Sie machen sich Sorgen, wenn jemand Stimmen hört. Die Frage 'Hören Sie Stimmen?' ist falsch gestellt. Eine bessere Frage wäre: 'Welche der vielen Stimmen spricht Sie am meisten an?' Psychiatrie ist wie mein schon lange verlorener Freund Karl Popper. Meinen Sie nicht, der Psychiatrie wäre durch eine Überprüfung ihrer Rhetorik mehr gedient?! Die Psychiatrie hat eine gewöhnliche Rhetorik gewählt. Warum keine vornehme Rhetorik?"

Mit einer schwungvollen Bewegung legte er mir „Geist und Natur" auf den Schoß und bestand darauf, daß ich dessen Inhalt erforsche. Zum erstenmal hatte ich nun das Gefühl, etwas zur Unterhaltung beitragen zu können. „Professor", sagte ich, „Sie müssen

on my colleague and friend, Michael White, who lives in Adelaide, Australia." He looked rather surprised and said that he had been under the impression that Karl Popper had "popper-ized" us. He said this was certainly the case in the universities he had visited. "Not in my family therapy," I replied. He said: "Yes, family therapy . . . I have met some family therapists here and there." He jokingly referred to his plan to climb Ayers rock the week after. I told him of your attempts to derive a therapy from the ideas of Bateson. He expressed keen interest. By the way, his name is Carl Auer. Be prepared: he's like no one I have ever met before. I hope you will offer him some of your generous hospitality. Your life may never be the same again.

Fond regards,

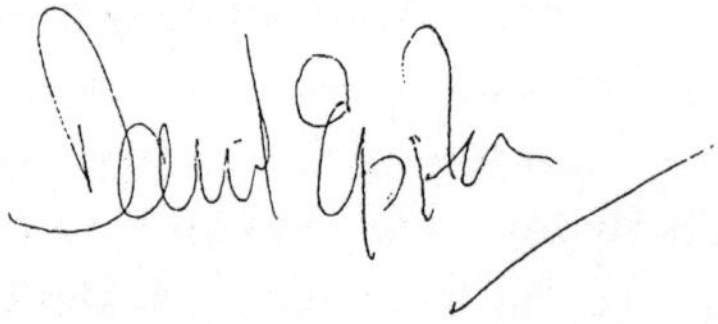

PS: Write back as soon as you can. Isn't it curious that Auer and Popper were at Canterbury University at the same time and I had never heard of him before. This cannot last forever, I assure you. One day, there will be a *festschrift* for Auer and New Zealand will be honored to realize it provided refuge for this man. He has had an influence on me that will only unfold over time. I hope you don't think I have gone crazy!

[1] Both are letters to Michael White, the answer to which has unfortunately been lost.

wissen, daß ich genau dieses Buch studiert habe und daß Bateson einen besonderen Einfluß auf meinen Kollegen und Freund Michael White, der in Adelaide in Australien wohnt, ausgeübt hat." Er schien ziemlich überrascht und sagte, er sei der Meinung gewesen, Karl Popper hätte uns „popperisiert". Er meinte, das sei auf jeden Fall so in den Universitäten, die er besucht habe. „Nicht in der Familientherapie", antwortete ich. Auer sagte: „Ja, Familientherapie … Ich bin hier und da einigen Familientherapeuten begegnet." Er erzählte mir noch, daß Adelaide auf seiner Reiseroute läge, und er erwähnte scherzhaft seinen Plan, in der darauffolgenden Woche Ayers Rock zu besteigen. Ich erzählte von Deinen Versuchen, aus Batesons Ideen eine Therapie abzuleiten. Er zeigte großes Interesse. Übrigens heißt er Carl Auer. Glaube mir, nie zuvor habe ich einen solchen Menschen kennengelernt. Ich hoffe, Du wirst ihm Deine großzügige Gastfreundschaft zuteil werden lassen. Danach wird Dein Leben wohl nie wieder das gleiche sein.

Beste Grüße

PS: Schreib' mir bitte, sobald Du Zeit hast. Ist es nicht merkwürdig, daß Auer und Popper zur gleichen Zeit in Canterbury waren und ich noch nie etwas über ihn gehört hatte? Ich versichere Dir, daß das nicht ewig so weitergehen kann. Eines Tages wird es für Auer eine Festschrift geben und Neuseeland wird sich geehrt fühlen, wenn es erfährt, daß es diesem Mann Zuflucht gewährt hat. Der Einfluß, den er auf mich ausgeübt hat, wird sich erst im Laufe der Zeit entfalten. Hoffentlich glaubst Du nicht, ich sei verrückt geworden!

[1] Es handelt sich hier um Briefe an Michael White. Dessen Antwortschreiben gingen leider verloren.

Auer Seen from a Woman's Point of View

Auer aus der Perspektive der Frauen

Vous Ne Risqueriez Rien - A Letter
Lynn Hoffman

Dear Gunthard:
Stimulated by Ernst von Glasersfeld, who of course knew Carl Auer well, I realized that my mother had met him when she was working for *Women's Wear* fashion magazine in Paris in 1929, and he was a young man of about 30. He was a small wiry person with piercing blue eyes as she recalled (she died in 1967, so I heard this story some years ago).

My mother, who was married at the time, met him at the "vernissage" of an exhibition of a friend of hers, I think Ossip Zadkine the sculptor. She told me that she was struck by this brilliant German expatriate who was also living in Paris and was studying at the studio of Fernand Léger where my mother had previously trained. Though he was at least five years younger than she was, they began conversing, found each other attractive, and he proposed that they go to bed together. She told him she was immensely complimented, but that she was pregnant with my younger sister and pointed to her stomach. She never forgot his reply, given in very bad French: "Mais c'est mieux comme ça! Vous ne risqueriez rien!" This reduced her to helpless laughter, and they ended up not going to bed but spending a wonderful evening at the Coupole, drinking Pernod and sharing anecdotes of the wonderful Paris they had come to love.

She never met him again, but occasionally, after she returned to the U. S., she would receive letters from him. She was touched at his devotion to "La Belle Américaine" despite his marriage to three women and his involvement with many others. Her eyes sparkled and her voice became especially gentle whenever she remembered

Vous ne risqueriez rien - Ein Brief
Lynn Hoffman

Lieber Gunthard,
angeregt durch Ernst von Glasersfeld, der Carl Auer natürlich gut kannte, erinnerte ich mich, daß meine Mutter ihn getroffen hatte, als sie für die Modezeitschrift „Women's Wear" 1929 in Paris arbeitete, und er ein junger Mann von etwa 30 Jahren war. Nach ihrer Erinnerung (sie starb 1967, also hörte ich diese Geschichte vor einigen Jahren) war er klein und drahtig und hatte stechende blaue Augen.

Meine Mutter, die damals verheiratet war, traf ihn auf der Vernissage eines ihrer Freunde, ich glaube es war Ossip Zadkine, der Bildhauer. Sie erzählte mir, sie sei von diesem brillanten, im Ausland lebenden Deutschen sehr angetan gewesen. Er habe auch in Paris gewohnt und bei Fernand Léger studiert, von dem meine Mutter früher ausgebildet worden war. Obwohl er mindestens fünf Jahre jünger war als sie, fingen sie an, sich zu unterhalten. Sie fanden sich attraktiv, und er schlug vor, miteinander ins Bett zu gehen. Sie antwortete, daß sie sich ungemein geschmeichelt fühle, allerdings mit meiner jüngsten Schwester schwanger sei, und deutete dabei auf ihren Bauch. Seine in sehr schlechtem Französisch gegebene Antwort hat sie nie vergessen: „Mais c'est mieux comme ça! Vous ne risqueriez rien!" Sie brach in schallendes Gelächter aus, was dazu führte, daß sie schließlich nicht miteinander ins Bett gingen, sondern einen wundervollen Abend zusammen im Coupole verbrachten. Sie tranken Pernod und erzählten sich Geschichten über das wundervolle Paris, das sie beide so sehr zu lieben begonnen hatten.

Sie hat ihn nie wieder gesehen, aber nachdem sie in die USA zurückgekehrt war, hat sie gelegentlich Briefe von ihm erhalten. Seine Hingabe an „La Belle Américaine" berührte sie sehr, obwohl er mit drei Frauen verheiratet war und mit vielen anderen Beziehungen hatte. Ihre Augen glänzten lebendig, und sie bekam eine besonders

the conversations with him. Maybe that's why his name got stuck in my mind.

My best love to all the Auer-Friends in Heidelberg,

Lynn Hoffman

sanfte Stimme, wenn sie sich immer wieder einmal an die Gespräche mit ihm erinnerte. Wahrscheinlich blieb mir deshalb sein Name so gut im Gedächtnis.

Allen meinen Heidelberger Auer-Freunden liebe Grüße

Lynn Hoffman

A Recollection of Carl Auer

Peggy Penn

I grew up surrounded by the undulating, bare black hills of a coal mining town in Western Pennsylvania. If you looked at their profile from my attic window you would see a large sleeping hunchback around whom over night a toy town of grey houses, all exactly the same, had mushroomed - as though to claim this ill-starred man as the best their fortunes could tender. It was a jerry-built town made to last as long as the coal or the men who mined it, no longer. There were many of these towns and they all had names that spoke the aspirations of the people who inhabited them; Grey, Red Onion, Blow By, Acosta, etc. They conveyed a sense of despairing immanence; this moment in time is all which fortune or God may offer, for tomorrow the mine may fall in, severing lives and handicapping any future.

My father was the one doctor in town and had come directly from medical school. His only experience around mines was shoveling iron ore down the silos for the Pittsburgh steel mills; an activity required to defray the cost of medical school during the Depression. His early practice was punctuated by the mine's catastrophes. The men who worked the mines were constantly in danger of the mine collapsing and of contracting black lung disease. The union was still almost non-existent and consisted of a few absent wags who made noise about organizing, but never, in my experience living their for five years, did they repair one structure in the mine or pay for the crippling of one man.

Eine Erinnerung an Carl Auer

Peggy Penn

Ich wuchs umgeben von den kahlen, schwarzen Hügeln einer Bergarbeiterstadt im Westen Pennsylvanias auf. Betrachtete man ihr Profil von meinem Dachfenster aus, sah man einen großen, schlafenden Buckligen, um den sich über Nacht eine Spielzeugstadt aus grauen, gleichförmigen Häusern ausgebreitet hatte, als wäre dieser vom Unglück verfolgte Mann das Beste, was ihnen ihr Schicksal anzubieten hätte. Es war eine schlampig gebaute Stadt, die mit der Kohle und den Männern, die sie abbauten, wieder verschwinden würde. Von diesen Städten gab es viele, und alle trugen Namen, die von der Hoffnung ihrer Bewohner zeugten: Grey, Red Onion, Blow By, Acosta usw. vermittelten ein Gefühl verzweifelnder Immanenz. Dieser Augenblick ist vielleicht alles, was das Schicksal oder Gott zu bieten haben, denn morgen stürzt das Bergwerk womöglich ein und zerstört Leben und Zukunft.

Mein Vater war der einzige Arzt in der Stadt und er war geradewegs von der medizinischen Fakultät hierher gekommen. Seine einzige Erfahrung mit Bergwerken hatte er gesammelt, als er Eisenerz in die Silos der Stahlwerke von Pittsburgh schaufelte, um sich während der Weltwirtschaftskrise sein Medizinstudium zu finanzieren. Die ersten Jahre der Praxis waren von den Katastrophen des Bergwerks überschattet. Die Männer, die in der Zeche arbeiteten, waren ständig in Gefahr, vom Berg begraben zu werden oder sich eine Lungenkrankheit zuzuziehen. Eine Gewerkschaft gab es praktisch nicht. Sie machte sich nur durch einige abwesende Witzbolde bemerkbar, die über das Organisieren faselten, aber soviel ich in den fünf Jahren, die ich dort lebte, mitbekommen konnte, haben sie keine einzige Konstruktion repariert oder einen zum Krüppel gewordenen Bergmann unterstützt.

I always knew when the mine collapsed. I heard the screaming of the women, "doctor! doctor!" I ran into the street and they streamed from between the rows of houses like a sudden flood. I stood perfectly still and they parted around me, screaming, "the doctor, where is the doctor?" Some women tore their dresses open in front, some tore at their hair, for time was off the essence; everyone must be quickly alarmed to save the men. I, too, looked for my father and often found him already running in the crowd, headed for the mine, his black bag clutched to his chest. Never sure which way to go, I usually fled into my house and sat under the dining room table which my mother told me we were so lucky to have, trying to control my violent trembling and somewhere on the verge of knowing I was afraid for my father's life. What if the mine collapsed again while he was in it? Who would save him? Who would save the rest of us and me? All night I could hear constant moaning in the small room attached to our house which was my father's office. The lights burnt all night as he treated the limbs, heads, and wounds of the survivors. I stayed awake until I could no longer smell the burnt coffee or hear the dark moaning and talking. Finally I slept praying to wake to the familiar occurrence of morning, nothing more. On the days when all was well I sat with my exhausted father at breakfast, watching him cut and chew every bite as though without my scrutiny he would not survive. But one morning all had not gone well. My father stood in his black suit in the hall, waiting for my mother to finish dressing. They told me Mr. Kapuchinsky had been hurt in the mine collapse and not survived. They were going to a church service for him. This was unbelievable; Mr. Kapuchinsky was a man whom I had helped in May and June to make dandelion wine. We picked all the dandelions we could find and put them in big vats along with orange and apple halves and special field flowers only he knew about. He prided himself on his recipe and when the wine was ready everyone in town came to taste it. They all received half a cup of wine and they toasted him, teasing him for his recipe. He would wink at me and say only he and I knew it and neither of us could write. On that day he made me a crown of dandelions and wildflowers which I kept until the fall when it turned to brown dust. After my parents left I went to his house and looked for him in every familiar place; his pipe smoking chair, his garden, and his small kitchen, but he was not present. Always forbidden to go to church alone because I had to cross the railroad tracks, today I did:

Ich wußte jedesmal, wenn ein Einsturz passiert war. Ich hörte das Schreien der Frauen: „Doktor, Doktor!“ Ich lief auf die Straße, wo die Menschen wie eine Springflut zwischen den Häuserreihen hervorgespült wurden. Ich blieb wie angewurzelt stehen. Sie teilten sich und strömten an mir vorbei und riefen: „Doktor, wo ist der Doktor?“ Manche Frauen zerrissen sich die Kleider, andere rauften sich die Haare, denn die Zeit war sehr kostbar: Um die Männer zu retten, mußten alle schnellstmöglichst alarmiert werden. Ich suchte meinen Vater und fand ihn oft schon mitten unter der Menge in Richtung Bergwerk rennen, seine schwarze Tasche an die Brust gepreßt. Da ich den Weg nicht genau kannte, rannte ich gewöhnlich heim und verkroch mich unter dem Eßzimmertisch, den zu besitzen - wie meine Mutter sagte - wir uns glücklich schätzen könnten, und versuchte, mein heftiges Zittern zu kontrollieren, ahnend, daß ich um das Leben meines Vaters bangte. Was, wenn es im Bergwerk noch einmal zum Einsturz käme, während er dort unten war? Wer würde ihn retten? Wer würde uns retten und mich? Die ganze Nacht hindurch hörte ich ununterbrochenes Stöhnen aus der Praxis meines Vaters, die sich in einem kleinen Anbau befand. Das Licht brannte die ganze Nacht, während er die Gliedmaßen, Köpfe und Wunden der Überlebenden behandelte. Ich blieb wach, bis ich den angebrannten Kaffee nicht mehr riechen und das dunkle Stöhnen und Reden nicht mehr hören konnte. Schließlich schlief ich ein und betete nur, daß ich beim Anbruch eines gewöhnlichen Tages wieder aufwachen würde. An den Tagen, an denen alles in Ordnung war, saß ich mit meinem erschöpften Vater beim Frühstück, schaute ihm zu, wie er jeden Bissen schnitt und kaute, als ob er ohne meine forschenden Blicke nicht überleben könnte. Eines Morgens war nicht alles in Ordnung. Mein Vater stand mit seinem schwarzen Anzug im Flur und wartete, daß sich meine Mutter fertig ankleidete. Sie erzählten mir, Herr Kapuchinsky sei beim Bergwerkseinsturz verletzt worden und habe nicht überlebt. Sie gingen zu einem Gottesdienst, der für ihn gehalten wurde. Das war unfaßbar. Herr Kapuchinsky war ein Mann, dem ich im Mai und Juni geholfen hatte, Löwenzahnwein zu machen. Wir pflückten soviel Löwenzahn, wie wir finden konnten und füllten ihn in große Bottiche, zusammen mit Orangen- und Apfelhälften und bestimmten Feldblumen, die nur er kannte. Er war sehr stolz auf sein Rezept, und als der Wein fertig war, kam die ganze Stadt zur Weinprobe. Jeder erhielt ein halbes Glas Wein. Sie tranken auf sein Wohl

I could not believe Mr. Kapuchinsky was "dead." I sat on the white fence in front of the church looking through the open door and listening to the long swells of organ music mixed with crying. I decided to join the family in the church so I too could see him and say goodbye. My parents were shocked when I walked down the aisle behind the distraught family, stood in front of the coffin and said, "I looked for you at home because I wanted to say good-bye Mr. Kapuchinsky, and I hope I see you again." This was my only social farewell, taught to me by my mother.

Leaving the church ahead of my parents, I went straight to a meadow in front of the woods behind my house; stretched out in the autumn grasses like a fallen angel and floated to my secret future when I would plant my own meadow with dandelions for Mr. Kapuchinsky, but in a new town without a mine.

Often I walked to a favorite family house in a different row from ours. A Polish family house where the entire first floor was a busy kitchen. Since I was not four I couldn't attend Kindergarten and so, I prided myself on my "job" - helping Mrs. Jandor prepare the four o'clock dinner for her family. The mine whistle blew at 3:45 p.m. and supper was served in every home by four. My job was to plough with my hands through sacks of beans, picking out the bad ones and reserving only the good ones to soak for tomorrow's dinner. Mrs. Jandor put all the soaked beans from yesterday in a big black pot on the wood stove and made a fire. Then we went outside and picked "greens," dandelion greens, or beet greens if available, for flavor. If times were good, a slab of bacon with almost no meat on it went into

und neckten ihn wegen seines Rezeptes. Er blinzelte mir zu und sagte, nur wir beide wüßten es, und keiner von uns könnte schreiben. An jenem Tag machte er mir eine Krone aus Löwenzahn und wilden Blumen, die ich bis zum Herbst aufbewahrte, bis sie sich in braunen Staub verwandelte. Nachdem sich meine Eltern auf den Weg gemacht hatten, ging ich zu seinem Haus und suchte ihn an allen bekannten Orten. Bei seinem Stuhl, in dem er Pfeife zu rauchen pflegte, in seinem Garten und in seiner kleinen Küche, aber er war nicht da. Obwohl es mir wegen der Bahnlinie, die ich überqueren mußte, verboten war, alleine zur Kirche zu gehen, ging ich heute trotzdem. Ich konnte nicht glauben, daß Herr Kapuchinsky „tot" war. Ich setzte mich auf den weißen Zaun, schaute durch die offene Tür und lauschte der mit Weinen vermischten an- und abschwellenden Orgelmusik. Ich entschloß mich, zu meiner Familie in die Kirche zu gehen, um ihn auch zu sehen und um mich von ihm zu verabschieden. Meine Eltern waren schockiert, als ich hinter der verzweifelten Familie durch den Mittelgang nach vorne ging, vor dem Sarg stehenblieb und sagte: „Ich habe Sie zu Hause gesucht, weil ich Ihnen Lebewohl sagen wollte, Herr Kapuchinsky. Ich hoffe, ich sehe Sie wieder." Dieses waren die einzigen Abschiedsworte, die mir meine Mutter beigebracht hatte.

Ich verließ die Kirche vor meinen Eltern und ging geradewegs zu einer vor dem Wald gelegenen Wiese hinter meinem Haus, streckte mich im herbstlichen Gras wie ein gefallener Engel aus und entschwebte in meine heimliche Zukunft, in der ich meine eigene Wiese mit Löwenzahn für Herrn Kapuchinsky bepflanzen würde, aber in einer neuen Stadt ohne Bergwerk.

Ich lief oft zu einem Reihenhaus in einer anderen Straße, in dem eine polnische Familie wohnte. Das gesamte Erdgeschoß bestand aus einer vielbenutzten Küche. Da ich noch keine vier Jahre alt war, durfte ich noch nicht in den Kindergarten, und deshalb war ich ausgesprochen stolz auf meinen „Job", Frau Jandor bei der Zubereitung der Vier-Uhr-Mahlzeit für ihre Familie zu helfen. Die Bergwerkssirene heulte um 15.45 Uhr, und in jedem Haus wurde um 16.00 Uhr das Abendessen serviert. Meine Arbeit bestand darin, mit den Händen durch Säcke voller Bohnen zu pflügen, um die schlechten auszulesen und nur die guten zum Einweichen für das morgige Essen aufzuheben. Frau Jandor schüttete alle eingeweichten Bohnen von gestern in einen großen schwarzen Topf auf dem Holzofen und machte Feuer.

the pot. Then she baked nine loaves of bread; one for each member of her family and some left over to pack in their lunches tomorrow. I felt such urgent directions from my stomach that I did my best to make myself useful enough to hang around until supper time when they would offer me a small bowl of beans and a piece of dipping bread. It all tasted like ambrosia to me but it was hard to explain to my parents why I didn't eat my own dinner at 5:30. They must have figured out where I spent my afternoons for my father made me a "special" sign to wear. Not sensing any villany I wore it proudly. However, as time went by, my job deteriorated and Mrs. Jandor didn't need me so much, especially around supper time. I waylaid her daughter on the way home from school and asked her to read my sign. She burst out laughing and read, "Please do not Feed!"

It was into this world at this time in my life that Carl Auer came. At first I thought he was a relative. He was introduced as a distant cousin of my mother's - a euphemism usually reserved for relationships that are hard to explain. He arrived in a shiny blue car, the only other car I had ever seen except my father's which was by now unpainted and rattled from the chains he kept in the trunk for winter "calls." But here was a car that came from an outside life I knew nothing about. I thought a lot about changing my life in those days. Now that I was almost four, I knew I would probably never be any smarter so I'd better make plans. I listened intently as my parents talked to Carl Auer. Their conversations were full of laughter as they planned picnics, swimming jaunts, drives; unheard of activities in our usual world. To the first picnic my mother wore a gauzy dress with raffles at the hem and my father's face smiled at her all afternoon. I wanted unbearably to be my mother that summer day!

Dann gingen wir nach draußen und pflückten Grüngemüse: Löwenzahn- oder Rübenblätter, wenn es welche gab, für den Geschmack. Waren die Zeiten gut, kam eine dicke, fast fleischlose Scheibe Speck in den Topf. Dann buk sie neun Laibe Brot, einen für jedes Familienmitglied und ein paar für das morgige Pausenbrot. Ich erhielt von meinem Magen derartig dringende Anweisungen, daß ich mich nach Kräften bemühte, mich nützlich zu machen, um bis zur Abendbrotzeit dableiben zu können. Gewöhnlich boten Sie mir dann eine kleine Schüssel Bohnen und ein Stück Brot zum Eintunken an. Für mich schmeckte alles wie Ambrosia. Allerdings fiel es mir nicht leicht, meinen Eltern zu erklären, warum ich Zuhause um 17.30 Uhr beim Abendbrot nichts aß. Sie müssen herausbekommen haben, wo ich meine Nachmittage verbrachte, denn mein Vater fertigte für mich ein „besonderes" Schild zum Tragen. Da ich nichts Böses ahnte, trug ich es voller Stolz. Mit der Zeit gab es bei meinem „Job" nicht mehr viel zu tun, und Frau Jandor brauchte mich nicht mehr so häufig, vor allem nicht um die Abendbrotzeit. Auf dem Heimweg von der Schule fing ich ihre Tochter ab und bat sie, mir vorzulesen, was auf meinem Schild stand. Sie fing an zu lachen und las: „Bitte nicht füttern!"

Zu dieser Zeit ist Carl Auer in mein Leben getreten. Zuerst hielt ich ihn für einen Verwandten. Er wurde mir als entfernter Cousin meiner Mutter vorgestellt - ein Euphemismus, der gewöhnlich verwendet wurde, wenn Beziehungen schwer zu erklären waren. Er kam in einem glänzenden blauen Auto an, das einzige andere Auto, das ich außer dem meines Vaters jemals gesehen hatte. Bei dem war aber die Farbe völlig abgeblättert und wegen der Ketten, die er für die Hausbesuche im Winter im Kofferraum aufbewahrte, klapperte es. Hier kam jedoch ein Auto aus einer fremden Welt, über die ich nichts wußte. Ich habe in jener Zeit viel darüber nachgedacht, mein Leben zu ändern, und da ich schließlich fast vier war, war mir klar, daß ich vermutlich nie viel schlauer sein würde und deshalb am besten mal Pläne machen sollte. Ich hörte aufmerksam zu, wenn sich meine Eltern mit Carl Auer unterhielten. Es wurde viel gelacht, wenn sie Picknicks, Badeausflüge und Fahrten in die Umgebung planten; Aktivitäten, die in unserer gewohnten Welt gänzlich unbekannt waren. Zum ersten Picknick trug meine Mutter ein hauchdünnes Kleid mit Rüschen am Saum, und mein Vater strahlte sie den ganzen Nachmittag an. Ich hatte das sehnsüchtige Verlangen, an diesem Sommertag meine Mutter zu sein!

Carl Auer sat in my meadow and read to us all from a book; sometimes his eyes just focused on the horizon for a long time, other times he would catch my eye and smile with what I thought to be pure radiance. The words in some odd way, seemed shaped to fit each other, like a song. How was I to know that these young people who were my parents and Carl Auer were reading poetry. Every sentence he read filled my lungs like a bellows. The day expanded. I suddenly knew that words like these, that language, could plant fields and fields of dandelions and that language could reach into the mine to become another form of rescue for Mr. Kapuchinsky, for Mrs. Jandor, for my father and for us all. Carl Auer was a poet at this time in his life and my first friend after Mrs. Jandor.

Over the next 30 years our exchanges were usually in the form of a poem. At first they encouragingly came from him to me, but somewhere before adolescence I wrote some lines I found the courage to send. I know he lived in Europe before the war and then took his family to New Zealand, vowing never to live through another world war. At this point Carl Auer, the inner poet, agreed with Robert Bly when he wrote, "We make war like a man anointing himself."

In New Zealand he put poetry aside and pursued the life sciences, determined that the outer man must now preserve the world whatever inner refusals that entailed. I lost track of him in the Pacific wideness but I heard that he and his wife lost a child and they never entirely recovered. I still gratefully remember the day he read to us and if I could send them one last poem it would be this one I wrote after my mother died:

My Mother Read Wordsworth

My mother read Wordsworth and, closing her life,
put the book on a shelf.
I had thought her mid-bed too mussed up for poetry;
as well as her iron whimsy too frail

Carl Auer saß auf meiner Wiese und las uns allen aus einem Buch vor; manchmal richtete sich sein Blick lange auf den Horizont, dann wieder schaute er mir, wie mir schien, mit einem strahlenden Lächeln in die Augen. Auf eine seltsame Art und Weise schienen die Worte so geformt zu sein, daß sie wie ein Lied zusammenpaßten. Wie sollte ich auch wissen, daß diese jungen Leute, die meine Eltern waren, und Carl Auer Gedichte lasen. Jeder Satz, den er las, füllte meine Lungen wie ein Blasebalg. Der Tag dehnte sich aus. Ich wußte plötzlich, daß solche Worte, daß Sprache Felder um Felder mit Löwenzahn bepflanzen konnte und daß Sprache in das Bergwerk hinunterreichen konnte, um für Herrn Kapuchinsky, Frau Jandor, meinen Vater und uns alle zu einer anderen Art der Rettung zu werden. Zu jener Zeit seines Lebens war Carl Auer Dichter und, nach Frau Jandor, mein bester Freund.

Die nächsten 30 Jahre bestand unser Austausch vorwiegend aus Gedichten. Am Anfang sandte er mir ermutigende Gedichte, aber irgendwann vor meiner Adoleszenz schrieb ich einige Zeilen und fand meinerseits den Mut, sie ihm zu schicken. Ich weiß, daß er vor dem Krieg in Europa lebte und dann mit seiner Familie nach Neuseeland ging und sich schwor, nie wieder einen Krieg durchzumachen. An dieser Stelle stimmte Carl Auer, der innere Dichter, mit Robert Bly überein, der schrieb: „Wir machen Krieg wie ein Mann, der sich selbst die letzte Ölung gibt."

In Neuseeland gab er das Dichten auf und wandte sich den Humanwissenschaften zu, entschlossen, als Mann der Tat die Welt zu bewahren, ganz gleich, welche inneren Verweigerungen das nach sich ziehen würde. Ich verlor ihn in der pazifischen Weite aus den Augen, hörte aber, daß er und seine Frau ein Kind verloren hatten und sie sich davon nie mehr völlig erholten. Ich denke immer noch dankbar an den Tag, an dem er uns vorlas, und wenn ich ihnen ein letztes Gedicht senden könnte, wäre es dieses, das ich nach dem Tod meiner Mutter schrieb:

Meine Mutter las Wordsworth

Meine Mutter las Wordsworth und, ihr Leben abschließend,
legte sie das Buch ins Regal.
Ich hatte ihr Hirn zu verwirrt gewähnt für Gedichte;
und ihre eisernen Marotten zu brüchig,

for the disturbance of words.
But this accidental volume, resurrected,
shows she read Wordsworth.

I bore witness to this silent life,
her head always turned away
toward some filmy spirituality
she wore in studied reluctance,
a vow of silence toward us all.

Perhaps she gave her heart to Basil, an old love
whose Catholic plate my grandmother threatened to poison
if he ever came back. He didn't.
Nor did she give her heart to her father or to mine.
Rejected, both their hearts belonged to me.

Is there some alchemy to change
your basest dust to living gold?
A glowing light where I might catch
your eye on this illumined page
that you would look on me at last
and speak?

You lie so wordless here
without the thinnest metaphor as cover
in the cold and soundless wind.
I stretch out, my cheek damp on damp ground
my face toward your face - to ask a question:

Poetry comes from such a far place,
inarticulate and mossy
contrary to the printed page,
to this small volume I hold in my hand -
could you be there ? In the landscape no one knows?
And if words forgive us
could we meet somewhere
to shout our recognition, curse
all ends! and quicken time's embrace
in verse?

um durch Worte gestört zu werden.
Doch dieser zufällige Band, wieder belebt
beweist: sie las Wordsworth.

Ich war Zeugin dieses stillen Lebens,
ihr Gesicht ständig abgewandt
zu einer verschleierten Spiritualität
stellte sie ihre Abneigung zur Schau
ein Schweigegelöbnis gegenüber uns allen.

Vielleicht schenkte sie ihr Herz Basil, einer alten Liebe,
dessen katholischen Teller meine Großmutter zu vergiften drohte,
sollte er je zurückkommen. Er kam nicht.
Weder ihrem Vater schenkte sie ihr Herz noch meinem.
Abgewiesen, gehörten ihrer beider Herzen mir.

Gibt es eine Alchemie, um deinen gewöhnlichsten Staub
in lebendiges Gold zu verwandeln?
Ein glühendes Licht, um deinen Blick
auf diese beleuchtete Seite zu bannen
daß du endlich mich anschaust
und etwas sagst?

Du liegst so wortlos hier
ohne die dünnste Metapher als Decke
in dem kalten und tonlosen Wind.
Ich strecke mich aus, meine Wange feucht auf feuchter Erde
um Angesicht zu Angesicht eine Frage zu stellen:

Poesie kommt von so weit,
unverständlich und bemoost
ganz Gegensatz zu dem bedruckten Blatt,
zu diesem kleinen Band in meiner Hand -
bist du dort vielleicht? In der Landschaft, die keiner kennt?
Und wenn uns Worte vergeben,
könnten wir uns irgendwo treffen,
um unser Erkennen herauszuschreien,
alle Zwecke verfluchend! Und beflügelt wird die Zeit
mit Versen umarmt.

Jelena and Carl: The Usual is Penetrated by the Unusual

Rosmarie Welter-Enderlin

As far as Carl's and Jelena's residence in our house is concerned, my opinions and those of my brothers and sisters diverge considerably. Even Jelena, on a visit to Europe just a short while ago, could not decide whether it was in 1945 or 1946 when they moved in with us. What is known, is that the Auers left for America in 1949. It was just after Carl's 49th birthday, which we had celebrated with friends of the Auers and our large family until late in the summer night under the apple tree behind our house, presumably about the middle of August. The two rucksacks they had carried on their arrival several years before were stowed in one of the many boxes, which we elder children then carted to the station. "Just in case," said Jelena, as she folded the empty rucksacks. "Who knows what use they might still be in this century of mass migration. Perhaps one day we'll be fleeing in the other direction, from West to East."

Searching for Tracks

It is well known, and yet still irritating: The experience of how differently people - in this case brothers and sisters - tell the same story. When visiting my brothers and sisters over the past few months to talk to them about our recollections of Jelena and Carl, it seemed to me that we must have grown up in completely different worlds. The kind of things we remembered showed that the pictures that have stuck in our minds can be pure fiction for others who shared the same world their whole childhood long. "You have always been known for your vivid imagination," one of my brothers said as I related my recollections of the Auers, "a real fibber. Remember how you used to

Jelena und Carl: Der Einbruch des Außergewöhnlichen ins Gewöhnliche

Rosmarie Welter-Enderlin

Die Meinungen unter uns Geschwistern gehen, was die Zeit von Carls und Jelenas Aufenthalt in unserem Haus betrifft, auseinander. Selbst Jelena, vor kurzem zu Besuch in Europa, konnte sich nicht entscheiden, ob es 1945 oder erst 1946 war, als sie bei uns einzogen. Fest steht, daß die Auers 1949 nach Amerika abreisten. Es war kurz nach Carls 49. Geburtstag, den wir unter dem Apfelbaum hinter dem Haus bis spät in die Sommernacht mit Freunden der Auers und unserer großen Familie gefeiert hatten, vermutlich gegen Mitte August. Die zwei Rucksäcke, die sie bei ihrer Ankunft Jahre zuvor getragen hatten, wurden irgendwo in einer der vielen Kisten verstaut, die wir älteren Kinder dann zur Bahnstation karrten. „Für alle Fälle", sagte Jelena, als sie die leeren Rucksäcke zusammenfaltete. „Wer weiß, wozu die noch gut sein werden in diesem Jahrhundert der Völkerwanderung. Vielleicht werden wir einmal noch umgekehrt, vom Westen in den Osten fliehen."

Spuren suchen

Altbekannt, und doch erneut irritierend: Die Erfahrung, wie unterschiedlich Menschen - in diesem Fall Geschwister - dieselbe Geschichte erzählen. Als ich in den letzten Monaten meine Schwestern und Brüder besuchte, um mit ihnen über unsere Erinnerungen an Jelena und Carl zu reden, war mir, als wären wir in völlig verschiedenen Welten aufgewachsen. Die Art unseres Erinnerns zeigte, daß das, was sich an Bildern in mir festgesetzt hat, für andere, welche eine Kindheit lang in derselben Welt lebten, reine Erfindung sein kann. „Du warst schon immer bekannt für deine lebhafte Phantasie", sagte einer meiner Brüder, als ich von meinen Erinnerungen an die Auers

tell us ghost stories at night, when we slept in the haye during the holidays, till we all actually saw and heard them? I wonder how you deal with reality professionally. . . ."

This divergence between the world of living and the world of meaning amongst my brothers and sisters and myself was painful, even at that time. The differing recollections of women and men as diverse possibilities of truth; gender as the fundamental organizational pattern of reality-construction? Is it possible that the women in our family, as in many others that I meet every day, had to develop a different memory for family history than the men? A memory that enables them to search for tracks in the labyrinth of myths and norms with their noses to the ground in order to find a place for themselves to which they are not unquestionably entitled as are the sons? Or did we simply need this different form of memory in order to free ourselves from the wonderfully luxurious yet at the same time overwhelmingly strong "family-we"? In the sense that our grass grew on the same childhood meadow, but in order to grow up we had to store the hay in different lofts? Does love mean perceiving similarities in unsimilar things and at the same time drawing nourishment from common roots for the appreciation of the differences, for the pleasure in the varied development of brothers and sisters, of men and women?

My mother's notes on the empty pages of our discarded exercise books - diary would be a much too ambitious word for it - which I discovered among her things after her death, helped me get by. In the post-war entries, for which she normally noted only day and month, the names Jelena and Carl appear shortly after the death of our Aunt Lisette, the woman who travelled alone to the World Exhibition in Paris in the last century and who was punished for it by her husband, who left her, and which she told us children without anger when she showed us a tiny Eiffel Tower she had bought with her last Francs. I remember that we put an advertisment in the newspaper to let her flat in the upstairs of our old house with the remark "furnished", which was obviously a handicap at that time. For this reason the flat was still empty when we received a letter from Marie, who had served an apprenticeship as gardener with my father before the war. She wrote

erzählte, „ein richtiges Lügenkind. Weißt du noch, wie du uns nachts im Heulager in den Ferien immer Gespenstergeschichten erzähltest, bis wir alle sie leibhaftig sahen und hörten? Ich würde nur gerne wissen, wie du es in deinem Beruf mit der Realität hältst ..."

Dieses Auseinanderklaffen von Lebens- und Bedeutungswelt unter uns Geschwistern war schon damals schmerzlich. Die unterschiedlichen Erinnerungen von Frauen und Männern als vielfältige Möglichkeiten der Wahrheit; Geschlecht als fundamentales Organisationsmuster unserer Wahrnehmung und Wirklichkeitskonstruktion? Könnte es sein, daß die Frauen in unserer Familie, wie in vielen andern, denen ich täglich begegne, ein anderes Gedächtnis für Familiengeschichte(n) entwickeln mußten als die Männer? Ein Gedächtnis, das ihnen ermöglicht, mit der Nase am Boden im Dickicht von Mythen und Normen Spuren zu suchen, um einen Platz für sich zu finden, der ihnen nicht fraglos zusteht wie den Söhnen? Oder brauchten wir die unterschiedliche Art des Erinnerns einfach, um uns zu befreien aus dem wunderbar üppigen und gleichzeitig überwältigend starken Familien-Wir? Etwa in dem Sinn, daß zwar unser Gras auf derselben Wiese der Kindheit gewachsen ist, daß wir aber, um erwachsen zu werden, das Heu auf verschiedenen Heubühnen lagern mußten. Bedeutet Liebe, Ähnliches an Unähnlichem wahrzunehmen und gleichzeitig aus den gemeinsamen Wurzeln Nahrung zu ziehen für die Anerkennung der Unterschiede, die Lust an der Vielfalt der Entwicklung von Brüdern und Schwestern, von Frauen und Männern?

Die Notizen meiner Mutter auf den unbeschriebenen Seiten unserer abgelegten Schulhefte - Tagebuch wäre ein zu hohes Wort dafür -, die ich in ihrem Nachlaß fand, halfen mir weiter. In den Eintragungen aus der Nachkriegszeit, die sie meistens nur mit Tag und Monat versah, erscheinen die Namen von Jelena und Carl kurz nach dem Tod unserer Tante Lisette, der Frau, die im letzten Jahrhundert allein zur Pariser Weltausstellung gereist war und zur Strafe dafür von ihrem Mann verlassen wurde, was sie uns Kindern ohne Zorn erzählte, als sie uns einmal einen winzigen Eifelturm zeigte, den sie mit ihren letzten Francs gekauft habe. - Ich erinnere mich, daß wir ihre Wohnung oben in unserm alten Haus in der Zeitung zur Vermietung ausgeschrieben hatten mit dem Vermerk „möbliert", was damals offenbar ein Hindernis bedeutete. So war die Wohnung noch frei, als ein Brief von Marie bei uns eintraf, die vor dem Krieg eine

from Tyrol that she was looking for a flat in Switzerland for a couple they had hidden from the Nazis on their alpine pasture at the beginning of the war and who were hoping to find work in Zurich. Before the war both the Auers had been 'reds', she had to inform us of this straight away for the sake of honesty, but they were educated and very respectable people nevertheless. The fact that Jelena was Jewish and had already fled from Serbia must have tipped the scales, as my mother's notes revealed. "After all the guilt we Swiss took upon ourselves when we closed our borders and sent these people to their deaths," she wrote, "the least we can do is to say yes to this."

The fact that our parents decided this way and no other has had a sustained influence on my life. I don't know which path I would have taken without Jelena and Carl, but I do know that I am still drawing from what they both awakened in me. They came to us from a world which had been almost completely destroyed as far as its material characteristics are concerned, but they brought an intellect and culture with them which blew into our tradition-bound life in the frugality of a small town like a fresh wind. Not that intellect and culture were altogether lacking in our family. But in the struggle for existence at a time when market-garden flowers were only being bought for weddings and funerals, and vegetables had to be grown instead, my parents had lost all interest in culture. In this they were not alone. The demon of wartime and the post-war period dried up the already barren land for culture in Switzerland completely. During the war there had been pockets of resistance such as the playhouse. Wolfgang Langhoff played Brecht. He met the Auers later when he was buying vegetable seedlings for his country garden in the nursery. But after the war Wilhelm Tell was put on again, compulsory for all higher school classes, in celebration of the defeat of tyranny. People were proud of the national establishment of armed neutrality and fostered myths which promote a sense of community as the historical truth, without questioning whether the overthrown tyrant had possibly spared the country because he was impressed by the comfortable stability and the secret bank accounts rather than by the rifle in every Swiss citizens' wardrobe. And it was certainly not the case that the free democratic attitude they were virtually born with gave everyone an equal chance to start anew. It served rather to isolate the

Gärtnerinnenlehre bei meinem Vater gemacht hatte. Sie schrieb aus Tirol, daß sie in der Schweiz eine Wohnung suche für ein jüngeres Paar, welches sie zu Beginn des Krieges oben auf ihrer Alm vor den Nazis versteckt gehalten hätten und das auf Arbeit in Zürich hoffe. Beide Auers seien vor dem Krieg Rote gewesen, das müsse sie uns der Ehrlichkeit halber gleich mitteilen, aber gebildete und hochanständige Leute, dennoch. Daß Jelena Jüdin und schon aus Serbien geflohen war, muß, wie aus den Notizen meiner Mutter hervorgeht, das Zünglein an der Waage gewesen sein. „Nach allem, das wir Schweizer geleistet haben, als wir unsere Grenzen abriegelten und diese Menschen in den Tod schickten", schreibt sie, „ist es das Geringste das wir tun können, wenn wir hier ja sagen."

Daß unsere Eltern sich so und nicht anders entschieden, hat mein Leben nachhaltig geprägt. Ich weiß nicht, wie mein Weg ohne Jelena und Carl verlaufen wäre, aber ich weiß, daß ich nach wie vor aus dem schöpfe, was beide in mir geweckt haben. Sie kamen aus einer Welt zu uns, die zwar in ihrer materiellen Ausprägung fast ganz untergegangen war, aber sie brachten einen Geist und eine Kultur mit sich, die wie ein frischer Wind in unser traditionsgebundenes Leben in der Kargheit der Kleinstadt wehte. Nicht, daß Geist und Kultur in der Familie überhaupt fehlten. Aber im Kampf um die Existenz zu einer Zeit, als die Blumen aus der Gärtnerei bloß für Hochzeiten und Begräbnisse gekauft wurden und an ihrer Stelle Gemüse angebaut werden mußte, war meinen Eltern die Lust an Kultur vergangen. Nicht nur ihnen. Der Ungeist der Kriegs- und Nachkriegszeit ließ den ohnehin kargen Boden für Kultur in der Schweiz vollends austrocknen. Während des Krieges hatte es Nischen des Widerstandes wie das Schauspielhaus gegeben. Wolfgang Langhoff spielte dort Brecht und lernte die Auers kennen, als er in der Gärtnerei Gemüsesetzlinge für seinen Bauerngarten kaufte. Aber nach dem Krieg spielte man wieder Wilhelm Tell, Pflichtbesuch für alle höheren Schulklassen, zur Feier des gestürzten Tyrannen. Man war stolz auf die nationale Einrichtung der bewaffneten Neutralität und pflegte gemeinschaftsstiftende Mythen als geschichtliche Wahrheit, ohne sich zu fragen, ob der gestürzte Tyrann das Land vielleicht verschont hatte, weil ihn die komfortable Stabilität und die geheimen Bankkonten und weniger das Gewehr im Kleiderkasten jedes Schweizerbürgers beeindruckt hatten. Wobei es durchaus nicht so war, daß die quasi angeborene freiheitlich-demokratische Gesinnung die gleichen

privileged from the less privileged and in particular as exterior isolation, and everything foreign automatically became displeasing. The Auers moved in in this epoch characterized by the spirit of monotony, diligence and order.

I still remember how happy I was when the rucksacks with the personal things which Jelena and Carl brought with them were followed a few days later by a washing basket full of books. Together with the typewriter, an Underwood, they were moved into Aunt Lisette's living room. Just like everyone in our family who could read, I craved anything in print. For me reading and being read to were small respites from the frugality of everyday life, meant immersion in different realities. For that very reason reading was limited to peripheral hours and to Sundays, and half an hour after the evening meal was set aside for reading aloud from the daily newspaper or the weekly magazine, whereby the feature section with "to be continued" was the most exciting. Everybody knew that the reading ban had the opposite effect, and that we children positively devoured books under the blankets or during monotonous jobs. I even caught father often with an open book next to him on the work-bench in the greenhouse, pushing seedlings into the earth with an absent look. - And so now two people who read and wrote professionally, as their job, were living under the same roof as us. This was a completely new idea, a perspective that evoked magnificent pictures of the future, ones full of other things than order, propriety and the grind in garden and greenhouses. . . .

Jelena and Carl met each other in Vienna in the editorial office of a socialist newspaper. After Austria's Anschluss to the Third Reich Carl, biologist and anthropologist, and Jelena, a few years younger and a student of Philosophy, had stayed on in the editorial office until the last moment. I don't know how they managed to get to our Marie in the Stubai Valley, but I distinctly remember my heart pounding every time their last-minute escape was talked about. At that time the Second World War was not on the school curriculum, and even in the higher classes it was only mentioned in passing, as entrance ticket to Wilhelm Tell, so to speak. So I had to piece together my own world history from scraps of grown-up conversation.

Startchancen für alle ermöglichte. Sie diente eher zur Abkapselung der Privilegierten von den weniger Privilegierten und besonders zur Abkapselung nach außen, indem das Fremde gleichsam automatisch zum Befremdlichen wurde. In dieser vom Geist der Monotonie, des Fleißes und der Ordnung geprägten Epoche hielten die Auers bei uns Einzug.

Ich weiß noch, wie glücklich ich war, als den Rucksäcken mit den persönlichen Sachen, die Jelena und Carl bei ihrer Ankunft trugen, ein paar Tage später ein Waschkorb voller Bücher folgte. Sie wurden samt der Schreibmaschine, Marke Underwood, in Tante Lisettes Wohnzimmer eingeräumt. Wie alle in unserer Familie, die lesen konnten, war ich gierig auf Gedrucktes. Lesen und Vorlesen waren für mich die kleinen Fluchten aus der täglichen Kargheit, bedeuteten Eintauchen in andere Wirklichkeiten. Gerade deshalb war Lesen eingeschränkt auf Randstunden und auf den Sonntag, und für das Vorlesen von Tageszeitung oder Wochenmagazin, am spannendsten das Feuilleton mit „Fortsetzung folgt", blieb eine halbe Stunde nach dem Abendessen. Daß das Leseverbot das Gegenteil bewirkte und wir Kinder unter der Bettdecke oder während monotoner Arbeit Bücher verschlangen, wußten alle. Selbst Vater habe ich oft dabei ertappt, wie er auf dem Arbeitstisch im Gewächshaus ein offenes Buch neben sich liegen hatte und mit abwesendem Blick Setzlinge in die Erde drückte. - Und nun lebten also zwei Menschen mit uns unter demselben Dach, die Lesen und Schreiben als ihren Beruf und somit als Arbeit betrieben. Ein völlig neuer Gedanke, eine Perspektive, die herrliche Zukunftsbilder weckte, welche mit anderem als mit Ordnung, Anstand und der Plackerei in Garten und Treibhäusern erfüllt waren . . .

Jelena und Carl hatten sich in Wien auf der Redaktion einer sozialistischen Zeitung kennengelernt. Carl, Biologe und Anthropologe, und Jelena, einige Jahre jünger und Studentin der Philosophie, hatten nach dem Anschluß Österreichs ans dritte Reich bis zuletzt auf der Redaktion ausgeharrt. Ich weiß nicht, wie sie zu unserer Marie ins Stubaital gelangten, erinnere mich aber deutlich, daß ich jedesmal Herzklopfen bekam, wenn von ihrer Flucht in letzter Minute geredet wurde. In der Schule war der Zweite Weltkrieg kein Thema, damals, und er wurde auch in den obern Klassen später nur am Rande erwähnt, sozusagen als Eintrittskarte zu Wilhelm Tell. So mußte ich mir aus den Gesprächsfetzen der Erwachsenen meine eigene Welt-Geschichte zusammenstückeln.

In the Beginning was the Word

At first Jelena's and Carl's words seemed artificial to me. We spoke dialect, even in school, and for us German was a written language, never a spoken one. When Jelena and Carl ate with us, which became more and more a matter of course, as they frequently gave us a hand with our work, "in order to do something real for once," as they said, I always felt as if we were mounting a stage and slipping into a new role, like actors. By speaking high German everything seemed to change colour and meaning, the ordinary became extraordinary, the world transformed itself. At first, however, we stumbled over our heavy tongues, skated on thin ice, ashamed of our clumsiness. Step by step we learned to control ourselves and to play with words, hesitantly at first, then with more and more pleasure. Even while remembering, I can still feel the excitement of the new worlds which dawned on me in conversation with the Auers, when they put names to things that had been nameless for me until then. At that time I spoke high German to myself, alone on my way to school, and told myself stories that I had never heard that way before.

Words as the key to a different reality: the Auers gave me this key at a time when I soaked words up like a sponge, infatuated with language. I can still hear Jelena's voice when she caught me with a book in the stairwell, where I was supposed to be cleaning the stairs: "Don't put blind faith in the words, child. They can make the dead rise again, but they can also kill. At your age I was as much in love with words as you. Now I have become suspicious. I have experienced what effect words can have. It isn't events that determine the course of the world, but the way we imagine them and the words with which we describe them." - The fact that these sentences have stuck in my mind has less to do with their content, which I only understood by way of suggestion, than with Jelena's attitude, which suited the way I lived at that time. The invention of reality through language, the little respites through stories, building castles in the air - "Build castles in the air, children, it doesn't cost anything, and who knows what will become of them," our father used to say, - all this was part of my childhood and was now respected and legitimized by our guests.

Am Anfang war das Wort

Für mich waren Jelenas und Carls Worte vorerst Kunstworte. Wir redeten Dialekt, auch in der Schule, und Deutsch war für uns eine geschriebene, nie eine gesprochene Sprache. Wenn Jelena und Carl mit an unserm Tisch aßen, was sich immer selbstverständlicher ergab, da sie häufig bei unserer Arbeit mit Hand anlegten, „um auch einmal etwas Rechtes zu tun“, wie sie sagten, war mir immer, als ob wir eine Bühne bestiegen und als Schauspieler in eine andere Haut schlüpften. Durch das Reden in Hochdeutsch bekamen die Dinge neue Farben und Bedeutungen, wurde das Gewöhnliche außergewöhnlich, verwandelte sich die Welt. Vorerst allerdings stolperten wir über unsere schweren Zungen, gerieten aufs Glatteis, schämten uns über unsere Unbeholfenheit. Schritt für Schritt lernten wir uns aufzufangen und mit Worten zu spielen, zögernd zuerst, dann immer lustvoller. Noch in der Erinnerung fühle ich die Erregung über die neuen Welten, die mir im Gespräch mit den Auers aufgingen, wenn sie Dinge benannten, die für mich bis anhin namenlos gewesen waren. In jener Zeit redete ich auf dem Schulweg laut Hochdeutsch vor mich hin und erzählte mir dabei Geschichten, die ich so noch nie gehört hatte.

Das Wort als Schlüssel zu einer andern Wirklichkeit: Jelena und Carl schenkten mir diesen Schlüssel zu einer Zeit, als ich Worte aufsaugte wie ein Schwamm, vernarrt war in Sprache. Ich habe noch Jelenas Stimme im Ohr, als sie mich einmal mit einem Buch im Treppenhaus ertappte, wo ich die Stiegen hätte wischen müssen: „Glaub den Worten nicht einfach, Mädchen, sei vorsichtig. Sie können die Toten auferstehen lassen, aber sie können auch töten. In deinem Alter war ich so verliebt in Worte wie du. Inzwischen bin ich mißtrauisch geworden. Ich habe erlebt, was Worte bewirken können. Denn es sind nicht die Ereignisse, die den Lauf der Welt bestimmen, sondern die Vorstellungen, die wir von ihnen haben, und die Worte, mit denen wir sie beschreiben.“ - Daß mir diese Sätze haften blieben, hat wohl weniger mit ihrem Inhalt, den ich nur andeutungsweise verstand, als mit Jelenas Haltung zu tun, welche zu meiner damaligen Lebenswelt paßte. Die Erfindung von Wirklichkeit durch Sprache, die kleinen Fluchten durch Geschichten, durch das Bauen von Luftschlössern - „Baut Luftschlösser, Kinder, das kostet nichts, und wer weiß, was aus ihnen wird“, pflegte Vater zu sagen, - das alles war Teil

Carl

As time passed we learnt that Carl's works, typed on the Underwood on the top floor, were attracting attention in the outside world. Carl was given a teaching post at the Swiss Institute of Science and Technology and was only at home evenings. Letters came for him from America, and from the conversations at table it became apparent that he had published a paper that imparted a new view of biology, a new way of viewing mankind. I had no idea what that meant, but once overheard an excited conversation between Carl and our father, the hobby biologist. It had to do with father's hobby, evolution and genetics, that I remember distinctly. Father not only read anything he could find on this subject, he also told us children about it and aroused our curiosity about the purple rose he was hoping to cultivate. While we waited - in vain - and were certain that he would give it the names of his three daughters, we proudly showed our friends the five sorts of apple that he had grafted on to the "Fürst Bismarck" tree next to the place where we sat, one sort for each apple month. - I vaguely remember Carl reproaching my father for his "blind belief in progress," when my father vehemently supported his idea that mankind would naturally develop to a higher stage of morality, which would render a war such as the one just experienced unimaginable in thousands (or was it hundreds of thousands?) of years. "Just look at your much praised dolphins," he said to Carl. "They are so peaceful because their brain has had far more time to develop than that of man." I didn't quite understand Carl's arguments. I, 10 or 12 years old, only heard that he was extremely concerned when he spoke of the development of the human mind, which, due to a terrible mistake, equated progress with the destruction of the world it lived in and had now - in contrast to the dolphins - caused the basis for a peaceful development to sway. The expression "It is five minutes to twelve or later," which I afterwards heard throughout my childhood, sometimes aroused fear in me, but even more the strength to resist.

meiner Kindheit und bekam nun Anerkennung und Legitimation durch unsere Gäste.

Carl

Mit der Zeit erfuhren wir, daß Carls Schriften, die er auf der Underwood im obersten Stockwerk tippte, in der Welt draußen Aufmerksamkeit erregten. Carl erhielt einen Lehrauftrag an der Eidgenössischen Technischen Hochschule und war nur noch an den Abenden im Haus. Es trafen Briefe für ihn aus Amerika ein, und aus den Tischgesprächen wurde klar, daß Carl eine Arbeit veröffentlicht hatte, die eine neue Sicht der Biologie, eine neue Sichtweise des Menschen, vermittelte. Ich hatte keine Ahnung, was damit gemeint war, überhörte aber einmal ein erregtes Gespräch zwischen Carl und unserm Vater, dem Hobby-Biologen. Es ging um Vaters Steckenpferd, Evolution und Vererbungslehre, daran erinnere ich mich genau. Nicht nur, daß Vater alles las, was es für ihn zu diesem Thema zu lesen gab, er erzählte auch uns Kindern davon und machte uns neugierig auf die violette Rosensorte, die er zu züchten hoffte. Während wir - vergeblich - darauf warteten und sicher waren, daß er ihr die Namen seiner drei Töchter geben würde, zeigten wir unsern Kameraden aber mit Stolz die fünf Apfelsorten, die er auf den „Fürst Bismarck"-Baum neben dem Sitzplatz gepfropft hatte, für jeden Apfelmonat eine. - Vage habe ich in Erinnerung, daß Carl bei jenem Gespräch meinem Vater seinen „blinden Fortschrittsglauben" vorwarf, als dieser sich vehement für die Idee einsetzte, daß der Mensch sich natürlicherweise zu höhern Stufen der Moral entwickeln würde, die in Jahrtausenden (oder waren es Hunderttausende?) einen Krieg wie den eben erlebten unvorstellbar machen würden. „So schau doch deine vielgerühmten Delphine an", sagte er zu Carl, „sie sind so friedfertig, weil ihr Hirn viel länger Zeit gehabt hat zu seiner Entwicklung als das des Menschen." Ich verstand Carls Argumente nicht ganz, hörte mit meinen 10 oder 12 Jahren nur, daß er zutiefst besorgt war, als er von der Entwicklung des menschlichen Geistes redete, der durch einen schrecklichen Irrtum Fortschritt mit Zerstörung seiner Lebenswelt gleichsetzte und nun - im Gegensatz zu den Delphinen - die Grundlagen für eine friedliche Entwicklung ins Wanken gebracht habe. Der Ausdruck „Es ist fünf vor zwölf oder später", den ich nachher eine Kindheit lang hörte, hat in mir manchmal Angst, aber vor allem die Kraft des Widerstands geweckt.

As Carl's star began to shine, Jelena seemed strangely ill-humored. She went to philosophical lectures at the University in Zurich, wrote as well, although no-one seemed interested in printing her work. To earn money for them both she worked in the Central Library, preferably Saturdays and Sundays, as she got double pay on those days. It wasn't until later that I heard that she had helped Carl write the papers that made him famous and had then translated them into English too. She supported his scientific discoveries with the formal logic of philosophy, and together with him developed a language which was able to express complex matters in a simple and elegant way, for which he was soon to become famous.

Once, it must have been 1948, Jelena returned from Zurich very agitated. Mother and I met her on the way home from the station, and mother asked her what was wrong. Jelena usually spoke rather thoughtfully in her soft, slavic way, but now her voice cracked."I went to visit Milena, she's Einstein's divorced wife, from Novi Sad like me, and a distant relation of my family. It's tragic the way she is vegetating in Albert's shadow. She's a highly talented mathematician! She subordinated her whole life to her husband's work, and now she's 73, alone and very ill. More in mind than in body, it seems to me, but she won't live much longer. . . . Do you know that Milena deserves a place in the history of science for her experiments in the physical laboratory and for her mathematical contribution to the development of Albert's theories? A place equal to that of her husband! And where did she end up? In his shadow, lonely, unknown, without importance. But worst of all, do you know what's worst of all? She still doesn't understand a thing, she still thinks it's natural that it's the way it is, and accepts the responsibility for her name not being included on their mutual works. She still only talks about Albert, although she hasn't seen him for years. He did bequeath her the money he received for the Nobel Prize, for he is a benevolent person. But what is that to her? And what is it to him that he never understood these correlations?"

Not until later, much later, did I understand Jelena's indignation. There was something else that united "us women," Jelena, my mother

Jelena schien in der Zeit, als Carls Stern zu leuchten begann, seltsam verstimmt. Sie ging zu philosophischen Vorlesungen an die Universität in Zürich, schrieb ebenfalls, doch schien niemand Interesse zu haben daran, ihre Arbeiten auch zu drucken. Um Geld für beide zu verdienen, arbeitete sie in der Zentralbibliothek, am liebsten Samstag und Sonntag, weil da der doppelte Lohn bezahlt wurde. Später erst habe ich gehört, daß sie Carls Arbeiten, mit denen er berühmt wurde, mit ihm geschrieben und dann auch ins Englische übersetzt hatte. Sie unterstützte seine naturwissenschaftlichen Entdeckungen mit der formalen Logik der Philosophie und entwickelte mit ihm eine Sprache, welche höchste Komplexität auf einfache und elegante Art auszudrücken vermochte, für die er bald einmal berühmt wurde.

Einmal, es muß 1948 gewesen sein, kam Jelena aufgewühlt von Zürich zurück. Mutter und ich begegneten ihr auf dem Weg vom Bahnhof nach Hause, und Mutter fragte sie, was denn los sei. Jelena, die in ihrer weichen slawischen Art sonst eher bedächtig sprach, überschlug es die Stimme. „Ich war bei Milena zu Besuch, das ist die geschiedene Frau von Einstein, aus Novi Sad wie ich, und weitläufig mit meiner Familie verwandt. Eine Tragödie, wie sie im Schatten von Albert vegetiert. Diese hochbegabte Mathematikerin! Sie hat ihr ganzes Leben der Arbeit ihres Mannes untergeordnet, und nun ist sie 73, allein und schwer krank. Mehr im Gemüt als am Körper, scheint mir, aber sie wird nicht mehr lange leben ... Wißt ihr, daß Milena mit ihren Versuchen im physikalischen Labor und mit ihrem mathematischen Beitrag an die Entwicklung von Alberts Theorien einen Platz in der Geschichte der Wissenschaft verdient hätte? Einen Platz, der dem ihres Mannes ebenbürtig ist! Und wo ist sie gelandet? In seinem Schatten, vereinsamt, unbekannt, ohne Bedeutung. Aber das Schlimmste, wißt ihr, was das Schlimmste ist? Sie versteht noch immer nichts, sie findet es immer noch natürlich, daß es so ist, und nimmt die Verantwortung dafür, daß ihr Name in den gemeinsamen Schriften fehlt, auf sich. Noch immer redet sie nur von Albert, obwohl sie ihn jahrelang nicht gesehen hat. Er hat ihr zwar das Geld, das er für den Nobelpreis erhielt, vermacht, denn er ist ein wohlwollender Mensch. Aber was hat sie nun davon? Und was hat er davon, daß er diese Zusammenhänge nie verstanden hat?

Später, sehr viel später erst, habe ich Jelenas Empörung verstanden. Es war da noch etwas anderes, was „uns Frauen" miteinander ver-

and I. In our house we only had "running cold and cold water", so every Saturday evening we had to go through the ritual in the bathroom extension, which also served as washroom. In turn we children were allowed to heat up the copper boiler with firewood and the contents of the waste paper baskets. I loved this job. As soon as the fire had caught, I would sit on the four-wheeled cart that spent the winter in the bathroom, soon cosily enveloped in steam, and go through the waste paper baskets in search of interesting scraps, looking for tracks through words, feeling for paths into the unknown. Curious about the connections grown-ups never thought to explain to the child, suspecting secret stories and tying loose ends into a fabric. The "fibber" is probably not far from the truth. . . From the time the Auers moved into our house the search for clues really became exciting. I understood little of what was on the manuscript pages or notes that were thrown away. What interested me most of all were Jelena's handwritten notes. I must have left several of them lying around, smoothed out. For Jelena's protection apparently, my mother put them in her note books, where I found them again decades later. It cannot be coincidence that she kept scraps on which I now read:

"Noted while translating Carl's book: German is a good language for the simple reason that it contains two words for the term 'reality': 'Wirklichkeit' and 'Realität.' I wonder whether both existed before Kant? Must trace it back."

- "Really nice that in German 'Mensch' is not identical with 'man.° Nice? Who over the centuries has answered the question: 'Lord, what is man?' Masters and men who were able to brood in their studies, while the other half of mankind prepared their daily bread in the kitchens. Mankind = man. Talking of daily bread: I am going to stop feeding Carl so diligently every day, with bread and with admiration, and feed myself better instead. In Rilke I read something in the *Cornet* which I feel to be a woman's poem rather than a soldier's:

> Rest. Just for once to be a guest. Not always compelled to satisfy one's own needs with meagre fare. Not always grasping with hostile hands. But just for once let everything happen, and know whatever happens will be good."

band, Jelena, meine Mutter und mich. In unserem alten Haus gab es nur „fließend kalt und kaltes Wasser", aber dafür jeden Samstagabend das Ritual in der angebauten Badestube, die auch als Waschküche diente. Wir Kinder durften abwechslungsweise den kupfernen Badeofen einheizen, mit Kleinholz und dem Inhalt der Papierkörbe. Ich liebte diese Arbeit. Sobald das Feuer entfacht war, setzte ich mich auf den Vierräderwagen, der in der Badestube überwinterte, bald einmal wohlig eingehüllt in Wasserdampf, und durchforstete die Papierkörbe nach interessanten Fetzen, Spuren suchend durch Worte, auf ihnen Wege ins Unbekannte ertastend, neugierig auf Zusammenhänge, die Erwachsene dem Kind nie zu erklären dachten, heimliche Geschichten ahnend und lose Fäden zu einem Gewebe knüpfend. Mit dem „Lügenkind" wird es wohl seine Richtigkeit haben . . . Seit die Auers im Haus wohnten, wurde die Spurensuche erst richtig lustvoll. Zwar verstand ich das wenigste auf den weggeworfenen Manuskriptseiten oder Notizblättern. Was mich interessierte, waren vor allem Jelenas handgeschriebene Zettel. Glatt gestrichen, ließ ich wohl einige davon liegen. Meine Mutter hat sie, offenbar um Jelena zu schützen, in ihre Notizhefte gelegt, wo ich sie Jahrzehnte später wieder fand. Es kann kein Zufall sein, daß sie Fetzen aufbewahrte, auf denen ich lese:

„Beim Übersetzen von Carls Buch gemerkt: Das Deutsche ist nur schon deshalb eine gute Sprache, weil in ihr zwei Wörter vorkommen für den Begriff „Reality": Wirklichkeit und Realität. Ich frage mich, ob es die beiden auch schon gab vor Kant? Muß dem nachgehen."

- „Eigentlich schön, daß 'Mensch' auf Deutsch nicht identisch ist mit 'Mann'. Schön? Wer hat denn über Jahrtausende die Frage beantwortet: 'Herr, was ist der Mensch?'Herren und Männer, die in ihren Studierstuben sinnieren konnten, während die andere Hälfte der Menschheit für sie in der Küche das tägliche Brot zubereitete. Mensch = Mann. A propos tägliches Brot: Ich will aufhören, Carl täglich so fleißig zu füttern, mit Brot und mit Bewunderung, und mich dafür selber besser nähren. Bei Rilke lese ich im „Cornet" etwas, was ich eigentlich eher als Frauengedicht als das eines Soldaten empfinde:

> Rast. Gast sein einmal. Nicht immer selbst seine Wünsche bewirten mit kärglicher Kost. Nicht immer feindlich nach allem fassen, einmal sich alles geschehen lassen und wissen: Was geschieht, ist gut!"

Jelena, who had words for things that even my mother only vaguely suspected at that time, how thankful I am for her words and pictures! She planted suspicions in me that later became, and indeed still become, knowledge. She approved of my curiosity and doubts at a time when plain, unquestioning conformity was far more desirable, particularly in a girl. The casualness with which she dug in the soil with her hands when planting vegetables, the pleasure with which she rolled out pasta dough on the kitchen table or plucked a freshly slaughtered chicken on her knees taught me that clear thinking, provocative questioning and sensuousness are possibilities of one and the same person, provided he or she refuses to be limited to the typically male or typically female characteristics. Not that this was the easier path, either for her or for me, but whoever sets out on this path finds no way back.

A picture emerges which has fixed itself in my mind forever. One day in Autumn my younger sister came running home from school through thick fog, into the house where I was preparing the evening meal with Jelena. In tears she threw herself at Jelena. "I was so frightened," she sobbed. "All of a sudden I didn't know whether this house and all of you existed, or whether I'm just dreaming it all and will suddenly wake up and be all on my own. . . ." The abyss that opened up at such a moment was already known to me from my own terrifying experience. For we don't live in the world, but in the pictures we make of it in our heads, and children know this, even if they hardly ever talk about it and so cannot be consoled in anyone's arms, as my sister was in Jelena's that time.- Later I learnt to connect the incredibility of this image with the realization that our dreams and ideas can also imply freedom. But the feeling of the abyss that is connected with freedom remained. Possibly the only consolation for the fact that "the thing-in-itself" doesn't exist, can only really be found in the loving embrace of another person.

Epilogue

The thread between the Auers and us never snapped completely, even though we sometimes lost touch with one another for years. I

Jelena, die eine Sprache hatte für Dinge, die wohl auch meine Mutter damals nur dunkel geahnt hat, wie bin ich ihr dankbar für Worte und Bilder! Sie hat in mir Ahnungen gesät, die später zu Wissen wurden und immer noch werden, sie hat meine Neugier und meine Zweifel gutgeheißen zu einer Zeit, als brave, fraglose Anpassung vor allem für Mädchen weitaus wünschenswerter war. Durch die Selbstverständlichkeit, mit der sie die Hände in die Erde grub, um Gemüse zu pflanzen, die Lust, mit der sie auf dem Küchentisch Nudelteig auswellte oder auf ihren Knien frischgeschlachtete Hühner rupfte, hat sie mir gelehrt, daß klares Denken, provokatives Fragen und Sinnlichkeit Möglichkeiten ein- und derselben Person sein können, wenn sie sich weigert, sich auf typisch männliche oder weibliche Merkmale einengen zu lassen. Nicht, daß es der einfachere Weg wurde, weder für sie noch für mich, aber wer einmal darauf gekommen ist, findet keinen Weg zurück.

Ein Bild taucht auf, das sich für immer in mir festgesetzt hat. An einem Herbsttag kam meine jüngere Schwester aus der Schule durch dicken Nebel ins Haus gerannt, wo ich mit Jelena das Abendessen richtete. In Tränen aufgelöst, warf sie sich Jelena an den Hals. „Ich hab so Angst gehabt", schluchzte sie. „Auf einmal wußte ich nicht mehr, ob es dieses Haus und euch alle überhaupt gibt, oder ob ich das alles nur träume und plötzlich erwache und ganz allein bin . . ." Den Abgrund, der sich in jenem Moment auftat, kannte ich bereits aus eigener schrecklicher Erfahrung. Wir leben ja nicht in der Welt, sondern in den Bildern, die wir uns von ihr im Kopf machen. Kinder wissen das, auch wenn sie fast nie darüber reden und darum auch nicht tröstend in die Arme genommen werden, wie damals meine Schwester von Jelena. - Später habe ich gelernt, die Bodenlosigkeit dieser Vorstellung zu verbinden mit der Erkenntnis, daß unsere Träume und Vorstellungen auch Freiheit bedeuten können. Aber das Gefühl des Abgrunds, der mit der Freiheit verbunden ist, blieb. Vielleicht liegt der einzige Trost dafür, daß wir die „Dinge an sich" nicht erkennen können, wirklich nur in der liebevollen Umarmung durch einen andern Menschen?

Epilog

Der Faden zwischen den Auers und uns riss nie ganz, auch wenn wir uns manchmal für Jahre aus den Augen verloren. Ich traf Carl noch

met Carl once more, exactly thirty years after our farewell at our home town train station. It wasn't easy to find him in Arcosanti, in the Arizona desert, where he was planning the 'new city' with Paolo Soleri and a young mexican architect. We finally managed to contact him through Jelena, who was living in Europe again. In Phoenix, Milton Erickson pointed out the way and showed us dozens of cast iron bells on the trees in his garden which had been cast in a workshop in Arcosanti. One of these hangs on the tree behind our house now, and when its ringing keeps me awake on stormy nights pictures well up in me, memories of the meeting with these two old men on the edge of the desert.

Carl had become famous. I read his name again and again in the works in my own vocational field, applied social sciences and systemic therapy. It's strange that a natural scientist should become a kind of saint in our territory, Carl thought so too. He had of course thought about the Condition Humaine, not only about the evolution of cells, he said, but he could provide no formulas for a better life or for how people could solve their problems.

But in spite of this he enjoyed visits from his disciples, even if this has the aura of a typical male organization about it. "Sometimes I feel quite ashamed," he said, "when a well-read young man comes to me who has accepted my ideas, sometimes quite loosely formulated, as the pure doctrine. And when he even starts making one of my essays into a theory on the essence of human beings and their possibility to change, which you therapists pack into your first aid kits as hand tools for all kinds of repair work, I can't help feeling a bit queasy. However, the people who come to you are presumably intelligent enough not to allow themselves to be patched like a water pipe. As you can see, I miss Jelena with her precise language and her superior housewife's common sense in many ways. I may be able to think systemically, but I have little aptitude to formulate systematically or to bother about the use of my insights in everyday life. This is one of the reasons I have come to the desert and am at last learning to use my hands."

einmal, genau dreißig Jahre nach unserem Abschied auf der heimatlichen Bahnstation. Es war nicht einfach, ihn in Arcosanti, in der Wüste Arizonas zu finden, wo er mit Paolo Soleri und einer jungen Architektin die „neue Stadt“ plante. Über Jelena, die wieder in Europa lebte, gelang es uns schließlich. In Phoenix wies uns Milton Erickson den Weg und zeigte uns Dutzende von gußeisernen Glokken an den Bäumen in seinem Garten, die in einer Werkstatt von Arcosanti gegossen worden waren. Eine davon hängt jetzt am Baum hinter unserem Haus, und wenn sie mich mit ihrem Läuten in stürmischen Nächten wachhält, steigen Bilder in mir hoch, Erinnerungen an die Begegnung mit den beiden alten Männern am Rande der Wüste.

Carl war berühmt geworden. Immer wieder las ich seinen Namen in den Arbeiten zu meinem eigenen Berufsfeld der angewandten Sozialwissenschaften und der systemischen Therapie. Seltsam, daß ein Naturwissenschaftler ausgerechnet in unserem Territorium zu einer Art Heiligem stilisiert worden war, das fand auch Carl. Natürlich habe er sich Gedanken gemacht über die Condition Humaine, nicht bloß über die Evolution von Zellen, meinte er, aber Rezepte zum besseren Leben oder dafür, wie Menschen ihre Probleme lösen könnten, seien ihm eigentlich fremd.

Und trotzdem genieße er es, wenn er von seinen Jüngern besucht werde, selbst wenn das so ein bißchen etwas Männerbündlerisches an sich habe. „Ich bin manchmal recht beschämt“, meinte er, „wenn so ein belesener junger Mann zu mir kommt, der meine manchmal doch recht unscharf formulierten Ideen als die reine Lehre aufgenommen hat. Wenn er dann aus einem meiner Essays gar eine Theorie über Wesen und Wandlungsmöglichkeiten von Menschen macht, die von euch Therapeuten quasi als Handwerkszeug ins Notfallköfferchen für allerlei Reparaturarbeit gepackt wird, kann ich mich eines mulmigen Gefühls nicht erwehren. Aber die Menschen, die zu euch kommen, werden schon intelligent genug sein, um sich nicht wie Wasserröhren flicken zu lassen. Du siehst, Jelena mit ihrer präzisen Sprache und ihrem überlegenen Hausfrauenverstand fehlt mir an allen Ecken und Enden. Ich mag wohl systemisch denken, aber systematisch formulieren oder mich um die Anwendung meiner Erkenntnisse im Alltag kümmern, liegt mir weniger. Ein Grund, warum ich in die Wüste gekommen bin und hier endlich lerne, meine Hände zu gebrauchen.“

Carl, over seventy meanwhile, still told stories as enchantingly as before and still permitted my questions to tempt him to tell stories. I was most interested in how he dealt with women. "They don't come often," he said with a wink. "Of course I enjoy being surrounded by willing hands, fortunately that is something that has never been lacking in my life, I am obviously the ideal father of ideal daughters. But in your field I seem to have a better reputation with the men than with the women." He didn't attempt an explanation until after his fourth Tequila: "Men like to shine in reflected glory. Maybe most women, apart from Jelena, can't believe in their own glory. They remain the great women behind the great men. Could that be?"

Jelena - "Jelänger-Jelieber," as my father used to call her somewhat adoringly, the popular name for honeysuckle (Lonicera) and symbol of loyalty, wrote a long letter from the Californian hills every summer, where she spent the holidays with Carl and the two children, Carl Anton and Nina. "You will hardly understand it," she wrote after many years, "but Carl and I have separated. We might stay that way, each in his own way, more faithful to each other than if we were living together. What has been, what we have given each other and meant to each other in the 20 years we were together cannot be lost."

Jelena has emerged from Carl's shadow, late but not too late. When almost fifty she wrote a textbook on European Philosophy in the 19th and 20th Century, from a female viewpoint, as she assures us. It has become compulsory reading for female and male students, not only in American Women's Colleges, and enabled her to look forward to an old age free of cares. Now and then she teaches as a guest at American universities, and has produced a television film with her daughter Nina on the advantages of non-coeducative women's training, where apparently far more female students take the examination for their doctorate than at the so-called integrated colleges.

Not long ago we met Jelena in Venice, in February, in front of the Teatro Fenice. Her friend Claudio had just conducted Mahler's *Kindertotenlieder* - in the dying city in which in winter, when its inhabitants are almost on their own, a vitality and happiness flares up, similar to what I've experienced at the bedside of the dying, when gradually the tremendous medicalbustle becomes senseless and then

Carl, mittlerweile über siebzig, erzählte so faszinierend wie damals und ließ sich von meinen Fragen zu Geschichten verführen, wie damals. Am meisten interessierte mich, wie er es denn mit den Frauen halte. „Sie kommen selten," meinte er augenzwinkernd, „natürlich genieße ich es, von dienstbaren Geistern umgeben zu sein, daran hat es mir in meinem Leben zum Glück nie gefehlt, offenbar bin ich der ideale Vater idealer Töchter. Aber ich scheine in eurem Feld einen besseren Namen zu haben bei den Männern als bei den Frauen." Erst nach dem vierten Tequila der Versuch einer Erklärung: „Men like to shine in reflected glory. Vielleicht trauen die meisten Frauen, außer Jelena, sich eigenen Ruhm schon gar nicht zu. Sie bleiben die großen Frauen hinter den großen Männern. Könnte das sein?"

Jelena - „Jelänger-Jelieber", wie mein Vater sie damals - ein bißchen verliebt wohl - genannt hatte, der Volksname für das Geißblatt (Lonicera) und Symbol für Treue, schrieb jeden Sommer einen langen Brief aus den Hügeln Kaliforniens, wo sie mit Carl und den beiden Kindern Carl Anton und Nina die Ferien verbrachte. „Ihr werdet es kaum verstehen", schrieb sie nach Jahren, „aber Carl und ich haben uns getrennt. Vielleicht bleiben wir so, jeder auf seine Weise, einander treuer, als wenn wir miteinander leben würden. Was war und was wir uns gegeben und bedeutet haben in den 20 Jahren unseres Zusammenseins, kann nicht verloren gehen."

Jelena ist aus Carls Schatten herausgetreten, spät, aber nicht zu spät. Sie hat, als sie fast fünfzig war, ein Textbuch über europäische Philosophie des 19. und 20. Jahrhunderts geschrieben, aus weiblicher Sicht, wie sie versichert. Es ist, nicht nur an amerikanischen Women's Colleges, zur Pflichtlektüre für Studentinnen und Studenten geworden und ermöglichte ihr, sorgenfrei dem Alter entgegen zu sehen. Hin und wieder unterrichtet sie als Gast an amerikanischen Universitäten und hat mit Tochter Nina einen Fernsehfilm über die Vorteile der nicht-koedukativen Frauenausbildung gedreht, wo offenbar viel mehr Studentinnen ihr Doktorat machen als an den sogenannt integrierten Colleges.

Kürzlich trafen wir Jelena in Venedig, im Februar, vor dem Teatro Fenice. Ihr Freund Claudio hatte eben Mahlers „Kindertotenlieder" dirigiert - in der sterbenden Stadt, in welcher im Winter, wenn ihre Bewohner fast unter sich sind, eine Lebendigkeit und Fröhlichkeit aufflackert, wie ich sie schon am Bett von Sterbenden erlebt habe, wenn nach und nach die ungeheure medizinische Geschäftigkeit

there is space and time for memories. Dazed, we stood in the dusk with wet faces, and held one another in our arms, just like that time long ago, in face of the abyss.... Jelena, magnificently dressed in blue, her eyes still sparkling, had emerged from Carl's shadow and yet spoke kindly of him. Later, at dinner in the almost empty "Fioretta", the four of us told each other about our lives, about the children. "You're bound to laugh, but Carl Junior now writes his name Karl and is the owner of a wholesale bakery in San Francisco, where they make European pastries. . . . The only way to distinguish himself from his famous father. Instead of books, he reads the Dow Jones Index, and is happy doing it."

And now for the story, the quite wonderful story I've saved till last for you because I know how mad you are about stories: On Carl's 90th birthday his son gave him a present which couldn't have been more phantastic if he'd dreamt it. He founded an academic publishing house in Heidelberg that bears his name, the Carl Auer Publishing House. You should have seen us when we invented it on a convivial Californian night. Of course the address could only be Heidelberg, stronghold of Humanism and Idealism, vision of higher education for everyone on the other side of the Atlantic, the perfect fiction. With many bottles of Zinfandel, Karl, Nina, their friends and I created the publishing team, the chosen sons of Carl the Great, a beautiful male organization with purely noble German names. All of them highly talented, and also good looking men in their prime, each one of them uniquely creative. Of course we designed robot photos for each one and fed them to the laptop computer Karl Jr. always carries with him. Sometime, when they have broken away from Carl, which will hopefully not happen for a long time, we will publish their collected biographies, with robot photos, you can do that nowadays. By the way, after a lot of thought we gave them a female colleague, a really good woman, warm and clever, to represent the female aspect. So far as I have heard even in Europe there's nothing doing without it.

Of course, Karl Jr. keeps a firm watch on things; considering all the money he has invested, this is very important. Since he cannot supervise everything from California he's found a competent scien-

sinnlos wird und auf einmal Raum und Zeit aufgehen für Erinnerungen. Benommen standen wir in der Dämmerung, mit feuchten Gesichtern, und hielten uns wie damals in den Armen, einmal mehr im Angesicht des Abgrundes . . . Jelena, prächtig in Blau gekleidet, mit ihren immer noch strahlenden Augen, hervorgetreten aus Carls Schatten und liebevoll von ihm erzählend. Später, beim Essen zu viert im fast menschenleeren „Fioretta", berichteten wir einander über unser Leben, über die Kinder. „Ihr werdet lachen, aber Carl Junior schreibt sich jetzt Karl und ist Besitzer einer Großbäckerei in San Francisco, wo europäisches Brot fabriziert wird . . . Die einzige Möglichkeit wohl, sich von seinem berühmten Vater abzugrenzen. Statt Bücher liest er den Dow Jones Index und ist glücklich dabei."

Und die Geschichte, die ganz wunderbare Geschichte, die ich bis zum Schluß für euch aufgespart habe, weil ich weiß, wie gierig ihr auf Geschichten seid: Zu Carls 90. Geburtstag hat sein Sohn ein Geschenk gemacht, wie er es sich phantastischer nicht hätte träumen können. Er hat nämlich in Heidelberg einen wissenschaftlichen Verlag gegründet, der seinen Namen trägt, den Carl Auer Verlag. Ihr hättet uns sehen sollen, als wir ihn in einer feuchtfröhlichen kalifornischen Nacht erfunden haben. Natürlich kam als Adresse nur Heidelberg in Frage, Hochburg von Humanismus und Idealismus, Traumbild höherer Bildung für alle auf der anderen Seite des Atlantik, die perfekte Fiktion. Bei vielen Flaschen Zinfandel schufen Karl, Nina, ihre Freunde und ich das Herausgeberteam, die auserwählten Söhne Carls des Großen, einen wunderschönen Männerbund mit lauter edlen deutschen Namen. Alles hochbegabte, übrigens auch gutaussehende Männer im besten Alter, jeder für sich einzigartig kreativ. Wir haben natürlich Robotbilder für jeden einzelnen entworfen und in den Computer eingefüttert, den Karl Jr. immer als Laptop bei sich trägt. Irgendwann, wenn sie sich von Carl abgelöst haben werden, was hoffentlich noch lange nicht der Fall sein wird, werden wir ihre gesammelten Biographien veröffentlichen, mit Robot-Fotos, das kann man heute. Übrigens: Nach langem Hin und Her haben wir ihnen eine Kollegin beigegeben, eine wirklich gute Frau, warm und gescheit, die den weiblichen Aspekt vertritt. Wie ich höre, geht selbst in Europa nichts mehr ohne diesen.

Natürlich hat Karl Jr. das Ganze fest in Händen; bei dem vielen Geld, das er da investiert hat, natürlich wichtig. Weil er von Kalifornien aus aber nicht alles übersehen kann, hat er sich einen tüchtigen

tific journalist as manager, one with European and American roots, extremely suited to repeating great ideas on either side of the Atlantic, and madly mixed up in the nepotism of the natural and social science clique. Carl would have preferred fictitious sons to a manager, you know how romantic he is, but Junior's American pragmatism convinced him in the end."

And then all that remained was for us to drink a toast with a drop from the area around Alba: Long live the Carl Auer Publishing House!

[1] Jerome Bruner, *Actual Minds, Possible Words*. Harvard University Press, Boston, Mass., 1986.
[2] Desanka Trbuhovic-Gjuric, *Im Schatten Albert Einsteins*. Verlag Haupt, Bern und Stuttgart,1983.
[3] Rosmarie Welter-Enderlin, "Wer hat Angst vor Virginia Woolf, und vor wem hat sie Angst? Gedankensplitter zu Frauen, Männern und zum Schreiben," *Zeitschrift für systemische Therapie*, 7. Jg (2) April 1989.

Wissenschaftsjournalisten als Manager geholt, einen mit europäischen und amerikanischen Wurzeln, bestens geeignet zum Nacherzählen großer Ideen, hüben und drüben, und herrlich verfilzt im natur- und sozialwissenschaftlichen Klüngel. Carl hätte zwar die fiktiven Söhne einem Manager vorgezogen, du weißt, wie romantisch er ist. Aber des Juniors amerikanischer Pragmatismus hat ihn schließlich überzeugt."

Darauf blieb uns nur noch, mit einem Tropfen aus der Gegend von Alba anzustoßen: Lang lebe der Carl Auer Verlag!

[1] Jerome Bruner, *Actual Minds, Possible Worlds*. Harvard University Press, Boston, Mass., 1986.
[2] Desanka Trbuhovic-Gjuric, *Im Schatten Albert Einsteins*. Verlag Haupt, Bern und Stuttgart, 1983.
[3] Rosmarie Welter-Enderlin, „Wer hat Angst vor Virginia Woolf, und vor wem hat sie Angst? Gedankensplitter zu Frauen, Männern und zum Schreiben", *Zeitschrift für systemische Therapie*, 7. Jg (2) April 1989.

On the Shoulders of Auer

Auf den Schultern von Auer

Shit Happens

Steve de Shazer

It is high time that the rest of the world recognizes the importance of Carl Auer as Milwaukee did long ago. After his first visit here, the city fathers named a street after him: Auer Avenue. It was planned as a grand avenue, not just another street, but - in keeping with Carl Auer's way of thinking - it became just a mean city street without any distinction whatsoever.

Carl Auer can best be described as an itinerant philosopher. It has never been clear whether he felt forced to travel in order to spread his ideas or his spreading his ideas resulted in his being forced to travel. Regardless, his compulsive traveling meant that he found little or no time to write except on napkins he picked up in pubs and restaurants. Therefore, although often quoted, the central ideas of his philosophy are infrequently given proper citation. In fact, credit is usually given to someone else. (Which is, of course, in keeping with Auerian philosophy.)

I first met Carl in a pub near the Marquette University campus in Milwaukee. The owner and barkeep (known as Professor Le Claire), who was born in Colorado and had worked as a cowboy (with my father) in his youth, was educated in Philosophy at the Sorbonne. Here, discussions of "things philosophical" would frequently continue - with schnapps in hand - long after the pub closed.

1. Auer's central idea can be simply stated using just two words: ***shit happens.*** This aphorism is now showing up in the U. S. as a bumpersticker! However 999,999,999 out of 1,000,000,000 have no idea that this is Carl Auer's claim to fame. This is lack of credit is

Scheiß passiert

Steve de Shazer

Es ist höchste Zeit, daß die Welt die Bedeutung Carl Auers erkennt, was Milwaukee schon lange tut. Nach seinem ersten Besuch hier benannten die Stadtväter eine Straße nach ihm: die Auer-Avenue. Sie sollte eine Prachtstraße werden, die nicht aussah wie jede andere Straße. Ganz Carl Auers Denkart entsprechend wurde sie aber eine ganz gewöhnliche Straße, die sich in rein gar nichts von anderen unterscheidet.

Carl Auer kann am besten als umherreisender Philosoph beschrieben werden. Es wurde nie klar, ob er sich zum Reisen gedrängt fühlte, um seine Ideen zu verbreiten, oder ob die Verbreitung seiner Ideen eine Folge seines dranghaften Umherreisens war. Jedenfalls führte dieses zwanghafte Reisen dazu, daß er wenig oder keine Zeit zum Schreiben fand, und wenn, dann notierte er sich was in Kneipen oder Restaurants auf Papierservietten. Aus diesem Grunde werden, obwohl er öfters erwähnt wird, die zentralen Ideen seiner Philosophie selten angemessen und richtig zitiert. Im Gegenteil, sie werden gewöhnlich anderen zugeschrieben (was natürlich wiederum im Sinne der Auerschen Philosophie ist).

Zum ersten Mal traf ich Carl in einer Kneipe nahe der Marquette-Universität in Milwaukee. Der Besitzer und Barkeeper (auch bekannt als Professor Le Claire), der in Colorado geboren wurde und (mit meinem Vater) in seiner Jugend als Cowboy arbeitete, hatte an der Sorbonne Philosophie studiert. In dieser Kneipe wurde nachts noch lange nach der Sperrstunde bei Schnaps über „philosophische Dinge" weiterdiskutiert.

1. Auers zentraler Gedanke kann ganz einfach in zwei Worten zusammengefaßt werden: ***Scheiß passiert.*** Dieser Aphorismus taucht in den USA. zur Zeit als Autoaufkleber auf. 999.999.999 von 1.000.000.000 haben keine Ahnung, daß Carl Auer Anspruch darauf

exactly what Carl meant by ***shit happens***. This idea, i. e., ***shit happens***, struck me as very profound in and of itself. Little do people understand that it only takes two (2) words to rid us of the tyranny of causation.

As we discussed this most profound thought over beer and sausage and its effect on both linear and circular causality, Auer's idea became clear. Once ***shit happens*** human beings can only react and sometimes the reaction turns out right (***Glück = good luck***, which in the Milwaukee dialect is "good shit") and sometimes it turns out wrong (***Pech = bad luck*** [in Milwaukee, it's "bad shit"]) and sometimes it turns out even worse (***Unglück = worse luck*** [in Milwaukee, it's "worse shit"]). Recursively, one can only react to these reactions. But, importantly, Auer believed that a reaction does not "cause" the following reaction (or re-reaction or meta-reaction). Each reaction to some shit's happening is just one more example of Shit's Happening which must be reacted to.

2. Therefore, regardless of which way one reacts, ***that's life*** (another uncited Auerian principle). Life is an endless string of linear pairs:

Shit happens -> Reaction

The worse the reaction, the worse the next round of shit happens and, therefore, things go from bad to wurst, rather worse.

3. One night, during an argument about the distinction between "philosophical truth" and "scientific truth," Carl Auer startled me and everyone else in the pub by claiming, and I quote: ***"An easily understood, workable falsehood is more useful than a complex, but incomprehensible truth."*** It was only years later, when doing therapy with a family (the eldest son was said to be schizophrenic), did I begin to understand.

4. Carl Auer's ideas influenced the humorist James Thurber rather profoundly as indicated by the "Thurber aphorism": There is not a hell of a lot of difference between a) bending over backwards and b) falling flat on your face.

hätte, damit berühmt zu werden. Dieser Mangel an berechtigter Anerkennung ist genau das, was Carl mit ***Scheiß passiert*** meint. Diese Idee - ***Scheiß passiert*** - an sich beeindruckte mich durch ihre Tiefgründigkeit. Die Menschen verstehen nur wenig davon, daß es nur dieser zwei (2) Wörter bedarf, um der Tyrannei des Kausalitätsprinzips zu entgehen.

Als wir diesen höchst inhaltsschweren Gedanken und seine Auswirkung sowohl auf die lineare als auch auf die zirkuläre Kausalität bei Bier und Würstchen diskutierten, wurde Auers Idee zunehmend einleuchtender. Wenn ***Scheiß passiert,*** können Menschen nur reagieren, und manchmal stellt sich die Reaktion als richtig heraus ***(Glück = Good luck,*** im Milwaukee-Dialekt „guter Scheiß"), manchmal erweist sie sich als schlecht ***(Pech = bad luck),*** was in Milwaukee „schlechter Scheiß" heißt und gelegentlich kommt es noch schlimmer ***(Unglück = worse luck*** [in Milwaukee schlimmer Scheiß]). Rekursiv kann man nur auf diese Reaktionen reagieren. Aber, was entscheidend ist, Auer war davon überzeugt, daß eine Reaktion die darauffolgende nicht „verursacht" (oder die Rück-Reaktion oder die Meta-Reaktion). Jede Reaktion auf passierenden Scheiß ist nur ein weiteres Beispiel eines Scheißereignisses, auf das reagiert werden muß.

2. Deshalb, egal wie man reagiert: ***that's life*** (ein weiteres nicht zitiertes Auer-Prinzip). Leben ist ein endloses Band der linearen Paare:

Scheiß passiert -> Reaktion

Je schlechter die Reaktion, um so schlimmer ist die nächste Runde des passierenden Scheißes und deshalb sieht es ziemlich schlecht aus, wenn's um die Wurst geht.

3. Eines Nachts, während einer Auseinandersetzung über die Unterscheidung von „philosophischer Wahrheit" und „wissenschaftlicher Wahrheit", verblüffte Carl Auer mich und alle anderen in der Kneipe mit dem Satz, ich zitiere: ***„Eine leicht verständliche, brauchbare Unwahrheit ist nützlicher als eine komplexe, unverständliche Wahrheit."*** Erst Jahre später begann ich das in einer Therapie mit einer Familie (der älteste Sohn, meinte man, sei schizophren) zu verstehen.

4. Carl Auers Ideen beeinflußten den Humoristen James Thurber, wie der folgende „Thurber-Aphorismus" zeigt, ziemlich nachhaltig: Es macht keinen Unterschied, a) ob man sich nach hinten bückt oder b) der Länge nach auf die Nase fällt.

5. Carl Auer once remarked to me that 20 minutes waiting for a bus was shorter than 20 minutes waiting to have a tooth pulled and that both were different from 20 minutes in bed with a woman. He said that it was not just that time was relative but that many things could happen simultaneously or sequentially or randomly. After much thought he concluded that time was very strange indeed and finally figured out the truth: ***Time is only nature´s way of preventing everything from happening at once.***

6. One night, in this same pub, the discussion between us and Professor Le Claire led to the relationships between "truth/falsity" and "simplicity/complexity" and "profundity/triviality." The French philosopher pushed for an "either/or" distinction in all three sets, while I pushed for a "both/and" distinction, but Carl insisted that we were both wrong and were being stupidly dogmatic. The relationship in all three cases is "both either/or and both/and" because the distinction was false. He said that pairs of this sort were always a shorthand way of saying something profound yet hidden which can be stated in this way (and again I quote): ***"It is a simple task to make things complex but a complex task to make things simple."***

(It was never clear to me when and where Carl Auer was born except for one fact: He was born in a brewery just at the time the first barrel of Maibock [of some year] was being opened.)

5. Carl Auer bemerkte mir gegenüber einmal, daß 20 Minuten auf einen Bus zu warten kürzer ist, als 20 Minuten darauf zu warten, daß einem ein Zahn gezogen wird, und daß beides sich von 20 Minuten mit einer Frau im Bett unterscheidet. Er sagte, daß es nicht nur darum geht, daß die Zeit relativ sei, sondern darum, daß viele Dinge gleichzeitig oder nacheinander oder zufällig passieren könnten. Nachdenkend kam er zu dem Schluß, daß Zeit etwas wirklich Merkwürdiges sei, und äußerte schließlich folgende Erkenntnis: ***Zeit ist nur ein Mittel der Natur, um zu verhindern, daß alles gleichzeitig passiert.***

6. In derselben Kneipe führte uns eines Nachts die Diskussion mit Professor Le Claire zum Verhältnis von „Wahrheit und Unwahrheit", „Einfachheit und Komplexität" und „Tiefe und Trivialität". Der französische Philosoph vertrat eine „Entweder/Oder"-Unterscheidung bei allen drei Paaren, während ich für eine „Sowohl-als-auch"-Unterscheidung plädierte. Carl jedoch bestand darauf, daß wir beide schief lägen und dümmlich dogmatisch seien. Die Beziehung sei in allen drei Fällen „sowohl entweder/oder als auch sowohl-als-auch", weil die Unterscheidung falsch sei. Er sagte, solche Gegensatzpaare seien immer nur verkürzte Versuche, etwas Grundsätzliches aber Verborgenes auszudrücken, das folgendermaßen zusammengefaßt werden könnte (und ich zitiere wieder): ***„Es ist eine einfache Aufgabe, Dinge komplex zu machen, aber eine komplexe Aufgabe, Dinge zu vereinfachen."***

(Ich weiß nicht, wo und wann Carl Auer geboren wurde, ich weiß nur eines: Er wurde in einer Brauerei gerade zu dem Zeitpunkt geboren, als das erste Faß Maibock eines Jahrgangs angestochen wurde.)

Conversation about Carl Auer

Luigi Boscolo and his team (Paolo Bertrando, Gabriela Boi, Paola Fiocco, Meri Palvarini, Jacqueline Pereira)

LUIGI: As you well know, our meetings take place in the office. This evening, I invited you to my home to discuss a matter of great interest: the work and life of Carl Auer whom we certainly all know, directly or indirectly.

On the occasion of his 90th birthday this year, I was asked to write something about him and his contribution to the field of systemic theory, cybernetics, constructivism. According to our model based on systemic epistemology, teamwork is the best way to reach a systemic view: six points of view are better than one.

I would like to open the discussion by asking each one of you to talk about Carl Auer, hoping that (as it happens in our therapy sessions) different punctuations by the team members will lead to "patterns which connect", as old Greg (Bateson) would say. Through this process I hope we shall arrive at a comprehensive systemic view of Carl Auer's life and work, which will finally do justice to this great man.

PAOLO: As far as I know, Carl Auer influenced, even though in an indirect way, all the most important achievements in systemic therapy. What puzzles me is the question how he managed to find such great minds who would develop his ideas. It seems he had a remarkable instinct for good whisky and talented people. . . .

LUIGI: This brings to my mind a passage from von Domarus' autobiography. He tells how his principle of identity through the predicates

Gespräch über Carl Auer

Luigi Boscolo und sein Team (Paolo Bertrando, Gabriela Boi, Paola Fiocco, Meri Palvarini, Jacqueline Pereira)

LUIGI: Normalerweise treffen wir uns ja am Arbeitsplatz. Heute abend habe ich euch aber zu mir nach Hause eingeladen, um eine höchst interessante Angelegenheit mit euch zu diskutieren: das Leben und das Werk von Carl Auer, den wir sicher alle direkt oder indirekt kennen.

Aus Anlaß seines 90. Geburtstags in diesem Jahr bin ich gebeten worden, etwas über seinen Beitrag zum Bereich der Systemtheorie, der Kybernetik und des Konstruktivismus zu schreiben. Unserem Modell entsprechend, das auf der systemischen Epistemologie basiert, ist Teamarbeit der beste Weg, zu systemischen Sichtweisen zu gelangen. Sechs Standpunkte sind besser als einer.

Ich möchte die Diskussion damit eröffnen, daß ich jeden von euch bitte, etwas über Carl Auer zu erzählen. Dabei hoffe ich, daß (wie es in unseren Therapiesitzungen passiert) unterschiedliche Interpunktionen der Teammitglieder zu „Mustern, die verbinden" führen, wie der alte Greg (Bateson) sagen würde. Durch diesen Prozeß, so hoffe ich, werden wir zu einem so umfassenden systemischen Verständnis von Carl Auers Leben und Werk gelangen, daß es diesem großen Mann endlich gerecht wird.

PAOLO: Soweit ich weiß, beeinflußte Carl Auer, wenn auch in indirekter Art und Weise, alle wichtigen Errungenschaften in der systemischen Therapie. Was mir Rätsel aufgibt, ist die Frage, wie es ihm gelang, so große Geister zu finden, die seine Ideen weiterentwickelten? Er scheint einen bemerkenswerten Spürsinn für guten Whiskey und talentierte Menschen gehabt zu haben ...

LUIGI: Dies erinnert mich an einen Abschnitt aus von Domarus' Autobiographie. Er erzählt, wie ihm sein Prinzip der Identität durch

rather than through the subjects in a syllogism, characteristic of schizophrenic thinking, had been suggested to him at a bar in Vienna. A certain Carl told him about his eccentric Aunt Mary who, in hot situations, would claim to be the Blessed Mother because she was a virgin. That very night, von Domarus conceived his famous principle which was picked up by others as being central in the pathogenesis of schizophrenia.

There is a link between Carl Auer and von Domarus' principle as well as between Carl Auer and Bateson's double-bind theory.

MERI: Then we still don't understand why Carl Auer never wanted these discoveries to be linked to him. He even begged Bateson not to mention his name, and never told his last name to von Domarus. It's quite mysterious. . . .

PAOLO: They also say that he wrote a fundamental treatise, but never wanted to get it published. Who knows why?

PAOLA: As far as I know, he has thrown it away.

JACKIE: Personally, I recall a very strange episode. While sitting on my father's lap, in Haiti - my country of origin - he used to tell me about this mysterious white man who was in Haiti in 1949. His name was Charles d'Auer. Charlie (as they called him in town), was very loved by the vodoo priests because he had revealed to them the secret of zombification.

GABRIELA: In fact, he was a chemist. . . .

JACKIE: Yes, but until this very day the voodoo priests hold this secret which was not only chemical, but coupled with techniques for influencing people.

PAOLO: Strange! In 1951 Carl Auer was in Phoenix, Arizona, where they say he taught hypnosis to a young medical doctor by the name

die Prädikate statt durch die Subjekte eines Syllogismus, was für eine schizophrene Denkweise typisch ist, in einer Wiener Kneipe suggeriert wurde. Ein gewisser Carl erzählte ihm von seiner exzentrischen Tante Mary. Diese behauptete in spannenden Situationen, sie sei die heilige Maria, weil sie noch Jungfrau war. In derselben Nacht entstand von Domarus' berühmtes Prinzip, das von anderen als zentral für die Pathogenese der Schizophrenie angesehen wurde.

Es gibt also sowohl eine Verbindung zwischen Carl Auer und dem Domarus-Prinzip, als auch zwischen Carl Auer und Batesons Double-Bind-Theorie.

MERI: Was wir dann aber nicht verstehen ist, warum es Carl Auer ablehnte, daß diese Entdeckungen mit seinem Namen verknüpft wurden. Er bat Bateson sogar inständig, seinen Namen nicht zu erwähnen und teilte von Domarus nie seinen Nachnamen mit. Es ist ziemlich mysteriös ...

PAOLO: Und man sagt, daß er eine grundsätzliche wissenschaftliche Abhandlung schrieb, es aber ablehnte, sie veröffentlichen zu lassen. Wer weiß warum?

PAOLA: Soweit ich weiß, warf er sie fort.

JACKIE: Ich selbst erinnere mich an merkwürdige Geschehnisse. Als ich in Haiti, meinem Heimatland, auf meines Vaters Schoß saß, pflegte dieser mir von einem mysteriösen Weißen zu erzählen, der sich 1949 in Haiti aufhielt. Sein Name war Charles d'Auer. Charlie (wie man ihn in der Stadt nannte) wurde von den Voodoo-Priestern sehr geliebt, weil er ihnen das Geheimnis der Wiederbeseelung offenbarte.

GABRIELA: Er war ja ein Chemiker ...

JACKIE: Ja, aber selbst heute bewahren die Voodoo-Priester noch dieses Geheimnis, und dieses ist nicht nur chemischer Natur, sondern mit bestimmten Techniken verknüpft, Menschen zu beeinflussen.

PAOLO: Seltsam! 1951 war Carl Auer in Phoenix, Arizona, wo er, wie man sich erzählt, einem jungen Arzt namens Milton Erickson Hyp-

of Milton Erickson. And hypnosis is a technique for influencing people. Maybe Erickson does not even remember since this happened in front of three bottles of Jack Daniel's, which had fogged their mind a bit.

Luigi: If we pass from the simple hypothesis to more general ones, I see a link between these observations. It seems as if Carl Auer prefered to operate behind the scene. He was interested in manipulating, obtaining an effect on people: he was always thinking of communication, of the indirect influence. At this point, the question of his influence upon von Bertallanfy comes to my mind. . . .

Paola: I am sure that Carl Auer taught chemistry in Vienna at the same time as von Bertallanfy was teaching biology.

Gabriela: What is still unclear is Carl Auer's real thinking. We know that he has stimulated the development of the ideas he had *in nuce*. But none of these ideas were his real thinking. They are only fragments. And I believe that he never wrote for one reason: his thinking was too advanced to be fully expressed and understood. Thus, it was necessary for his thoughts to emerge from the praxis gathered by people ready enough to pick them up.

Paola: Among these people, there is Humberto Maturana, the Chilean biologist who got the idea of his well-known study, "What the frog's eye tells the frog's brain," when he invited Carl Auer to Santiago. As they were having coffee in his living room, Maturana noticed something odd: Auer put the sugar in a fish bowl resting on a table behind him (180° from the coffee cup). Observing Carl Auer's crossed eyes, the movement of his hand and the cup, Maturana had the brilliant intuition to turn the frog's eye 180°, so that the frog would strike its tongue 180° backwards from the worm put in front of it.

nose beibrachte. Hypnose ist eine Technik, um Menschen zu beeinflussen. Vielleicht konnte Erickson sich selbst kaum daran erinnern, weil sich das alles bei drei Flaschen Jack Daniels abspielte, die ihre Sinne etwas vernebelt hatten.

LUIGI: Wenn wir von dieser einfachen Hypothese zu umfassenderen übergehen, so sehe ich einen Zusammenhang zwischen diesen Beobachtungen. Carl Auer scheint es vorgezogen zu haben, hinter den Kulissen wirksam zu sein. Er scheint daran interessiert gewesen zu sein, in bestimmter Art und Weise auf Menschen einzuwirken: Er dachte immer über Kommunikation nach, über indirekte Beeinflussungen. An diesem Punkt kommt mir die Frage in den Sinn, inwieweit Carl Auer auch von Bertallanfy beeinflußt hat.

PAOLA: Ich bin mir sicher, daß Carl Auer zur selben Zeit in Wien Chemie lehrte, als von Bertallanfy dort Biologievorlesungen hielt.

GABRIELA: Was bisher noch nicht klar in Erscheinung tritt, ist Carl Auers wirkliches Denken. Wir wissen, daß er die Entwicklungen von Ideen die er *in nuce* hatte, stimulierte. Aber keine dieser Ideen repräsentiert sein wirkliches Denken. Es sind nur Fragmente, und ich nehme an, daß er nur aus einem Grunde nie schrieb: Sein Denken war zu fortgeschritten, um vollständig ausgedrückt und verstanden werden zu können. So ist es notwendig, seine Gedanken an Hand der Praxis derjenigen zu erschließen, die bereit und hinreichend fähig waren, sie aufzunehmen.

PAOLA: Einer dieser Menschen ist Humberto Maturana, der chilenische Biologe. Dieser lud Carl Auer nach Santiago ein und entwickelte während dessen Besuch die Idee zu seiner bekannte Studie: „Was das Auge des Frosches dem Gehirn des Frosches mitteilt." Als sie im Wohnzimmer gemeinsam Kaffee tranken, bemerkte Maturana, daß Carl Auer komischerweise den Zucker in ein Goldfischglas schüttete, das auf einem Tisch hinter ihm stand (180° von der Kaffeetasse). Carls Silberblick, die Bewegung seiner Hand und die Tasse beobachtend, hatte Maturana die brillante Idee, das Froschauge um 180° zu drehen. Der Frosch schlug dann seine Zunge 180° rückwärts nach dem Wurm, der vor ihm lag.

LUIGI: This led to Maturanas development of the theory that there is no difference between perception and illusion, that is, the theory of objectivity in parenthesis. A psychoanalytic interpretation could relate his theory to an unconscious defense from Carl Auer's anxiety-inducing influence. In this way, he unconsciously put Carl Auer in parenthesis.

PAOLO: What a powerful master! . . .

LUIGI: This brings to my mind how his strabism gave us the idea of circular questioning. The Milan quartet, Selvini, Boscolo, Cecchin, and Prata, met him at a conference. As we were all chatting in the hall, we noticed that every time Carl Auer asked one of us a question, the other would answer.

JACKIE: It's amazing how Carl Auer used his body to get to people. This incident happened in Vienna: while sipping a schnapps at the bar and conversing on cybernetics with a certain Carl who had a cast on his left leg, Heinz von Foerster asked him about the reason for his cast. Carl explained that he had made a jump from the second to the first floor (a jump of levels). It was then that von Foerster got the idea of the cybernetics of "the first and second floor," which became of "the first and second order."

GABRIELA: But this does not help us understand Carl Auer as a person. I think that, in order to comprehend his thinking, we should first understand the man.

LUIGI: We should get into his life's story and idiosyncrasis.

MERI: There must be a reason why Carl Auer assumed the role of stimulator and observer of a whole community of thinkers.

LUIGI: There are some wild speculations about his family of origin. For instance, they say that he was Einstein's first cousin, and that he was

Luigi: Das führte dazu, daß Maturana die Theorie entwickelte, daß es keinen Unterschied zwischen Wahrnehmung und Illusion gibt, genauer gesagt, zu seiner Theorie der Objektivität in Anführungszeichen. Psychoanalytisch gedeutet könnte man diese Theorie mit einer unbewußten Abwehr gegen Carl Auers angstinduzierenden Einfluß in Zusammenhang bringen. Auf diese Weise setzte er Carl Auer unbewußt in Anführungszeichen.

Paolo: Welch ein machtvoller Meister! ...

Luigi: Dies erinnert mich daran, wie sein Schielen uns auf die Idee des zirkulären Fragens brachte. Das Mailänder Quartett (Selvini, Boscolo, Cecchin und Prata) begegnete ihm während einer Tagung. Als wir im Foyer gemeinsam plauderten, bemerkten wir, daß jedesmal, wenn Carl Auer einem von uns eine Frage stellte, ein anderer antwortete.

Jackie: Es ist schon erstaunlich, wie Carl Auer seinen Körper als Zugang zum Menschen nutzte. Folgendes Vorkommnis ereignete sich in Wien: Einen Schnaps trinkend und mit einem gewissen Carl, der am linken Bein einen Gips trug, in ein Gespräch über Kybernetik vertieft, fragte Heinz von Foerster schließlich nach dem Grund für den Gipsverband. Carl erklärte, daß er einen Sprung vom zweiten in den ersten Stock (einen Sprung von einer Ebene zur nächsten) gemacht habe. Das brachte Heinz von Foerster auf die Idee, der Kybernetik „der ersten und zweiten Etage", die später zur Kybernetik „erster und zweiter Ordnung" wurde.

Gabriela: Das hilft uns jedoch noch nicht, die Person Carl Auers zu verstehen. Ich denke, daß wir sein Denken erst dann erfassen können, wenn wir den Menschen verstehen.

Luigi: Ja, wir sollten seine Lebensgeschichte betrachten und seine persönliche Eigenart.

Meri: Es muß doch einen Grund dafür geben, warum Carl Auer die Rolle des Beobachters und Anregers einer ganzen Gemeinschaft von Denkern übernahm.

Luigi: Einige wilde Spekulationen über seine Herkunftsfamilie sagen aus, daß er ein Cousin Einsteins sei und auf dessen Erfolg sehr

very jealous of Einstein's success. He knew that it was impossible for him to become as famous as his cousin. That's why he avoided expressing his ideas directly and chose to have them circulate through others.

JACKIE: There is a rumor attributing the cause of all this to the very strong, almost morbid tie between Carl Auer's mother and Einstein's mother who feared that her son could have been overshadowed by Carl's brilliancy.

LUIGI: Some say that Carl Auer was the illegitimate son of a famous Italian opera singer. His secrecy could be related to his will to protect his family secret.

MERI: There are people who swear that his mother, the famous opera singer, had been analysed by Freud. It was this "case" that gave Freud the idea of utilizing a couch!

PAOLO: But Carl Auer's inability to reveal himself because he wanted to protect some members of his family must have contributed to his existential doubts. At one point, he must have asked himself who he was and whether or not he was Einstein's cousin.

PAOLA: Really, Carl Auer was much more advanced than Einstein. Deep down, Einstein continued to think that reality existed, while Carl Auer had freed himself from this prejudice long before. He understood that "reality" was a radical construction.

PAOLO: He understood it so well that, at times, he doubted his own existence! What counts for Carl Auer is that there be "ideas" in the systems, a thesis taken up by Bateson. It seems as if Carl Auer said to himself, "Even if I never existed, my ideas would still be important."

PAOLA: He was obsessed with the idea of not existing. Also, due to his crossed eyes, he was always getting answers from people to whom he had not asked a question. He probably asked himself: "Is it really I who is asking questions or is it someone else?"

eifersüchtig war. Er wußte, daß er unmöglich so berühmt wie sein Cousin werden konnte. Aus diesem Grunde vermied er es, seine Ideen direkt auszudrücken und wählte den Weg, sie durch andere verbreiten zu lassen.

JACKIE: Ein weiteres Gerücht sieht den Grund für all dies in der krankhaften Beziehung zwischen der Mutter Carl Auers und Einsteins Mutter, welche befürchtete, daß ihr Sohn in Gefahr war, durch die Brillanz Carls in den Schatten gestellt zu werden.

LUIGI: Einige behaupten, Carl Auer sei ein unehelicher Sohn einer berühmten italienischen Opernsängerin. Sein Im-Verborgenen-Bleiben könnte auf seine Absicht hinweisen, dieses Familiengeheimnis zu hüten.

MERI: Es gibt Leute, die schwören, daß die berühmte Opernsängerin von Freud analysiert wurde und daß es dieser „Fall“ gewesen sei, der Freud auf die Idee brachte, eine Couch zu benutzen.

PAOLO: Aber das Bestreben, unerkannt zu bleiben, um Familienmitglieder zu schützen, mußte zu den existentiellen Zweifeln Carl Auers beigetragen haben. Irgendwann muß er sich selbst gefragt haben, wer er war, und ob er nun Einsteins Cousin war oder nicht.

PAOLA: Carl Auer war wirklich viel weiter als Einstein. In seinem Innersten fuhr Einstein fort, an eine Realität zu glauben, während Carl Auer sich lange zuvor von diesem Aberglauben befreit hatte. Er hatte verstanden, daß „Realität“ eine radikale Konstruktion war.

PAOLO: Er verstand dies so gut, daß er manchmal an seiner eigenen Existenz zweifelte. Für Carl Auer zählen die „Ideen“ in den Systemen, eine These, die von Bateson übernommen wurde. Es scheint als hätte Carl Auer sich gesagt: „Auch wenn ich nie existierte, würden meine Ideen immer noch wichtig sein.“

PAOLA: Weil er wegen seines Silberblicks auf seine Fragen immer von Leuten Antworten bekam, die er nicht gefragt hatte, war er ständig mit der Frage beschäftigt, ob er existiert. Er fragte sich dann wahrscheinlich selbst: „Bin ich es wirklich, der die Fragen stellt, oder ist es jemand anderes ?“

Paolo: . . . He even thought that he was asking questions of no one; therefore, no one exists.

Gabriela: And it was just to demonstrate his own existence that he persisted in this hard work of stimulating other people's minds. And, perhaps, his ultimate goal was to produce this book to which we are contributing, and which will demonstrate in the end that he exists.

Luigi: Let's hope! . . . Let's hope that all these contributions will convince him that he exists. In this way, we will finally give back to Carl Auer everything he has given to us.

Milan, May 1989

Paolo: ... Er dachte sogar, daß er an niemanden Fragen richtete und daß deshalb niemand existierte.

Gabriela: Gerade um seine Existenz zu beweisen, fuhr er mit seiner schwierigen Arbeit, andere geistig anzuregen, unbeirrt fort. Vielleicht war es sein höchstes Ziel, dieses Buch, zu dem wir einen Beitrag leisten, entstehen zu lassen, weil das schließlich den Nachweis seiner Existenz erbringt.

Luigi: Hoffentlich! ... Laßt uns hoffen, daß all diese Beiträge ihn davon überzeugen werden, daß es ihn gibt. Auf diese Weise geben wir schließlich Carl Auer alles zurück, was er uns gegeben hat.

Mailand, Mai 1989.

Things are not What They Are: A Letter

Dear Gunthard,
Mr. Carl Auer was never in Chile in my living room. The event of which Paolo and Luigi speak may have occurred in relation to Dr. Roger Sperry who is the person who did in 1942 the experiment of rotating the eye of a newt and of a frog's tadpole. I repeated the experiment as a student sometime in the mid-fifties, but I did not understand what it revealed until many years later, 1965, when I developed my theory of relativistic color coding and became concerned with the question of cognition.

Mr. Carl Auer was a friend of my mother's before I was born, but I never met him even if I knew him as a child, which I do not know. My mother used to say that Carl Auer would say if contradicted, "Things are not as they are, and, in fact, even when they are they are not." After that my mother would add of her own: "Whatever things are even if they are not, is your responsibility."

Mr. Carl Auer must have been 26 or 27 when he was in Chile in 1926 or 1927, and he did in Chile many things that he did not do, and at the same time he did not do many things that he did. Whichever is the case, according to my mother, whatever he did or did not do, he did not do it or did it doing it or not doing it as his responsibility. And, of course, this is what you are showing by recollecting all these memories about him and his doings and not doings.

Finally, I must add that although I never met Carl Auer, I never met a person who was like him so totally responsible of whatever he did or did not do. It is for this that I admire Mr. Carl Auer and that I

Die Dinge sind nicht wie sie sind: Ein Brief

Lieber Gunthard,
Herr Carl Auer war niemals in meinem Wohnzimmer hier in Chile. Paolo und Luigi sprechen wohl von einem Ereignis, das mit Dr. Roger Sperry zusammenhängt. Er hat nämlich 1942 das Experiment ausgeführt, das Auge eines Wassermolches und einer Kaulquappe zu rotieren. Ich wiederholte das Experiment als Student irgendwann Mitte der 50er Jahre, habe allerdings erst viele Jahre später seine Bedeutung begriffen, als ich 1965 meine Theorie der relativistischen Farbkodierung entwickelte und mich mit der Frage der Wahrnehmung beschäftigte.

Herr Carl Auer war ein Freund meiner Mutter bevor ich geboren wurde. Ich habe ihn aber nie getroffen, selbst wenn ich ihn als Kind gekannt hätte, was ich nicht weiß. Meine Mutter sagte, daß, wenn ihm jemand widersprach, Carl Auer zu sagen pflegte: „Die Dinge sind nicht wie sie sind, und selbst wenn sie es sind, sind sie es nicht." Meine Mutter fügte dann von sich aus hinzu: „Was immer die Dinge sind, selbst wenn sie es nicht sind, du bist für sie verantwortlich."

Herr Carl Auer muß 26 oder 27 Jahre alt gewesen sein, als er 1926 oder 1927 in Chile war. Er hat in Chile viele Dinge getan, die er nicht tat, und hat gleichzeitig viele Dinge nicht getan, die er tat. Wie auch immer, nach den Erzählungen meiner Mutter, hat er, was immer er getan hat oder nicht getan hat, nicht getan oder getan, indem er es aus eigener Verantwortung tat oder nicht tat. Genau das ist es natürlich, was Du durch das Sammeln all dieser Erinnerungen über ihn und sein Tun und Nicht-Tun zeigst.

Schließlich muß ich hinzufügen, daß ich, obwohl ich Carl Auer niemals getroffen habe, niemals eine Person traf, die wie er so vollständig verantwortlich war für alles, was sie tat oder nicht tat.

have been willing to reveal to you so many intimate things as I have done in this letter.

Yours sincerely,

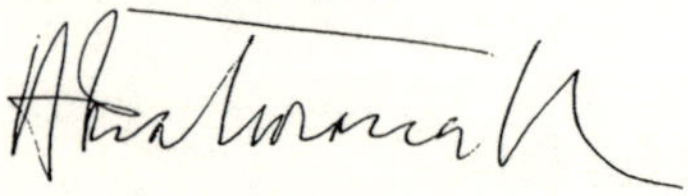

Humberto R. Maturana

Greetings!!

Greetings!!

Deshalb bewundere ich Herrn Carl Auer und deshalb war ich bereit, Dir in diesem Brief so viele intime Dinge zu enthüllen.

Mit freundlichen Grüßen

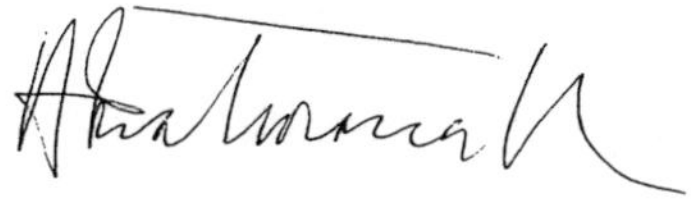

Humberto R. Maturana

Grüße!!

Grüße!!

The Galveston Experience (We Think)

Harold A. Goolishian and Harlene Anderson

The importance of Carl Auer to our development here at the Galveston Family Institute is difficult to describe and document. We must relate a long and complex history. We were young and naive clinicians at the time we first heard of his genius. The little information we had concerning his skill as a therapist and his capacities to relate the concepts of therapy to the highest order of scientific thinking, was so superlative that at first we did not believe in his existence and thought him to be a myth like Santa Claus.

We did not hear of him all at once. Quite the contrary, it was the knowing wink, the forced indifference, and the quick change of subject from our supervisors that forced us novice therapists to realize that our mentors knew of a higher order clinician than we were privileged to know. It was similar to the feeling we often had as children when the grown-ups would make remarks that somehow seemed exciting and yet forbidden. The telling of what we later learned to be off color stories too hot for small ears. That was what it was like when his name came up or when our supervisors would tell us that they knew what to do because he had said so. What we didn't realize was that his was such a powerful and overriding wisdom that we were being protected from a force we couldn't handle.

It was not until we met a clinical anthropologist, a young protegé of Carl Auer, that we actually could permit ourselves to believe in his existence and brilliance. We were talking one day (sometime in 1956) with our consultant from Palo Alto, Gregory Bateson. We had already begun our preliminary project in family therapy and had hopes that

Das Erlebnis von Galveston (glauben wir)

Harold A. Goolishian und Harlene Anderson

Es ist schwierig, die Bedeutung von Carl Auer für unsere Entwicklung hier am Galveston Family Institute zu beschreiben und zu dokumentieren. Wir müssen dazu eine lange und komplexe Geschichte erzählen. Wir waren junge und naive Therapeuten, als wir zum ersten Mal von seiner Genialität hörten. Das wenige, was wir über sein Geschick als Therapeut und seine Fähigkeit wußten, Therapiekonzepte mit den höchsten Ebenen wissenschaftlichen Denkens in Verbindung zu bringen, war so voll von Superlativen, daß wir zuerst nicht an seine Existenz glaubten und ihn, wie den Weihnachtsmann, für einen Mythos hielten.

Wir hörten nicht gleich etwas über ihn. Vielmehr war es das wissende Zwinkern, die gewollte Gleichgültigkeit und der rasche Themenwechsel unserer Supervisoren, der uns Anfänger spüren ließ, daß unsere Mentoren einen herausragenden Therapeuten kannten und daß wir dieses Privileg nicht hatten. Es war ein ähnliches Gefühl, wie wir es als Kinder oft hatten, wenn die Erwachsenen Bemerkungen machten, die uns aufregend aber auch verboten erschienen, wenn sie, wie wir später erfuhren, schlüpfrige Geschichten erzählten, die für kleine Ohren nicht geeignet waren. Das gleiche Gefühl war es, wenn sein Name erwähnt wurde oder unsere Supervisoren uns sagten, sie wüßten, was zu tun sei, weil er es gesagt habe. Wir begriffen allerdings nicht, daß seine Weisheit so mächtig und überwältigend war, daß wir vor einer gewaltigen Kraft geschützt wurden, mit der wir nicht umgehen konnten.

Erst als wir einen klinischen Anthropologen kennenlernten, einen jungen Protegé Carl Auers, konnten wir uns gestatten, an seine Existenz und Brillanz zu glauben. Eines Tages (irgendwann im Jahre 1956) unterhielten wir uns mit unserem Berater aus Palo Alto, Gregory Bateson. Wir hatten schon mit unserem frühen Familientherapie-

this thinker could help us find ways of describing what to us was inexplicable: a transference neurosis was not necessary to therapeutic change. Bateson told us he once knew of a clinical theoretician and philosopher who could help us puzzle through the apparent impossibility of our finding. He told us that this "person" he knew might be our only hope and only if he was still around.

We quickly asked who this miracle man might be. Bateson told us that he had already said more than he should and quickly obfuscated the subject by deliberating about differences that could make a difference even if you did not want them to. We were excited by his wisdom about differences. A little miffed, we wondered why he talked about a different subject when he knew who could answer our pressing question. Bateson with his infinite and patient obstructionism would only smile and mutter something about *obiter dictum*. Obviously we were very excited. Somewhere there was a great person, someone who had the answer to our terrifying finding and who would permit us the opportunity to enjoy a little in the way of therapeutic usufruction.

We are somewhat embarrassed to admit our next move. Our only excuse is our youth. This was over thirty years ago and perhaps we may also be excused for our infelicitous infringement by our excitement over the use of the new therapeutic technologies, our one-way mirrors and our hidden microphones. We had already become kind of benevolent "peeping toms" for our patients so we peeped on Gregory while he was sleeping. Without his knowing it, we bedded him in our therapy room made to look like an ordinary bedroom. We watched all night behind the one-way mirror.

We do not know if you have ever had the opportunity to see a great man sleep, it is an exciting event. Each snore, each breath, and each rolling over is filled with magnificent anticipation. Did he say

Projekt begonnen und hofften, daß uns dieser Denker helfen konnte, Methoden zu finden, um ein für uns unerklärbares Phänomen zu beschreiben; nämlich die Beobachtung, daß eine Übertragungsneurose für den therapeutischen Wandel nicht notwendig war. Bateson erzählte uns, er habe einst einen klinischen Theoretiker und Philosophen gekannt, der uns helfen könnte, unser offensichtlich unmögliches Ergebnis zu enträtseln. Er sagte uns, diese „Person", die er kenne, sei womöglich unsere einzige Hoffnung, und auch nur dann, wenn sie noch am Leben sei.

Rasch fragten wir, um wen es sich denn bei diesem Wundermann handle. Bateson antwortete, er habe schon mehr gesagt, als er eigentlich solle, und vernebelte schnell das Thema, indem er sich über Unterschiede ausließ, die selbst dann einen Unterschied machen, wenn man das gar nicht wolle. Seine Einsichten über Unterschiede begeisterten uns. Allerdings fühlten wir uns doch ein wenig auf den Schlips getreten und fragten uns, warum er ein anderes Thema anschnitt, wo er doch wußte, daß er unsere drängendste Frage beantworten konnte. Bateson, mit seiner grenzenlosen und geduldigen Obstruktionspolitik, lächelte nur und murmelte etwas von einer beiläufigen Bemerkung. Verständlicherweise waren wir ungemein aufgeregt. Irgendwo gab es einen großen Mann, jemand, der die Antwort hatte für unser erschreckendes Ergebnis, und der uns die Gelegenheit bieten könnte, ein wenig in den Genuß therapeutischer Nutznießung zu kommen.

Es ist uns ziemlich peinlich, unseren nächsten Schritt einzugestehen. Unsere Jugend ist unsere einzige Entschuldigung. Mehr als dreißig Jahre ist das her, und vielleicht läßt sich unser unpassendes Verhalten dadurch entschuldigen, daß wir wegen der Anwendung neuer therapeutischer Techniken, nämlich unserer Einwegspiegel und unserer versteckten Mikrophone, so übermütig wurden. Für unsere Patienten waren wir schon zu wohlwollenden Voyeuren geworden, und deshalb beobachteten wir auch Gregory heimlich, während er schlief. Ohne daß er es wußte, quartierten wir ihn in unserem Therapiezimmer ein, das wir in ein gewöhnliches Schlafzimmer verwandelt hatten. Wir saßen die ganze Nacht lang hinter dem Einwegspiegel auf Beobachtungsposten.

Wir wissen nicht, ob Sie jemals die Gelegenheit hatten, einen großen Mann schlafen zu sehen; es ist ein aufregendes Erlebnis. Jedes Schnarchen, jeder Atemzug und jedes Umdrehen ist von einer unge-

something, what will he say next? Bateson was an executant sleeper. We were not disappointed: he talked. At first it was difficult to know what he was saying, an experience that was not uncommon when listening to Bateson even while he was awake. Unfortunately our wire recorder got all tangled. We did not have audio-tape in those days so you must rely only on our constructed recollections. Bateson was talking to somebody called Carl Auer. As we put it together it seems that he was making promises. He promised not to make the same mistakes that Galileo made. He would publish in a way so as not to offend and yet to spread the truth of a fiction of Aristetolian essences and of linear reductionism.

We were frightened and not sure what we had witnessed. At first we thought Bateson was simply hallucinating. Then we thought we were. Then Carl Auer appeared. At least it seemed that he appeared or kind of appeared. There was a major transcendental influence in the bed (therapy) room that came right through the mirror. We could begin to hear clearly even though nothing was said. Carl Auer was insisting that Bateson not make the fundamental mistake that Galileo had made. He insisted that Bateson not reduce his wisdom to a mere twenty-four pages as Galileo had done in Florence. The reference here seemed to be to Galileo's paper, *The Starry Messenger*. This was the paper published in 1610 describing Galileo's observations of the satellites of Jupiter. Bateson understood. He repeated that he would always speak the truth with regard to the distinctions he made but always in such a way that it could not be reduced to a trivial twenty-four pages.

As we talked about this years later, we slowly understood that Carl Auer, the mentor of all scientific revolutions, Carl Auer, the spirit of Kuhn, was rightly concerned that too often the great insights of science are misunderstood because of the simplicity of the underlying notions. Bateson was not to do this. We knew that Bateson had fulfilled his promise to his transcendental mentor when we noted the posthumous publication of *Angels Fear*.

But that is ahead of our story. We had done the unforgivable. By peeping without explicit informed consent we had violated the

heuren Erwartung begleitet. Hat er etwas gesagt, was wird er als nächstes sagen? Bateson war ein sehr ausdrucksvoller Schläfer. Wir wurden nicht enttäuscht: Er redete. Am Anfang war es schwierig zu verstehen, was er sagte, eine Erfahrung, die man selbst dann oft machte, wenn er wach war. Unglücklicherweise verhedderte sich unser Drahtmagnetophon. Wir hatten damals kein Tonbandgerät, weshalb Sie sich auf unsere konstruierten Erinnerungen verlassen müssen. Bateson sprach mit jemandem, der Carl Auer hieß. So wie wir das verstanden, schien er Zusicherungen zu machen. Er versprach, nicht die gleichen Fehler zu begehen wie Galilei. Er würde publizieren, ohne Anstoß zu erregen, und dennoch die Wahrheit über die Fiktion der Aristotelischen Lehren und den linearen Reduktionismus verbreiten.

Wir hatten Angst und waren nicht sicher, was wir gesehen hatten. Zuerst glaubten wir, daß Bateson einfach halluzinierte. Dann dachten wir, wir halluzinierten selbst. Dann erschien Carl Auer. Zumindest hatte es den Anschein, daß er erschien oder etwas in der Art passierte. Im Schlaf- bzw. Therapiezimmer breiteten sich große transzendente Einflüsse aus, die durch den Spiegel zu spüren waren. Wir konnten deutlich etwas hören, obwohl nichts gesagt wurde. Carl Auer bestand darauf, daß Bateson nicht den fundamentalen Fehler Galileis wiederholen solle. Er betonte, Bateson solle vermeiden, seine Weisheit auf 24 Seiten zu reduzieren, wie Galilei das in Florenz getan hatte. Er schien sich hier auf Galileis Schrift „Der Sternbote" zu beziehen. In dieser 1610 veröffentlichten Schrift beschrieb Galilei seine Beobachtungen der Satelliten Jupiters. Bateson verstand. Er wiederholte, daß er in Bezug auf die Unterscheidungen, die er machte, immer die Wahrheit sagen werde, allerdings immer auf eine solche Art und Weise, daß sie nicht auf bloße 24 Seiten zu reduzieren sei.

Als wir uns Jahre später darüber unterhielten, verstanden wir allmählich, daß Carl Auer, der Mentor aller wissenschaftlichen Revolutionen, Carl Auer, der Geist Kuhns, zu Recht besorgt war, daß die großen Einsichten der Wissenschaft wegen der Einfachheit der zugrundeliegenden Ideen allzu häufig mißverstanden werden. Bateson sollte dies nicht tun. Wir wußten, daß Bateson sein Versprechen gegenüber seinem transzendentalen Mentor gehalten hatte, als wir von der postumen Veröffentlichung von „Angels Fear" hörten.

Aber das greift zu weit voraus. Wir hatten das Unverzeihliche getan. Indem wir ohne ausdrückliche Zustimmung heimlich zu-

confidential spiritual relationship between a great thinker and his source. We were dispondent and moribund. Bateson sensed something was wrong when he consulted with us the next day. We confessed, expecting the worst. To our surprise, our transgression was received with kindness and warmth. It was as if Bateson had wanted to share his lonely relationship with others but was afraid to reveal the story. Now we knew.

He sat us on his knee. He had large and bony knees, and he told us this metalogue:

"Do you know what a ghost is?" Gregory asked looking away as if to hide his opprobrious response to our predicted silly reply.

"Of course," we innocently replied. We had read *Webster's* from stem to stern. "A ghost is a spirit or demon."

"No," was Gregory's immediate and amused response.

We were confused and perplex. We had spent weeks studying the dictionary because we knew he would ask us something important and we hate to fail. "What is a ghost?" we asked in childish petulance.

"A ghost," he patiently replied, "is the opposite of epistemology."

The opposite of epistemology was not what we expected and we said so. What we did not confess was that we did not know what the word meant and could not have pronounced it if he had not said it. If it was in *Webster's*, we had not seen it.

"Epistemology," he spoke as if he were raptured, "is knowledge of knowledge. It is the sum and grand reflexive total of all the little differences that make the big difference."

"But the opposite of all this differences would be no difference," we spoke in our naive certainty.

"No," he half said as he retreated behind his big brows.

We waited with restrained patience, having finally learned to never interrupt a thinker. This was a principal which, as we only

schauten, hatten wir die vertrauliche spirituelle Beziehung eines großen Denkers zu seiner Quelle gestört. Wir waren bedrückt und wähnten uns zum Scheitern verurteilt. Bateson merkte, daß etwas nicht stimmte, als er uns am nächsten Tag sprach. Wir beichteten und erwarteten das Schlimmste. Zu unserer Überraschung wurde unser Verstoß mit Freundlichkeit und Wärme aufgenommen. Es war, als ob Bateson seine einsame Beziehung mit anderen habe teilen wollen, sich aber nicht traute, die Geschichte aufzudecken. Jetzt kannten wir sie.

Er setzte uns auf sein Knie. Er hatte große, knochige Knie und hielt uns diesen Metalog.

„Wißt ihr, was ein Geist ist?" fragte Gregory und schaute weg, als ob er seine verächtliche Reaktion auf unsere höchstwahrscheinlich dumme Antwort verbergen wollte.

„Natürlich", antworteten wir unschuldig. Wir hatten den *Webster's*[1] von vorne bis hinten gelesen. „Ein Geist ist ein Gespenst oder ein Dämon."

„Nein", lautete sofort Gregorys amüsierte Antwort.

Wir waren verwirrt und verblüfft. Wochenlang hatten wir das Lexikon studiert, weil wir ahnten, daß er uns eine wichtige Frage stellen würde, und wir haßten es, uns zu blamieren. „Was ist ein Geist?" fragten wir mit kindlichem Trotz.

„Ein Geist", antwortete er geduldig, „ist das Gegenteil von Epistemologie."

Das Gegenteil von Epistemologie, das hatten wir nicht erwartet und sagten das. Jedoch gaben wir nicht zu, daß wir nicht wußten, was das Wort bedeutete und es nicht hätten aussprechen können, wenn er es uns nicht gesagt hätte. Wenn es im *Webster's* stand, hatten wir es jedenfalls übersehen.

„Epistemologie", sprach er, als wäre er verzückt, „ist das Wissen über das Wissen. Es ist die Summe und das reflexive Gesamtergebnis aller kleinen Unterschiede, die den großen Unterschied ausmachen."

„Aber das Gegenteil all dieser Unterschiede wäre kein Unterschied", sprachen wir in unserer naiven Gewißheit.

„Nein", hätte er fast gesagt, als er sich hinter seine großen Brauen zurückzog.

Da wir inzwischen gelernt hatten, daß man einen Denker nicht unterbrechen darf, warteten wir geduldig. Erst einige Jahrzehnte

discovered several decades later, had therapeutic application when we noted that it was not good to interrupt our clients.

After some time - it was as if he had been talking to someone else - he said, "No, a ghost is truly akin to Geist."

"But what is Geist?" we asked in dismayed unity.

"Geist, ghost - it is life or rather the seat of life and therefore the seat of intelligence."

We were astounded at the enormity of the answer. Could this be it? If it was it, what was it? We sunk into a morass of complex obscurity. We had been shown the lock of life but had forgotten to ask for the key.

He let us soak in our abject stupidity until some hours later he said, "To know is to close off knowing. To not know is to know the need for a difference."

"Oh," we said, feigning brilliance.

By this time Bateson was in a self-induced Bali-like trance state. "I did not know this," he continued, "until the great mentor of all post-Copernicusian scientists, the little known Geist and Ghost of all that is ecologically error-proof, the wise old man who has taught me to struggle with failure, appeared to me in my youth. I speak of Carl Auer. He knew what I was doing when I did not. Had I known I would not have still needed to know it. It was Carl Auer who has kept alive the inspiration of the last two hundred years, the unity of mind and body. It was Carl Auer, who gave Lamarck the evolutionary theory. It was Carl Auer who gave to Blake the capacity to see through his eyes and not with them. It was Carl Auer who drove Butler to the brink of family therapy with a schizophrenogenic family. It is Carl Auer who knows what it is that we do not know and it is he that inspires me." He added, just as he was awakening from his trance state, ". . . and now he will inspire you."

"When, how?!" we shouted with impatience.

"I do not know," Gregory replied with tiredness in his voice, "Sometime, somewhere, somehow he will appear. You may not know

später entdeckten wir, daß dieser Grundsatz auch therapeutisch von Bedeutung war, als wir feststellten, daß es nicht gut war, unsere Klienten zu unterbrechen.

Nach einer Weile - es schien, als hätte er sich mit jemand anderem unterhalten - sagte er: „Nein, ein 'ghost' ist wahrhaftig mit Geist verwandt."

„Was ist denn Geist?" fragten wir.

„Geist, 'ghost' - es ist das Leben, oder vielmehr der Sitz des Lebens und somit der Sitz der Intelligenz."

Die Ungeheuerlichkeit der Antwort versetzte uns in Erstaunen. Könnte es das sein? Wenn es das war, was war es? Wir versanken in einem Sumpf komplexer Obskurität. Uns war das Schloß zum Leben gezeigt worden, doch wir hatten vergessen, nach dem Schlüssel zu fragen.

Er ließ uns einige Stunden in unserer erbärmlichen Dummheit schmoren, dann sagte er: „Zu wissen bedeutet, das Wissen abzuschotten. Nicht zu wissen bedeutet, zu wissen, daß ein Unterschied nötig ist."

„Aha", sagten wir, Klugheit vortäuschend.

Inzwischen befand sich Bateson in einem selbstinduzierten baliartigen Trance-Zustand. „Ich wußte das auch nicht", fuhr er fort, „bis mir in meiner Jugend dieser großartige Mentor aller post-kopernikanischen Wissenschaftler, der kaum bekannte Geist und 'Ghost' von allem, was ökologisch gegen jeden Irrtum gefeit ist, der weise alte Mann, der mich gelehrt hat, gegen Mißerfolge anzugehen, erschien. Ich spreche von Carl Auer. Er wußte, was ich tat, wenn ich es nicht wußte. Wenn ich es gewußt hätte, hätte ich es nicht mehr wissen müssen. Carl Auer war es, der die Inspiration der vergangenen zweihundert Jahre am Leben erhalten hat, die Einheit von Körper und Geist. Carl Auer gab Lamarck die Theorie der Evolution. Carl Auer gab Blake die Fähigkeit, durch seine Augen hindurch statt mit ihnen zu sehen. Er brachte Butler mit einer schizophrenogenen Familie an den Rand der Familientherapie. Carl Auer weiß das, was wir nicht wissen, und er inspiriert mich." Gerade als er aus seinem Trance-Zustand erwachte, fügte er hinzu: „. . . und jetzt wird er Euch inspirieren."

„Wann, wie?!" riefen wir voller Ungeduld.

„Ich weiß es nicht", antwortete Gregory mit müder Stimme. „Irgendwann, irgendwo, irgendwie wird er in Erscheinung treten.

him when you see him. You may think you see him when you do not. You may hear him when you do not see him. You may hear him when you see him and you may see him before you hear him. It is a little like 'who is on first '(if you have heard that story)."

"Oh," we said in grave sincerity, "but how will we know the message if the medium is so unknowable?"

"I can only say that the message system will be cybernetic and transform simple linear thinking."

These were words that we could not translate and Bateson would say no more.

Since that fateful day in the mid-fifties we have often talked with and been inspired by Carl Auer (we think). Like all our good teachers we have never seen him. He has never come to Galveston but he appears to us. Rumors are that he has appeared in person to others than Gregory Bateson. Someone once told us that the expression "bat-e-son" (used by some family therapists in their pre-celtic gang rituals of hypothesizing orgy) is really using a part of a little known liturgical chant that is thought to make this inspirational genius appear. Some say he is merely a construction. Some positivists say he is real. Popper says that some day we will disconfirm him. Hoffman thinks he may be the thing in the bushes. Some rumors claim that he was once actually seen by a professor in Heidelberg and that he appeared anorectic.

There is an amusing claim that he is only a solution while others claim him to be the problem solution. Dick Fisch is reported to have used his name in a masterful strategy while he was interdicting an hallucination. Dell denies that he is the true power. Minuchin claims he is not structural. Haley thinks he is organizational and perhaps the confusion between levels of our relationship system. Object relation theorists think he may be the bad mother. Wynne hopes that he may turn out to be the original pseudomutuality. Selvini et al. are quite convinced that he is the invariant prescription. Weakland knows that Carl has never received a degree and that if he did it would be in Chemical Engineering in order to better study anthropology. Someone whose name we cannot reveal once told us with absolute conviction

Ihr erkennt ihn vielleicht nicht, wenn Ihr ihn seht. Ihr meint vielleicht, ihn zu sehen, wenn er nicht da ist. Ihr hört ihn vielleicht, obwohl Ihr ihn nicht seht. Ihr hört ihn vielleicht, wenn Ihr ihn seht, oder Ihr seht ihn, bevor Ihr ihn hört. Es ist so ähnlich wie 'wer zuerst dran kommt' (falls Ihr diese Geschichte kennt)."

„Aha", sagten wir mit großer Aufrichtigkeit. „Wie werden wir aber die Botschaft erkennen, wenn das Medium so unfaßbar ist?"

„Ich kann nur sagen, daß das Informationssystem kybernetisch sein wird und einfaches, lineares Denken von Grund auf transformieren wird."

Das waren Worte, die wir nicht umsetzen konnten, doch sagte Bateson nichts weiter.

Seit jenem schicksalsschweren Tag Mitte der 50er haben wir oft mit Carl Auer gesprochen und uns von ihm inspirieren lassen (glauben wir). Wie alle unsere guten Lehrer haben wir ihn nie gesehen. Er ist nie nach Galveston gekommen, doch erscheint er uns. Gerüchten zufolge ist er außer Gregory Bateson auch anderen in Person erschienen. Man erzählte uns, daß der Ausdruck 'Bat-e-son' (von manchen Familientherapeuten in ihren vorkeltischen Bandenritualen der hypothetisierenden Orgie benutzt) in Wirklichkeit einen Teil eines kaum bekannten liturgischen Sprechgesangs verwendet, von dem behauptet wird, er lasse dieses inspirierende Genie erscheinen. Manche behaupten, er sei bloß konstruiert. Manche Positivisten sagen, er sei real. Popper meint, wir würden ihn eines Tages verleugnen. Hoffman glaubt, er könnte das Ding in den Büschen sein. Manchen Gerüchten zufolge wurde er tatsächlich einmal von einem Professor in Heidelberg gesehen, dem er anorektisch zu sein schien.

Es wird lustigerweise behauptet, daß er nur eine Lösung sei, während andere behaupten, er sei die Lösung des Problems. Dick Fisch soll seinen Namen in einer meisterhaften Strategie zum Verbot einer Halluzination benutzt haben. Dell bestreitet, daß er die wahre Macht sei. Minuchin behauptet, er sei nicht strukturell. Haley vertritt die Ansicht, er stelle Organisation und vielleicht die Verwirrung zwischen den Ebenen unseres Beziehungssystems dar. Objektbeziehungstheoretiker meinen, er sei die böse Mutter. Wynne hofft, er wird sich als die ursprüngliche Pseudo-Gegenseitigkeit herausstellen. Selvini et al. sind fest davon überzeugt, er sei die unveränderliche Verschreibung. Weakland weiß, daß Carl nie einen akademischen Grad erhalten hat, und wenn, dann wäre es in Chemotechnik,

that Whitaker talks with Carl Auer whenever he goes to sleep in a therapy session. We were assured that whenever Whitaker goes to sleep it is to consult and open conversation with Carl Auer. Bloch has wondered if he may not be Nathan Ackerman returning to see us straight. Bowen once said that Carl is the infinite source of non-individuation. Bowen's contention is that we must seek Carl Auer out and we must differentiate from him in order to truly know. Maturana, on the other hand, is convinced that Carl Auer is a distinction in the domain of Geist that has been brought forth by our pre-Columbian structure. Von Foerster has never observed him observing him but knows he is more than a trivial machine. Varela is said to have obtained his concepts on star logic by Carl Auer's continuing reference to Galileo's paper on stars. Keeney has attempted to put him to music in the form of an Italian Opera. The Norwegians are convinced that he is a reflective troll. Personal construct theorists are convinced he posed as Kelly, while the psychodynamic theorists know he was really Freud. An Australian once said that he thought Carl Auer was the paradigm lost. We do not know. For us, he is more than linear, he is more than circular, he is more than systemic, he is more than cybernetic, and he may be more than hermeneutic. We have talked with him often, we think.

We had a friend write a song once about "Galveston Oh Galveston" hoping that it would trap Carl Auer into transcendental materialistic ectoplasm. It did not work. I guess he heard it and ignored us for at least a decade. He came back, we think. He particularly likes foggy days. You can almost make him out in the mist but then you wipe your eyes and he is gone. We think you can hear his voice. When he talks, you hear through your ears and not with your ears. He sounds ontologically epistemological, a sound we can not imitate. Whenever we become desperate he helps (we think). In that with him "we do not know," we continue to make a few small differences. Perhaps someday he will favor us with a telekinetic smile and a huge difference will occur to us. The danger remains, however, that when and if he does smile, and when and if we see the big difference, it may turn out to be

um ihm das Studium der Anthropologie zu erleichtern. Einer, dessen Namen wir nicht enthüllen dürfen, erzählte uns, er sei fest davon überzeugt, daß Whitaker jedesmal mit Carl Auer spreche, wenn er während einer Therapiesitzung einschlafe. Es wurde uns versichert, daß Whitaker immer dann einschlafe, wenn er Carl Auer konsultieren und mit ihm ins Gespräch kommen wolle. Bloch hat sich gefragt, ob er nicht Nathan Ackermann sein könnte, der wiedergekommen sei, um uns den rechten Weg zu weisen. Bowen sagte einmal, Carl sei die unendliche Quelle der Nicht-Individuation. Er behauptet, wir müßten Carl Auer erforschen und uns von ihm differenzieren, um das wahre Wissen zu erhalten. Maturana andererseits ist davon überzeugt, Carl Auer sei eine Unterscheidung im Bereich des Geistes, die durch unsere vorkolumbianische Struktur hervorgerufen wurde. Von Foerster hat nie beobachtet, wie er ihn beobachtete, weiß jedoch, daß er mehr als eine triviale Maschine ist. Varela soll seine Vorstellungen über die Logik der Sterne von Carl Auers wiederholten Verweisen auf Galileis Schrift über Sterne erhalten haben. Keeney hat den Versuch unternommen, ihn in Gestalt einer italienischen Oper zu vertonen. Die Norweger sind davon überzeugt, er sei ein 'reflecting' Troll. Personenkonstruktivisten sind der Überzeugung, er gäbe sich als Kelly aus, während die psychodynamischen Theoretiker wissen, daß er in Wirklichkeit Freud war. Ein Australier sagte einmal, er sei der Meinung, Carl Auer sei das verlorene Paradigma. Wir wissen es nicht. Für uns ist er mehr als linear, mehr als zirkulär, mehr als systemisch, mehr als kybernetisch und womöglich sogar mehr als hermeneutisch. Wir haben oft mit ihm gesprochen, glauben wir.

Wir ließen einmal einen Freund ein Lied über „Galveston, oh Galveston" komponieren in der Hoffnung, das würde Carl Auer in transzendentales, materialistisches Ektoplasma einfangen. Es klappte nicht. Ich nehme an, er hörte es und ignorierte uns daraufhin mindestens ein Jahrzehnt lang. Er kam wieder, glauben wir. Nebeltage mag er besonders. Man kann ihn im Nebel fast erkennen, doch dann wischt man sich über die Augen, und er ist verschwunden. Wir glauben, daß man seine Stimme hören kann. Wenn er spricht, hört man durch die Ohren, nicht mit ihnen. Er hört sich ontologisch epistemologisch an, ein Klang, den wir nicht nachmachen können. Immer, wenn wir am Verzweifeln sind, hilft er (glauben wir). Dadurch, daß wir mit ihm „nicht wissen", machen wir ein paar kleine Unterschiede. Vielleicht beehrt er uns einmal mit einem telekinetischen

in the final judgment only the tautologically limited reduction to pre-Galilean social axiom and definition.

The truth is that the truth does not take more than twenty-four pages. As Carl Auer has taught us, however, nobody will believe it if it does not take more. What may be worse is that he has never indicated which twenty-four pages is the real truth.

So we are left to our conversations in the fog. These conversations with Carl Auer stimulate and reinforce our Geist and Ghost. They are never about what we know and we never know if we have it. We never know if we have heard him since we never know what it is that we do not yet know. Carl Auer is the guide that drives us on our restless search for the new paradigm. He is the living ghost that saves us from the apodictic certainty of the ordinary work of our systemic science. We have learned from our unpredictable but powerful contacts in the Galveston fog with this great meta-systemacist that the universe is one big test. We have also learned that the answers are always multiple choice.

Thank you Carl Auer from your foggy friends at the Galveston Family Institute.

Lächeln, und wir erleben dann einen großen Unterschied. Es besteht jedoch immer noch die Gefahr, daß, sollte er wirklich lächeln und sollte uns tatsächlich der große Unterschied auffallen, er sich letztendlich vielleicht als eine bloße, tautologisch beschränkte Reduktion auf vorgalileische soziale Axiome und Definitionen herausstellt.

Die Wahrheit ist, daß die Wahrheit nicht mehr als vierundzwanzig Seiten ausfüllt. Wie Carl Auer uns jedoch gelehrt hat, wird niemand sie glauben, wenn das alles ist. Was vermutlich noch schlimmer ist, ist die Tatsache, daß er noch nie auch nur angedeutet hat, welche vierundzwanzig Seiten die Wahrheit enthalten.

Uns bleiben also nur unsere Gespräche im Nebel. Diese Gespräche mit Carl Auer stimulieren und schärfen unseren Geist und „Ghost". Sie handeln nie von etwas, das wir wissen, und wir wissen auch nie, ob wir es haben. Wir wissen nie, ob wir ihn gehört haben, denn wir wissen nie, was es ist, das wir noch nicht wissen. Carl Auer ist der Führer, der uns bei unserer rastlosen Suche nach dem neuen Paradigma antreibt. Er ist der lebendige „Ghost", der uns vor der apodiktischen Gewißheit der gewöhnlichen Arbeit unserer systemischen Wissenschaft rettet. Von unseren unberechenbaren, jedoch mächtigen Kontakten mit diesem großen Meta-Systemiker im Nebel von Galveston haben wir gelernt, daß das Universum ein großer Test ist. Wir haben auch gelernt, daß die Antworten immer Multiple-choice-Antworten sind.

Carl Auer, die benebelten Freunde des Galveston Familieninstituts danken dir.

[1] *Webster's* ist ein in den Vereinigten Staaten sehr gebräuchliches einsprachiges Wörterbuch.

Gone to the Dogs

Auf den Hund gekommen

A Doggy Discourse with Carl Auer (or the Man I Think was Him)

Helm Stierlin

I first heard of Carl Auer about 40 years ago. At the time I was studying Philosophy and Medicine in Heidelberg. There was as yet hardly any sign of a Federal Republic. There were occupied zones with the respective victors. Adenauer, Globke and Heuss were making the headlines. The economic miracle and the Cold War existed side by side. Jaspers was teaching philosophical truth to an attentive community in the University assembly hall, while in Freiburg Heidegger was still banned from speaking. Freud could be read again, but was hard to get hold of. Konrad Lorenz held lectures on the loyalty of grey geese to their partners.

The zoologist Erich von Holst, a friend and colleague of Konrad Lorenz, also lectured in Heidelberg. Along with Jaspers, Victor von Weizsäcker and Radbruch he too was one of the stars of the University. Today he is regarded as the founder of biological cybernetics as a result of his discovery of the reafference principle. It was from him that I first heard of Carl Auer. Carl Auer was a pioneering researcher, thinker, biologist, psychologist and philosopher in one. After escaping from the Nazis under great difficulties, he had emigrated first to New Zealand and was now a psychological adviser in the service of the American military government. He had agreed to give a lecture on „The appearance and reality of instincts" for a small circle of listeners. Since I represented the cultural department of the Students' Union, I was allowed to take part. But the lecture was not held. Auer unexpectedly cancelled it. Von Holst consoled me with an awkward rhyme: "One day even you will realize: The further away our Auer, the more we feel his power." My response was then: „You can only say that of God." Von Holst: "Exactly."

My second chance to see Carl Auer came a few years later. I was then studying in Freiburg. I remember: sunny vineyards, mighty, still

Ein Hundediskurs mit Carl Auer (bzw. dem Mann, den ich dafür halte)

Helm Stierlin

Es war vor etwa 40 Jahren, als ich zum erstenmal von Carl Auer hörte. Ich studierte damals in Heidelberg Philosophie und Medizin. Von einer Bundesrepublik war noch wenig zu merken. Es gab Besatzungszonen mit darin zuständigen Siegern. Adenauer, Globke und Heuss machten Schlagzeilen. Wirtschaftswunder und Kalter Krieg koexistierten. In der Aula der Heidelberger Universität belehrte Jaspers eine andächtig lauschende Gemeinde über die Wahrheit, während Heidegger in Freiburg noch Redeverbot hatte. Freud durfte wieder gelesen werden, war aber schwer zugänglich. Konrad Lorenz hielt Vorträge über die Partnertreue der Graugänse.

In Heidelberg lehrte auch der Zoologe Erich von Holst, ein Freund und Mitarbeiter Konrad Lorenz'. Neben Jaspers, Viktor von Weizsäcker und Radbruch war auch er ein Star der Universität. Er gilt heute - wegen seiner Entdeckung des Reafferenzprinzips - als Begründer der biologischen Kybernetik. Von ihm hörte ich erstmals über Carl Auer. Dieser sei ein wegweisender Forscher und Denker, Biologe, Psychologe und Philosoph in einem. Er sei, den Nazis mit Mühe und Not entkommen, zuerst nach Neuseeland ausgewandert, stehe aber jetzt als psychologischer Berater im Dienst der amerikanischen Militärregierung. Er habe zugesagt, im kleinen Kreise einen Vortrag über „Sein und Schein des Triebes" zu halten. Da ich im ASTA das Kulturressort vertrat, durfte ich daran teilnehmen. Aber der Vortrag fand nicht statt. Auer sagte überraschend ab. Von Holst tröstete mich, etwas ungelenk kalauernd: „Auch Sie werden noch merken: Je ferner unser Auer, um so mehr wirkt er auf Dauer." Meine damalige Antwort: „Das läßt sich höchstens noch von Gott sagen." Darauf von Holst: „Eben."

Meine zweite Chance, Carl Auer zu sehen, kam einige Jahre später. Ich studierte damals in Freiburg. Ich erinnere mich: Sonnen-

healthy Black Forest pines, fun bathing in the Altrhein surrounded by swarms of mosquitos and croaking frogs, professors still doing their rounds as 'gods in white', me on internship in the Faculty of Internal Medicine, washing out countless urine bottles and taking blood pressures. Heidegger nearby, still banned from speaking, preparing his 'turn' (Kehre) in the peace and quiet of the Black Forest. I was studying Freud's theory of instincts, wanted to compare it with Konrad Lorenz's. What wouldn't I have given for a copy of Auer's essay, "The appearance and reality of instincts." I went to Otto Köhler, the well-known ethologist then occupying the chair for zoology at the University of Freiburg, and friend of Konrad Lorenz, for advice. Maybe he had a copy of Auer's lecture. He merely said: "Young man, a respectable scientist does not get mixed up with a swine like Freud."

At least I was permitted to participate in a symposium of ethologists, as an unofficial guest. Lorenz, von Holst, Tinbergen, Kortlandt and all the other pioneers of the first hour were present. The comparison with Freud's Wednesday conferences comes involuntarily to mind. Both involved a small group of researching outsiders, who subsequently created quite a stir scientifically throughout the world. Carl Auer was expected by this group too. He was the tip. I imagined him to be like this: A man in his mid-fifties with a kind face framed by an already greying beard, an intense and at the same time dreamy expression, who still spoke with a slight Austrian or Swabian accent in spite of many years spent in the USA, a powerful partner in dialogues, hitting the nail on the head in a flash.

Yet again the great man conveyed his apologies. He was in the country, but had suddenly become ill. (A particularly nasty form of gastric 'flu was raging in South Baden at the time. It was said to have been brought in by colored French soldiers in the occupying forces.)

I was disappointed, despondent even. Was I to miss the famous clandestine thinker and researcher yet again? I was still at an age when one is inclined to admire heroes, and in which such admiration grows with the degree of distance from the object of admiration (just as about one and a half decades later the transfiguration of Mao as a people's hero seemed to increase in proportion to his distance), yet cannot quite dispense with occasional contact with the hero altogether.

durchstrahlte Weinberge, mächtige, noch kerngesunde Schwarzwaldtannen, Badespaß am Altrhein inmitten von Mückenschwärmen und Froschgequake, die Professoren noch als Götter in Weiß ihre Visiten abhaltend, ich, in der Inneren Medizin famulierend, unzählige Uringläser spülend und Blutdrucke messend. Heidegger in der Nähe, noch immer mit Redeverbot, in der Stille des Schwarzwaldes seine „Kehre" vorbereitend. Ich studierte Freuds Trieblehre, wollte sie mit der von Konrad Lorenz vergleichen. Was hätte ich nicht für eine Kopie von Auers Aufsatz „Sein und Schein des Triebes" gegeben. Ich wendete mich um Rat an Otto Köhler, den bekannten Verhaltensforscher, damals Inhaber des Freiburger Zoologischen Lehrstuhles und Freund Konrad Lorenz'. Vielleicht hatte er eine Kopie des Auerschen Vortrages. Er sagte nur: „Junger Mann, mit einem Schwein wie Freud läßt sich ein anständiger Wissenschaftler nicht ein."

Immerhin: ich durfte bald darauf an einem Symposium der Verhaltensforscher teilnehmen, sozusagen als Zaungast. Lorenz, von Holst, Tinbergen, Kortland und wie die Pioniere der ersten Stunde alle hießen, waren dabei. Der Vergleich mit Freuds Mittwochsgesellschaft drängte sich auf. Beide Male ein Häuflein von forschenden Außenseitern, das dann weltweit wissenschaftliche Wellen schlug. Auch in dieser Gruppe erwartete man Carl Auer. Er war der Geheimtip. Ich machte mir ein Bild von ihm: Ein Mann, etwa Mitte 50, gütiges Gesicht, umrahmt von einem schon ergrauten Bart, der Blick zugleich intensiv und versonnen, trotz vieler in den USA verbrachter Jahre noch einen leicht österreichischen oder schwäbischen Akzent sprechend, als Dialogspartner mächtig, das Wesentliche mit Blitzeskraft treffend.

Aber auch diesmal ließ sich der große Mann entschuldigen. Er sei zwar im Lande, aber plötzlich erkrankt. (Es grassierte damals in Südbaden eine üble Form von Darmgrippe. Farbige französische Besatzungssoldaten, hieß es, hätten sie eingeschleppt.)

Ich war enttäuscht, ja niedergeschlagen. Sollte mir der geheimnisvolle, berühmte Denker und Forscher wieder entgehen? Ich war noch in einem Alter, das der Heldenverehrung zuneigt und bei dem solche Verehrung zwar mit dem Grad der Entfernung des Verehrungsgegenstandes wächst, (so wie etwa eineinhalb Jahrzehnte später die Verklärung eines Mao als Volkshelden im Maße seiner Ferne zuzunehmen schien), aber eben doch nicht ganz ohne einen gelegentlichen

At that time my hero could only be a hero of the mind - one of the format of a Carl Auer.

My semester in Freiburg was drawing to a close. Although it was rumoured that Carl Auer was staying in the Black Forest on a health cure, I had given up all hope of seeing him. But then - just before my return to Heidelberg - I did meet him, or at least I think I met him. It happened like this:

I had settled myself down at the edge of the forest. In front of me was a vineyard. The afternoon sun was wandering to the west, towards Alsace. Dragonflies were buzzing, and I was surrounded by the smell of fresh pinewood and ripe blackberries. I had opened Hegel's *Phenomenology of the Spirit* and was brooding on the philosopher's dubiously stimulating exposition on the relationship between "master and servant." My mind was wandering. Heidegger's wisdom got entangled in Hegel's dialectic jungle: "The being being nullifies the nullifying nothingness"... And then it happened. A hard push and, simultaneously, a strong smell of dog woke me from my philosophical daydreams. As I came to my senses I recognized the disturber of the peace: a huge Alsatian, which apparently had its eye not on me, but on a fieldmouse it had seen disappearing into a hole by my side. I just saw how the dog threw the mouse, by now a mere ball of grey hair and flesh, into the air one last time before swallowing it in one go.

And then he stood in front of me in person: the man I now presume, looking back, to have been Carl Auer. He corresponded almost exactly - which surely is seldom enough the case - to my inner picture of him. He actually did have a beard, even though it was red and not yet turning grey. His expression was both dreamy and intense. And although he spoke perfect German, there was just a hint of dialect which I assigned to the Bavarian- Austrian border countries.

He apologized for his Senta. She was still young, impetuous, a hothead, but a lovely creature, and for him a constant source of important discoveries besides. I was curious and asked him about these discoveries. He then sat down on the moss next to me, and that is how my only conversation - up till today - with the man I am ever more convinced was Carl Auer, developed. Whilst we talked, Senta went on hunting fieldmice.

Kontakt mit dem Helden auskommt. Mein Held konnte aber damals nur ein Held des Geistes - eben vom Format eines Carl Auer - sein.

Mein Freiburger Semester neigte sich dem Ende zu. Obschon die Rede davon war, daß Auer sich zu einer Kur im Schwarzwald aufhalte, hatte ich die Hoffnung aufgegeben, ihn noch zu sehen. Doch dann - es war kurz vor meiner Rückreise nach Heidelberg - traf ich ihn doch, oder meine zumindest, ihn getroffen zu haben. Und das ergab sich so:

Ich hatte es mir an einem Waldrand bequem gemacht. Vor mir ein Weinberg. Die Nachmittagssonne wanderte nach Westen zum Elsaß. Libellen summten, ein Geruch von frischem Tannenholz und reifen Brombeeren umfing mich. Ich hatte Hegels „Phänomenologie des Geistes" aufgeschlagen und sinnierte über des Philosophen dunkel anregende Ausführungen zum Verhältnis von „Herr und Knecht". Meine Gedanken wanderten. Heideggersche Weisheiten verfingen sich in Hegels dialektischem Dickicht: „Das seiende Sein nichtet das nichtende Nichts"... Und dann geschah es. Ein heftiger Stoß und gleichzeitiger scharfer Hundegeruch rissen mich aus meinen philosophischen Tagträumen. Als ich zur Besinnung kam, erkannte ich den Ruhestörer: Einen mächtigen Schäferhund, der es aber offenbar nicht auf mich, sondern auf eine Feldmaus abgesehen hatte, die er neben mir in einem Loch hatte verschwinden sehen. Ich sah gerade noch, wie der Hund die Maus, nunmehr ein graues Haar- und Fleischknäuel, ein letztes Mal in die Luft schleuderte und in einem Schluck hinunterschlang.

Und dann stand er selbst vor mir: der Mann, von dem ich im Rückblick annehme, daß es Carl Auer war. Er entsprach - was selten genug der Fall sein dürfte - nahezu vollständig meinem inneren Bild von ihm. Er trug in der Tat einen Bart, allerdings einen roten und noch nicht ergrauten. Sein Blick war zugleich versonnen und intensiv. Und er ließ, obschon fehlerfrei deutsch sprechend, einen Dialekt anklingen, den ich den bayerisch-österreichischen Grenzlanden zuordnete.

Er entschuldigte sich für seine Senta. Sie sei noch jung, ungestüm, ein Hitzkopf, aber doch ein liebes Geschöpf und dazu für ihn eine ständige Quelle wichtiger Erkenntnisse. Ich wurde neugierig, fragte ihn nach diesen Erkenntnissen. Er setzte sich daraufhin neben mich ins Moos, und so entspann sich mein - bis heute - einziges Gespräch mit dem Mann, von dem ich mehr denn je überzeugt bin, daß er Carl Auer war. Während wir uns unterhielten, jagte Senta weiter Feldmäuse.

I do not consider myself a dog lover. We had a dachshund at home, we called him Abel Müller. He stank in spite of the periodic dog baths our parents made us children give him. During a boxing match with my younger brother I once slipped in Abel's dog shit, and had to swallow defeat and humiliation at one and the same time. Thinking of Abel, I wasn't exactly enthralled by Senta. But it was obviously quite the contrary as far as Carl Auer (or the man I think was him) was concerned. He was a dog fan, in fact he had, as I was soon to realize, chosen the dog as the animal that not only taught him things of importance about the dog species, but also about homo sapiens. It could be said: What grey geese were for Lorenz, dolphins and octopi for Bateson, for Carl Auer it was dogs. This fact should make it more understandable that my only discourse with the man I thought was Carl Auer was a discourse about dogs. I hope the reader will forgive me for limiting the following short contribution to this volume to what I can still remember of this discourse (unfortunately a little muddled).

To begin with Auer spoke about the dog as an incitement - essential to many people - to take exercise. Without my Senta or another dog, I still hear him saying, I would hardly walk for an hour in the fresh air on the edge of the forest. And like me countless other people profit from this incitement to exercise. However, one can distinguish between people who have an external dog and those who have an inner dog to incite them to exercise. It is quite likely that the inner dog is superior to the external one, as it means less dependence, more autonomy, more self management. But the inner dog can also cause problems. It can be so inflexible, so fixed in its views that autonomy is reversed to slavery. He then went on to speak about a particular kind of inner dog that only exists in German-speaking countries, namely the inner *Schweinehund*. It is difficult to find a more striking phenomenon to explain the psychology of the Germans. Just consider, I hear him say with increasing emotion, just consider the Germans' recent past. Consider the millions of German warmongers, the Nazis and their passive followers who fought their inner *Schweinehund* day in and day out, thereby forgetting to ask how a man like Hitler could make them go to the dogs. The conversation then touched on Hitler himself. Auer mentioned Hitler's Alsatian. Just a few hours before he committed suicide, Hitler got married, and the

Ich empfinde mich nicht als Hundeliebhaber. Daheim hatten wir einen Dackel, den nannten wir Abel Müller. Aber er stank trotz der uns Kindern von den Eltern periodisch verordneten Hundewäsche. Einmal war ich auch, während eines Boxkampfes mit meinem jüngeren Bruder, in Abels Hundekot ausgerutscht und hatte zugleich Niederlage und Demütigung einstecken müssen. An Abel denkend, war ich auf Senta nicht gut zu sprechen. Aber bei Carl Auer (bzw. dem Mann, den ich dafür halte) war das offensichtlich anders. Er war ein Hundefan, ja hatte sich, so konnte ich bald erfahren, den Hund als das Tier auserkoren, das ihn nicht nur Wesentliches über die Spezies Hund, sondern auch die des Homo sapiens lehrte. Man konnte sagen: Was für Lorenz Graugänse, für Bateson Delphine und Octopi als Erkenntnislieferanten waren, das waren für Carl Auer Hunde. Diese Tatsache dürfte auch verständlicher machen, daß mein einziger Diskurs mit dem (mutmaßlichen) Carl Auer ein Diskurs über Hunde war. Der Leser möge mir also verzeihen, wenn ich mich in meinem folgenden kurzen Festschriftbeitrag auf das beschränke, was mir von diesem Diskurs in (leider ungeordneter) Erinnerung geblieben ist.

Auer sprach zunächst vom Hund als einem - für viele Menschen notwendigen - Bewegungsmacher. Ohne meine Senta oder einen anderen Hund, höre ich ihn noch sagen, würde ich täglich kaum eine Stunde lang in frischer Luft an Waldrändern spazierengehen. Und wie ich selbst, profitieren zahllose andere Menschen von solcher Bewegungsmache. Man kann jedoch, fuhr er fort, Menschen unterscheiden, die einen Außenhund und solche, die einen inneren Hund als Bewegungsmacher haben. Man könne sich vorstellen, daß der innere, bewegungsmachende Hund dem Außenhund sogar überlegen ist. Denn er bedeutet ja weniger Abhängigkeit, mehr Autonomie, mehr Selbststeuerung. Aber auch der innere Hund könne problematisch werden. Er könnte so starr, so unbelehrbar sein, daß sich die Autonomie wieder in Sklaverei verkehre. Er kam sodann auf eine besondere Art des inneren Hundes zu sprechen, den es nur im deutschsprachigen Raum gebe, nämlich den inneren Schweinehund. Für das Verständnis der Psychologie der Deutschen gebe es wohl kaum ein treffenderes Phänomen. Denken Sie, höre ich ihn mit zunehmender Bewegtheit sagen, denken Sie an die jüngste deutsche Vergangenheit. Denken Sie an die Millionen deutscher Krieger, Nazis und Mitläufer, die tagein, tagaus ihren inneren Schweinehund bekämpften und dabei sich zu fragen vergaßen, wie ein Mann namens

dog formed part of his family. Eva Braun and the dog were both bound in faith to Hitler and were rewarded with death. Death as the reward for loyalty - that too is something typically German.

As he said that he glanced at the book lying next to me, namely Hegel's *Phenomenology of the Spirit*. He was, of course, familiar with Hegel's exposition on the subject "master and servant" and even introduced the dog here as an elucidating element. I stammered something about my difficulties to understand Hegel's remarks on the relationship between master and servant and the balance of power conveyed by this relationship. For the man at my side this was the cue to turn to the subject of the allocation of power between "master and dog."

Take my Senta, he said. I agree: I am her master and she is my creature. So far, so good. Senta shows her dependence on me, she is more dependent than a child, as her speciality is loyalty. When I am angry with her and just frown slightly, she is overcome with remorse, lop-eared, a picture of misery. But do I really have power over my dog? And do I have the pleasure of power? I doubt it. When Senta whines at me remorsefully, I am filled with remorse, too. Loyalty for loyalty. She has the whip hand for triggering guilt. When I am travelling - and unfortunately I have to travel quite frequently at the moment - the thought of leaving Senta behind, pining, unhappy, feeling misunderstood by strangers, robs me of my sleep. In so far as I am a moral being, I feel monopolized, tied down, enslaved by Senta's love and loyalty.

As Auer, or the man I thought to be him, said this (probably exaggerating a little), an idea of the essence and meaning of relationships germinated in me, which I was to develop in my later writings. In a system dominated by doggish human relationships such as my interlocutor impressed on me, one could indeed barely make out who was master and who was servant, who was the culprit and who the victim. The deeds of one were the deeds of the other - a classic example of centripetal dynamics.

Spontaneously this brought to mind a contrary scene, stimulated by my recent reading of descriptions of travel in southern countries.

Hitler sie auf den Hund brachte. Das Gespräch kam dann auf Hitler selbst. Auer erwähnte Hitlers Schäferhund. Nur wenige Stunden vor seinem Selbstmord gründete Hitler eine Familie, und dazu gehörte der Hund. Dieser war, wie auch Eva Braun, Hitler in Treue verbunden und wurde dafür mit dem Tod belohnt. Der Tod als Lohn der Treue. Auch das typisch deutsch.

Als er dies sagte, fiel sein Blick auf das neben mir liegende Buch, nämlich Hegels „Phänomenologie des Geistes". Auch er war natürlich mit Hegels Ausführungen zum Thema „Herr und Knecht" vertraut und brachte nun auch hier den Hund als erhellendes Moment ein. Ich stammelte etwas von meinen Schwierigkeiten, Hegels Ausführungen zur Beziehung zwischen Herr und Knecht und den sich darin vermittelnden Machtverhältnissen zu verstehen. Das war dann für mein Gegenüber das Stichwort, um sich dem Thema der Machtverteilung zwischen „Herr und Hund" zuzuwenden.

Sehen Sie meine Senta, sagte er. Ich gebe zu: Ich bin ihr Herr und sie ist mein Geschöpf. So weit, so gut. Senta zeigt sich abhängig von mir, abhängiger als ein Kind, da auf Treue spezialisiert. Wenn ich böse mit ihr bin, nur leicht die Stirn runzele, wird sie zerknirscht, hängeohrig, ein Bild des Jammers. Aber habe ich wirklich Macht über meinen Hund? Und habe ich auch den Genuß der Macht? Ich bezweifle es. Wenn Senta mich zerknirscht anjammert, knirscht es auch in mir. Treue um Treue. Sie sitzt am längeren Hebelarm der Schuldauslösung. Wenn ich auf Reisen gehe - und leider muß ich das in letzter Zeit häufiger - raubt mir der Gedanke an die zurückgelassene Senta, die darbt, unglücklich ist, sich von Fremden mißverstanden fühlt, den Schlaf. Soweit ich ein moralisches Wesen bin, fühle ich mich durch Sentas Liebe und Treue vereinnahmt, gefesselt, ohnmächtig, geknechtet.

Als Auer, bzw. der Mann, den ich dafür hielt, dies (sicherlich leicht übertreibend) sagte, keimte wohl erstmals in mir eine Vorstellung von dem Wesen und der Bedeutung der Bindung, wie ich sie später in meinen Schriften entwickeln sollte. In einem hündisch-menschlich gebundenen System, wie es mein Gesprächspartner mir nahebrachte, war in der Tat kaum mehr auszumachen, wer Herr und Knecht, wer Täter und Opfer war. Das Tun des Einen war das Tun des Anderen. Das Musterbeispiel einer zentripetalen Dynamik.

Unwillkürlich stellte sich mir daraufhin ein gegenteiliges Szenario dar, angeregt durch meine kürzliche Lektüre von Reisebeschreibungen

(On visiting several of these at a later time, I found my ideas confirmed): A scene with countless stray dogs romping about in sundried streets in droves, shaggy, emaciated curs, mongrels, prowling around searching for rests in rubbish heaps, some lethargic, others suspicious and vicious, all thrown into the fight for survival in a cold, competitive world. These were the outcasts, the neglected, expression and result of centrifugal dynamics.

My partner seemed to have guessed my thoughts. We, Senta and I, he said, are a culprit, victim and projecting company and are undergoing coevolution.

I pricked up my ears once again. This was the first time I heard this word, which has now been adopted in our daily family therapy language. Even today I am unable to say whether Auer (or the man I thought to be him) passed the concept of coevolution on to his friend Bateson or took it over from him. It is possible that they both created a theory of coevolution independently, just as Wallace and Darwin developed one of evolution independently.

Whatever the case may be: The cue "coevolution" inspired the man next to me to further reflections relating to dogs. Today, looking back almost 40 years, they could almost be called prophetic. The coevolution of man and dog, he said, can now be traced over a period of four to five thousand years. However, it gives me little pleasure to contemplate it. After man had first tamed and domesticated the proud wild dog, he soon made a plaything out of it. He kept to the word of God, "Subdue the earth," and subdued the dog first. He bred dogs. And what dogs: monsters with screwed up building plans, doomed to waddling and to arthrosis after just a few years, dogs with floppy ears and bleary eyes, dogs like balls of wool and smaller than cats, dilatory, clumsy, childish melodramas, and also vicious and suspicious, sly monstrosities of dogs. Whatever was required, a live toy, substitute for a partner, something to dispel loneliness, a laboratory animal, the embodiment of their unrealized lust and wildness, they bred it in the dog.

südlicher Länder.. (Als ich später einige davon besuchte, fand ich meine Vorstellungen bestätigt:) Ein Szenario mit zahllosen herrenlosen Hunden, die sich zuhauf in sonnenverdorrten Straßen tummelten, struppige, abgemagerte Köter, Promenadenmischungen, herumstreunend, Müllhaufen nach Abfällen durchsuchend, manche lethargisch, manche argwöhnisch-bissig, alle hineingeworfen in den Überlebenskampf in einer kalten Konkurrenzwelt. Das waren die Ausgestoßenen, die Verwahrlosten, Ausdruck und Folge einer zentrifugalen Dynamik.

Es war, als hätte mein Partner meine Gedanken erraten. Wir, Senta und ich, sagte er, sind eine Täter-, Opfer- und Projektionsgemeinschaft und machen dabei eine Koevolution durch.

Wieder horchte ich auf. Das war das erstemal, daß ich dieses Wort, das inzwischen in unsere familientherapeutische Alltagssprache eingegangen ist, hörte. Bis heute vermag ich nicht zu sagen, ob Auer (oder der Mann, den ich dafür halte) den Begriff der Koevolution seinem Freunde Bateson zugespielt oder von diesem übernommen hatte. Möglicherweise schufen sie unabhängig voneinander eine Theorie der Koevolution so wie einst Wallace und Darwin unabhängig voneinander eine solche der Evolution entwickelt hatten.

Wie dem auch sei: Das Stichwort „Koevolution" regte mein Gegenüber zu weiteren hundbezogenen Betrachtungen an. Heute, im Rückblick von fast 40 Jahren, könnten sie fast prophetisch anmuten. Die Koevolution von Mensch und Hund, sagte er, läßt sich inzwischen über einen Zeitraum von vier- bis fünftausend Jahren verfolgen. Sie zu bedenken schafft mir jedoch wenig Freude: Nachdem der Mensch den stolzen Wildhund erstmals gezähmt und zu einem Haustier gemacht hatte, machte er ihn auch bald zu seinem Spielzeug. Er hielt sich an Gottes Wort: „Macht Euch die Welt untertan" und machte sich zunächst den Hund untertan. Er züchtete sich Hunde. Und was für welche: Ungetüme mit verkorksten Bauplänen, schon nach wenigen Jahren zu Watschelgang und Arthrose verurteilt, Hunde mit Schlappohren und Triefblick, Hunde wie Wollknäuel und kleiner als Katzen, saumselige, tolpatschige, kindliche Rührstücke, aber auch bissig-argwöhnisch verschlagene Monstrositäten von Hunden. Was immer Menschen sich als lebendes Spielzeug, als Partnerersatz, als Einsamkeitsverscheucher, als Labortier, als Verkörperung ihrer nicht ausgelebten Begierde und Wildheit wünschten, das züchteten sie sich im Hund.

After a little thought he added: Models, so to speak, of what man will do with man in a few decades. Breeding himself, he will celebrate orgies of breeding, the progress of medicine, in particular molecular biology, will make it possible. Brave new world.

My partner was brooding further : We can also find contrasting programs in man in so far as the attitude towards their offspring is concerned: On the one hand overplanning, overprotection, overbinding, overresponsibility; on the other hand the carefreeness of mating rabbits, who think: "God will take care of it." But I fear that God - let us assume that he exists and is looking down on such quagmires of human protoplasm as Lagos, Cairo, Calcutta or Mexico City - does not feel induced to judge or repair. (Translator's note: "richten" in German can also be used to mean 'do something up', 'fix', or 'repair'. The author uses the word in both senses.)

In answer to my bashful question as to whether he spent a lot of time thinking about God, he referred me to Meister Ekkehart, William Blake and Samuel Butler. They had already said it all. Take Samuel Butler, for instance, he added after a while. He said, "The designer was the design itself"! That is something to be taken into consideration.

It was, however, difficult for me to understand this. I am still puzzling over it today. (Again I am reminded of Bateson as I write this down. Did Bateson take his idea of God as a cybernetic nemesis over from Auer? Questions upon questions).

If I remember correctly, Auer then spoke of a planetary future in which there would be only three categories of living organisms or bio-matter: (1) The human bio-matter that had adapted to a human-made environment; (2) the bio-matter of the creatures subjugated and bred by man, i.e. the bio-matter of domesticated, zoo, laboratory animals and those bred for slaughter, and finally (3) the (dwindling) bio-matter of such creatures as rats, sparrows, cockroaches, lice, bacteria and viruses which have continually managed to outwit man in his subjugation and breeding game.

This was indeed a gloomy perspective. But Auer substantiated it by returning to his doggy theme. He said: In order to satisfy the many dog breeders and dog-lovers in our western world, the wild horses in

Und nach kurzem Nachdenken fügte er hinzu: Sozusagen Modellversuche für das, was in einigen Jahrzehnten der Mensch mit Menschen machen wird. Er wird auch hier, sich selbst züchtend, Züchtungsorgien feiern, die Fortschritte der Medizin und insbesondere der Molekularbiologie werden es ermöglichen. Wackere neue Welt.

Mein Partner sinnierte weiter: Auch wo es um die Einstellung zum Nachwuchs geht, finden wir beim Menschen Kontrastprogramme: Auf der einen Seite Überplanung, Überfürsorglichkeit, Überbindung, Überverantwortung, auf der anderen die Unbekümmertheit rammelnder Kaninchen, die da denken: „Der Herrgott wird´s schon richten." Aber, ich fürchte, der Herrgott - nehmen wir mal an, es gäbe ihn, und er schaute auf solche Wuselpfuhle menschlichen Protoplasmas wie Lagos, Kairo, Kalkutta oder Mexiko-City hinab - fühlt sich nicht zum Richten bewogen (Richten sowohl im Sinne von Rechtsprechen als auch im Sinne von Herrichten, Einrichten, wieder in Ordnung bringen).

Auf meine schüchterne Frage, ob er sich viele Gedanken über Gott mache, verwies Carl Auer mich auf Meister Ekkehart, William Blake und Samuel Butler. Die hätten schon das Wesentliche gesagt. Nehmen Sie z. B. Samuel Butler, fügte er nach einer Weile hinzu. Der sagte „The designer was the design itself"! Das sollte man bedenken.

Das war für mich jedoch schwer zu verstehen. Noch heute knobele ich daran. (Wieder muß ich, da ich dies niederschreibe, an Bateson denken. Hatte Bateson auch seine Idee von Gott als kybernetischer Nemesis von Auer übernommen? Fragen über Fragen.)

Wenn ich mich recht erinnere, sprach Auer dann von einer planetarischen Zukunft, in der es nur noch drei Kategorien von Lebewesen bzw. Biomasse geben werde: 1. Die menschliche, sich in einer von Menschen geschaffenen Umwelt einrichtende Biomasse; 2. die Biomasse der vom Menschen unterjochten und gezüchteten Geschöpfe, d. h. die Biomasse der Haus-, Zoo-, Labor- und Schlachttiere, und schließlich 3. die (schrumpfende) Biomasse solcher Kreaturen wie Ratten, Sperlinge, Kakerlaken, Läuse, Bakterien und Viren, die den Menschen bei seinem Unterwerfungs- und Züchtungsspiel weiterhin auszutricksen verständen.

Das waren in der Tat trübsinnig stimmende Perspektiven. Aber Auer untermauerte sie, indem er wieder zu seinem Hundethema zurückfand. Er sagte: Um die vielen Hundezüchter und Hunde-

the USA would have to cop it. They were being made into dog food. But soon beef will have to start being used more and more often too. That is being bred en masse in Brasil, on meadows that are quickly turning into steppe, where rain forests grew not so very long ago. That's where I admire the Chinese. They get along without dogs, they take their canaries into the streets instead. Instead of rearing dogs, they slaughter them young. Although - and he smilingly realized the contradiction he had talked himself into - I wouldn't have enjoyed my Senta, not even as a baby.

So you see, he said, kindly embarrassed, even I am a walking contradiction, but so is the rest of mankind. Man could be divided into two parts, by the way. Those who suffer in the face of contradictions, or who make others suffer to elude their own suffering. And the others, less in number, who enjoy contradictions. I hope you belong to this minority, or if not, that you will join it as soon as possible.

With these words he rose. Senta was still chasing fieldmice in the distance. The sun was about to disappear behind the Vosges Mountains. Auer's diminishing figure vanished into the forest. The very next day I left Freiburg. It was not only my attitude to dogs that was changed by this conversation.

liebhaber in unserer westlichen Welt zu befriedigen, müssen auch die Wildpferde in den USA dran glauben. Die werden nun zu Hundefutter verarbeitet. Daneben wird man aber mehr und mehr auf Rinder zurückgreifen müssen. Die werden auch schon massenhaft in Brasilien gezüchtet, auf schnell versteppendem Weideland, das vor kurzem noch einen Regenwald trug. Da lobe ich mir die Chinesen. Die kommen ohne Hunde aus, tragen stattdessen ihre Kanarienvögel auf die Straße. Anstatt sie großzuziehen, schlachten sie ihre Hunde, wenn sie noch jung sind. Allerdings - und lächelnd erkannte er den Widerspruch, in den er sich hineingeredet hatte - meine Senta hätte mir nicht gut geschmeckt, auch nicht als Baby.

Sie sehen, sagte er in liebenswürdiger Verlegenheit, auch ich bin ein wandelnder Widerspruch, ebenso wie der Rest der Menschheit. Man könnte die Menschen übrigens in zwei Teile aufteilen. Diejenigen, die am Widerspruch leiden oder, um solchem Leiden zu entgehen, andere leiden lassen. Und die anderen, weniger zahlreichen, die am Widerspruch Spaß haben. Ich wünsche Ihnen, daß Sie zu dieser Minderheit gehören oder, falls nicht, sich dieser möglichst bald zugesellen.

Mit diesen Worten erhob er sich. Senta jagte in weiter Ferne ihre Feldmäuse. Die Sonne schickte sich an, hinter den Vogesen zu verschwinden. Auers kleiner werdende Gestalt verlor sich auf einem Waldweg. Schon am folgenden Tag reiste ich von Freiburg ab. Nicht nur meine Einstellung zu Hunden hat sich durch dieses Gespräch geändert.

The Potential of Relationship

Paul Watzlawick

My only meeting with Carl Auer was purely coincidental: 1977 on the shore of Killaney Bay, south of Dublin. It was about 5 o'clock in the afternoon and I had just finished a two-day seminar. The participants were satisfied with my pearls of wisdom and the meeting dissolved itself in satisfaction, so to speak. Tired from those long hours of work, but even more so from the long flight and the time difference from San Francisco, I walked down the narrow path leading from the hotel to the sea and sat on one of the benches along the promenade. Probably like anyone who visits this area for the first time, I was struck by its almost Mediterranean beauty: a deep-blue, calm sea, embraced by two promontories, palm trees, flowering magnolias, the soft light of the setting sun from behind, warmth, silence. One of those rare moments when we feel *in tune* with it all - and when for once the intellect is not trying to find out what that "it" is.

And then suddenly, behind me, an ugly, unmistakable noise. Somebody has started kicking around an empty can. Does this always have to happen? - Every time that, for a brief moment, we are blessed to participate in that harmony, there comes some Neanderthal man and spreads acoustic stench from his transistor radio or rapes the silence with his motorcycle or with beer cans! I wait, hoping for the noise to cease, and eventually turn my head to murder this moron with my looks - and in the fraction of a second my mood turns into its opposite. For who is kicking that beer can around is a medium-sized, black dog. Never in my life have I seen an animal play with such abandon and virtuosity, with such total joy. I watch him until my neck starts to hurt and I turn my head again towards the sea. The noise

Die Möglichkeiten von Beziehungen

Paul Watzlawick

Meine einzige Begegnung mit Carl Auer war eine rein zufällige: 1977, am Ufer der Killaney-Bay, südlich von Dublin. Es war ungefähr fünf Uhr nachmittags, und ich hatte eben ein zweitägiges Seminar glücklich hinter mich gebracht. Die Teilnehmer waren mit den Perlen meiner Weisheit zufrieden gewesen, und die Versammlung hatte sich sozusagen in Wohlgefallen aufgelöst. Ermüdet von der Arbeit, aber noch mehr vom langen Flug und dem Zeitunterschied zu San Francisco, ging ich den schmalen Pfad vom Hotel hinunter zum Meer und setzte mich auf eine der Bänke an der Uferpromenade. Wie wohl jeder, der zum ersten Mal diese Gegend besucht, war ich von der fast mediterranen Schönheit der Landschaft überrascht: Ein blaues, stilles Meer, umarmt von zwei Landzungen, Palmen, blühende Magnolien, das weiche Licht der Abendsonne aus dem Westen, Wärme, Stille. Einer jener seltenen Augenblicke, in denen *es stimmt* und in denen der Intellekt einmal nicht herauszufinden versucht, was jenes „es" ist, das da „stimmt".

Und dann plötzlich, hinter mir, ein häßlicher, unverkennbarer Lärm. Jemand hat begonnen, mit einer leeren Bierdose Fußball zu spielen. Muß denn das immer so sein? Immer wenn man für kurze Zeit an der Harmonie teilhaben darf, kommen irgendwelche Neandertaler und verbreiten akustischen Gestank aus ihren Transistorradios oder vergewaltigen die Stille mit ihren Motorrädern oder eben Blechdosen. Ich warte, hoffe, daß der Lärm endlich wieder aufhört, und blicke schließlich nach hinten, um den Kerl mit meinen Blicken zu töten - und im Bruchteil einer Sekunde schlägt meine Wut ins Gegenteil um. Denn wer da mit der Bierdose Fußball spielt, ist ein mittelgroßer, schwarzer Hund. Noch nie habe ich ein Tier mit solcher Hingabe und Virtuosität spielen sehen, mit solcher Freude. Ich schaue

behind me goes on, just like before - *but now it is part of the harmony.* And then a sudden thought: you twerp - you manage to write learned books on the construction of realities, and when you catch yourself in the process, you are all surprised. . . .

The frail, elderly gentleman on the next bench must have been watching my face and its sudden change from icy anger to blissful delight. Oh no - now he thinks he has to start a conversation. His English has the same accent as mine, and therefore I answer in Austrian German. With this tactical mistake I really get him going. But what he says has somehow firmly remained in my memory.

"How is it possible that animals can have such power over us?" It is as if he were talking almost to himself; as if my presence were irrelevant. "I was seven years old when a stray tom cat invited himself into our house. A real beauty - silky black fur, unfathomably deep, yellow eyes. My first extrafamilial relationship object, as the psychologists would probably 'explain' it. Be that as it may, his arrival changed my world. Parents, relatives, school, priests, they all had been tampering with me in order to turn me into the person I 'should' be. The cat beat them all. With calm self-confidence he taught me how he wished to be treated, what he considered pleasant, what unpleasant. His purring, the way he rolled over on his back and stretched himself luxuriously, approving my caresses or correcting them, briefly touching my lips with his paw after having sat down on the book I was reading - no present and no demonstration of love on the part of the grown-ups came anywhere near what went on between the cat and me. Somehow he managed to take me into another world in which only he and I existed."

He falls silent, and I don't know what to say. Then: "Two years later he suddenly began to cough. There were no antibiotics yet in those days. One morning I found him dead on his little bed down in the basement." He is silent again; then in a shaky voice: "I remember that all I could think was: Never, never again must I permit myself to love like that. This pain is unbearable. - And yet, it was the beginning of my gradual understanding of the immense potential of and the inexhaustible 'realities' created by relationships. - And now, I look at

ihm zu, bis mir der Nacken zu schmerzen beginnt und ich mich wieder dem Meer zuwende. Der Lärm hinter mir geht weiter, wie früher - *aber nun ist er Teil der Harmonie.* Und dann plötzlich der Gedanke: Du Trottel, da schreibst du gelehrte Bücher über die Konstruktion von Wirklichkeiten - und wenn du dich selbst dabei erwischst, bist du ganz überrascht.

Der schmächtige, ältere Herr auf der Bank neben mir muß mir am Gesicht abgelesen haben, wie mein eisiger Zorn in Freude umschlug. Ach du liebe Zeit - nun glaubt er, Konversation machen zu müssen. Sein Englisch hat denselben Akzent wie meines; also antworte ich ihm in österreichischem Deutsch. Mit diesem taktischen Irrtum bringe ich ihn erst so richtig in Schwung. Und was er sagt, ist mir irgendwie fest im Gedächtnis geblieben.

„Worin liegt bloß die Macht, die Tiere über uns haben?" Er spricht es vor sich hin; fast als ob mein Zuhören belanglos sei. „Sieben Jahre war ich alt, als uns ein Kater zulief. Eine richtige Schönheit - seidiges schwarzes Fell, unergründlich tiefe, gelbe Augen. Mein erstes, nichtfamiliäres Beziehungsobjekt, wie die Psychologen dies vermutlich 'erklären' würden. Wie dem auch sei, mit seiner Ankunft änderte sich meine Welt. Eltern, Verwandte, Schule, Priester, sie hatten alle schon längst an mir herumgebastelt, um aus mir den Menschen zu machen, der ich sein 'sollte'. Der Kater schlug sie alle. In ruhiger Selbstsicherheit brachte er mir bei, wie er behandelt werden wollte, was ihm gefällig, was unangenehm war. Sein Schnurren, wie er auf den Rücken rollte, sich wohlig streckte und mein Streicheln akzeptierte, beziehungsweise es verbesserte, das kurze Auflegen seiner Tatze auf meine Lippen, nachdem er sich vor mir auf das Buch hingesetzt hatte, das ich las - kein Geschenk und keine Liebesbezeugung seitens der Erwachsenen war auch nur im entferntesten dem vergleichbar, was zwischen dem Kater und mir vorging. Er versetzte mich irgendwie in eine völlig andere Welt, in der nur er und ich lebten."

Er schweigt, und ich weiß nicht, was ich sagen soll. Dann: „Zwei Jahre später begann er plötzlich zu husten. Damals gab es noch keine Antibiotika. Eines Morgens fand ich ihn tot in seinem Bettchen im Keller." Wieder Schweigen; dann mit unsicherer Stimme: „Ich erinnere mich, daß ich nur eines denken konnte: Nie, nie wieder darf ich mir erlauben, so zu lieben. Dieser Schmerz ist unerträglich. - Und doch war es nur der Anfang meines langsamen Begreifens der enormen Möglichkeiten und der unerschöpflichen 'Wirklichkeiten', die in

today's youngsters and I shiver at the realization that their 'first extrafamilial relationship object' is the home computer and their source of inspiration the television screen. . . ."

The sound of an engine behind us; a short honk.

"Oh, my taxi." He gets up; a brief polite nod: "Carl Auer - good evening." And he hurries away.

What - *the* Carl Auer?? - I should have run after him . . .

Beziehungen liegen. - Und nun sehe ich mir die heutige Jugend an, und es schaudert mich, wenn ich daran denke, daß ihr erstes nichtfamiliäres Beziehungsobjekt der Computer, und die Quelle ihrer Inspiration der Fernseher ist . . ."

Motorengeräusch hinter uns; ein kurzer Hupton.

„Ah, mein Taxi." Er steht auf; ein kurzes, höfliches Nicken: „Carl Auer - guten Abend." Und eilig geht er weg.

Was - *der* Carl Auer?? - Ich hätte ihm nachlaufen sollen . . .

That Son-of-a-Bitch

Edgar H. Auerswald

Dear Fritz,

You can have no idea of how astonished I was to receive your letter and to discover that Carl Auer is still alive. Your revelation prompts me to share a part of my life which I have not shared with anyone except for my former analyst and one very close friend. I spent many years of my life looking for that son-of-a-bitch. There was a time when I wanted to expose him publicly - to let the world know that his concern with families and his work in that realm was a fraud carried out by a man who had shown by his behavior that he did not give a rat's ass for the well-being of families. For the past several years I have assumed he was dead.

In your letter you jokingly wrote that he might, after all, be some distant uncle of mine. Let me tell you that this is no joking matter. He is not a distant relative. He is a very close relative. In fact, he is my mother.

His name, before he underwent a sex change operation was Karla Auer. In 1924, at the very young age of 24, Karla married my father, Edgar Wald, who was ten years her senior. The two of them had immigrated to the U.S. from Germany immediately after their marriage and settled in Wisconsin. Seven months after their marriage and three months after their arrival in Wisconsin, I was born. Karla had insisted that her maiden name be included in their married name, and my father who was exceptionally progressive for his day agreed. They had become the Auer-Wald family, and this is the name that appears on my birth certificate. (Subsequently, my father, wishing to dissociate himself from his marriage for reasons I will explain, but

Dieser Hundesohn

Edgar H. Auerswald

Lieber Fritz,
Du kannst Dir nicht vorstellen, wie erstaunt ich war, Deinen Brief zu erhalten und herauszufinden, daß Carl Auer immer noch am Leben ist. Deine Enthüllung veranlaßt mich, einen Teil meines Lebens mit Dir zu teilen, über den ich mit niemandem außer meinem früheren Analytiker und einem sehr engen Freund gesprochen habe. Ich habe viele Jahre meines Lebens damit verbracht, nach diesem Hundesohn zu suchen. Es gab eine Zeit, in der ich ihn öffentlich bloßstellen wollte - um die Welt wissen zu lassen, daß sein Interesse an Familien und seine Arbeit in diesem Bereich ein Betrug war, ausgeführt von einem Mann, der durch sein Verhalten gezeigt hat, daß er keinen Rattenarsch für das Wohlergehen von Familien gibt. Seit einigen Jahren hatte ich angenommen, er sei tot.

In Deinem Brief schreibst Du scherzhaft, er könnte womöglich ein entfernter Onkel von mir sein. Laß Dir sagen, daß dies nichts ist, worüber man Scherze macht. Er ist kein entfernter Verwandter von mir. Er ist ein sehr naher Verwandter. Um die Wahrheit zu sagen: Er ist meine Mutter.

Sein Name war, bevor er sich einer Geschlechtsumwandlung unterzog, Karla Auer. Im Jahre 1924, im Alter von 24, heiratete Karla meinen Vater, Edgar Wald, der zehn Jahre älter war als sie. Unmittelbar nach ihrer Heirat waren die beiden aus Deutschland in die Vereinigten Staaten eingewandert; sie ließen sich in Wisconsin nieder. Sieben Monate nach ihrer Eheschließung und drei Monate nach ihrer Ankunft in Wisconsin wurde ich geboren. Karla hatte darauf bestanden, daß ihr Mädchenname in den Familiennamen aufgenommen werden sollte, und mein Vater, der außerordentlich fortschrittlich für seine Zeit war, hatte zugestimmt. Sie waren die Auer-Wald Familie geworden, und dies ist der Name, der auf meiner Geburtsur-

stuck with a variety of documents containing that name, inserted an "s" in place of the hyphen. I have used this name, Auerswald, ever since.)

As it turned out, Karla Auer, my mother, was an unfaithful wife. Her infidelities were particularly humiliating to my father because almost all of them were carried out, not with men, but with other women. After seven years of stormy marriage, Karla gave birth to my brother and promptly left for parts unknown. No one in my family has seen her since.

I was, I must say, luckier than most children born to such a mother. Before and after Karla deserted us, I spent most of my days in the home of my father's sister, Bertha, a young and childless widow who dwelt in a house only a stone's throw away from our own. Bertha was warm and loving, and I never lacked mothering. In fact, she was so good at mothering that, when Karla left, my anger was not profound.

The same, however, cannot be said for my father and my brother. My father was devastated by her treatment of him. His reaction to his discovery of her many infidelities was to gradually withdraw from the world of shared reality and to construct his own. In his private reality, he was a psychiatrist. When Karla left, he went public with that reality. Even though he had never received the degrees and training required to practice the profession, he ultimately rented an office, printed cards (on which he substituted the "s" for the hyphen in Auer-Wald), and set himself up as a psychiatrist. For ten years he lived in that reality with his patients. He even became mildly famous as the architect of a standardized system of psychiatric diagnosis which he called DSM 1 $^1/_2$. When, ten years later, he was discovered and taken to court for practicing without a license, his lawyer convinced him to agree to an insanity defense.

Ironically, his own diagnostic system was used by the psychiatrists who examined him, and he was ultimately declared not guilty,

kunde erscheint. (Später fügte mein Vater, der sich selbst aus Gründen, die ich noch erklären werde, von seiner Ehe distanzieren wollte, aber durch eine Vielzahl von Dokumenten, die auf diesen Namen lauteten, gebunden war, das „s" an die Stelle des Bindestrichs. Diesen Namen, Auerswald, habe ich seither immer benutzt.)

Wie sich herausstellte, war Karla Auer, meine Mutter, ein treuloses Weib. Ihre eheliche Untreue war für meinen Vater deswegen besonders verletzend, weil sie fast immer nicht mit Männern, sondern mit anderen Frauen die Ehe brach. Nach sieben Jahren einer stürmischen Ehe gebar Karla meinen Bruder und verschwand sofort mit unbekanntem Ziel. Niemand in meiner Familie hat sie seither gesehen.

Ich hatte mehr Glück, muß ich sagen, als die meisten Kinder, die solch einer Mutter geboren werden. Bevor und nachdem Karla uns im Stich ließ, verbrachte ich die meisten meiner Tage bei der Schwester meines Vaters. Bertha war eine junge und kinderlose Witwe, deren Haus nur einen Katzensprung von unserem entfernt war. Sie war herzlich und liebevoll und an mütterlicher Fürsorge fehlte es mir nie. Offen gesagt: Sie war so gut im Bemuttern, daß meine Wut, als Karla verschwand, nicht sehr tief reichte.

Dasselbe kann allerdings nicht für meinen Vater und meinen Bruder gesagt werden. Mein Vater war von der Art, wie sie ihn behandelte hatte, ganz niedergeschmettert. Seine Reaktion auf die Entdeckung ihres vielfachen Betrugs war ein allmählicher Rückzug aus der Welt der gemeinsamen Wirklichkeit und die Konstruktion einer eigenen. In seiner persönlichen Realität war er Psychiater. Als Karla verschwand, ging er mit dieser Realität an die Öffentlichkeit. Obwohl er nie die notwendige Ausbildung und die akademischen Titel erhalten hatte, die erforderlich sind, um diesen Beruf auszuüben, mietete er sich eine Praxis, druckte Visitenkarten (auf denen er das „s" an die Stelle des Bindestrichs in Auer-Wald setzte), und ließ sich als Psychiater nieder. Zehn Jahre lang lebte er mit seinen Patienten in dieser Realität. Er wurde sogar ein wenig berühmt als der Architekt eines standardisierten Systems psychiatrischer Diagnosen, das er DSM 1 $^1/_2$ nannte. Als er zehn Jahre später entlarvt und wegen des Praktizierens ohne Lizenz vor Gericht gestellt wurde, überredete ihn sein Anwalt, auf Unzurechnungsfähigkeit zu plädieren.

Ironischerweise verwandten die Psychiater, die ihn untersuchten, sein eigenes diagnostisches System, und er wurde schließlich für

but insane. The judge committed him to a mental hospital where he remained until his death. Trapped as he was in his own reductionist diagnostic reality, he spent his years in the hospital developing finer and more detailed diagnostic categories. His goal was to develop a system which would allow for pathological diagnosis of all humans. He succeeded. By the time death claimed him, he had developed a decision tree leading to 480 generic diagnoses, 2021 subdiagnoses, and 40089 subsubdiagnoses.

My brother fared no better. When he was deserted by Karla the day after his birth, our father had already entered his psychiatric reality, and hoping, I guess, to create a self-fulfilling prophecy, he named my brother Normal. For eighteen years as he grew up, my brother tried valiantly to live up to that name. I shall never forget his anguish when, on his eighteenth birthday, he confessed to me that he had no sense of identity because he had never been able to figure out what Normal meant. My suggestion that he could at least consider himself a point at the apex of a bell curve seemed to be of no use to him. In fact, when I made the suggestion, he hit me. On his twenty-first birthday he committed suicide, leaving a note in which he wrote that he had finally discovered the definition of Normal and thus had discovered his identity. The word, he wrote, was synonymous with boring and his identity was that of a totally boring human being. Death, he had decided, was a better fate than normality. To this day I regret that it never occurred to me to suggest to him that he change his name.

I have always been convinced that neither my father nor my brother would have met with such disaster in their lives had it not been for the actions of Karla Auer. However, the woman who mothered me, my aunt Bertha, taught me to seek meaning in my own life and activities without excessive attention to adversity or resort to blame. It is, therefore, probable that I would have swallowed my anger at my mother and proceeded with my life with no further concern for her whereabouts, had not the following chain of events intervened.

nicht schuldig, aber geistesgestört erklärt. Der Richter überwies ihn in eine Nervenheilanstalt, wo er bis zu seinem Tod blieb. Gefangen in seiner eigenen, reduktionistischen diagnostischen Realität, verbrachte er seine Jahre in der Anstalt damit, immer feinere und detailliertere diagnostische Kategorien zu entwickeln. Sein Ziel war es, ein System zu entwickeln, das eine Pathologiediagnose aller Menschen erlauben würde. Er hatte Erfolg. Zu dem Zeitpunkt, als der Tod ihn abrief, hatte er einen Entscheidungsbaum entwickelt, der zu 480 Hauptdiagnosen, 2021 Unterdiagnosen und 40089 Unterunterdiagnosen führte.

Meinem Bruder ging es nicht besser. Als er von Karla am Tage nach seiner Geburt im Stich gelassen wurde, war unser Vater bereits in seine psychiatrische Wirklichkeit eingetreten; und er gab meinem Bruder, vermutlich in der Hoffnung auf eine selbsterfüllende Prophezeiung, den Namen Normal. Während der ersten 18 Jahre seines Lebens versuchte mein Bruder heroisch, diesem Namen gerecht zu werden. Nie werde ich seine Seelenqual vergessen, als er mir an seinem 18. Geburtstag gestand, er habe keinerlei Identitätsgefühl, da er nie fähig war herauszufinden, was Normal bedeutet. Mein Vorschlag, er könne sich zumindest als Punkt auf dem Gipfel einer Glockenkurve betrachten, schien für ihn nicht von Nutzen zu sein. Um ehrlich zu sein, schlug er mich, als ich meinen Vorschlag machte. An seinem 21. Geburtstag beging er Selbstmord; er hinterließ eine Notiz, in der er schrieb, daß er endlich die Definition von Normal und damit seine Identität entdeckt hätte. Das Wort, so schrieb er, war synonym mit langweilig, und seine Identität war die eines vollkommen langweiligen menschlichen Wesens. Tod, so hatte er entschieden, war ein besseres Schicksal als Normalität. Bis heute bedaure ich, daß mir nie die Idee kam, ihm vorzuschlagen, seinen Namen zu ändern.

Ich war immer überzeugt, daß weder mein Vater noch mein Bruder in ihrem Leben so vom Unglück getroffen worden wären, wären nicht Karla Auers Taten gewesen. Wie dem auch sei, die Frau, die für mich die Mutterrolle übernahm, meine Tante Bertha, lehrte mich, Sinn in meinem eigenen Leben und meinen eigenen Aktivitäten zu suchen, ohne übermäßige Aufmerksamkeit auf ein mißliches Schicksal zu richten oder Zuflucht darin zu nehmen, die Verantwortung abzuschieben. Es ist daher wahrscheinlich, daß ich den Zorn auf meine Mutter hinuntergeschluckt hätte und mein Leben weitergelebt hätte, ohne mich weiter um ihre Lebensumstände zu kümmern, wäre es nicht zu folgender Kette von Ereignissen gekommen.

During the years that my father was practicing psychiatry, I ran across a set of the collected works of Sigmund Freud on the shelves of his office. The inscriptions on the cover page of each book stated that they were owned, not by my father, but by my mother, Karla, and each copy had been signed by Sigmund Freud himself. I asked my father about this, but he was unwilling to talk with me about my mother, who he thought all of us should try to forget. I read these books from cover to cover, and was much impressed by them. By the time I finished reading the last of them, I had decided that I would myself pursue a career as a psychoanalyst.

Years later, in 1956, as I lay on my training analyst's couch one day, expressing my anger at my mother, I told my analyst (who I shall call Dr. P.) about the volumes of Freud's work that I had found in my father's office and that they had, in fact, belonged to my mother. Something about this revelation seemed to offend him. He not only broke his silence, but, as it turned out, he lost his cool. Actually, he mumbled to himself, but his mumbling was quite loud, loud enough for me to hear. "Too bad she never read them!" is what I heard. At first, I took this to mean that he thought she would have been a better mother if she had read them, but this outburst was so uncharacteristic of him that I could not let it pass. I told him that I had heard what he had said under his breath and had wondered what he had meant. I got no immediate answer. He remained silent until a few minutes later he announced that my time was up.

Although I thought some about this incident between sessions, it seemed of minor import. I was to learn otherwise. When I next entered Dr. P.'s office, to my surprise he directed me not to lie on the couch, but rather to sit in a chair facing him. He then told me that he had decided, after some agonizing thought, that he could not continue as my analyst. He asked me to seek out another training analyst. The reason for this decision, he said, was that he could not maintain his objectivity to the degree necessary for him to conduct my analysis. He lost his objectivity, he confessed, whenever I spoke of my mother.

Während der Jahre, in denen mein Vater Psychiatrie praktizierte, stieß ich im Bücherregal seines Arbeitszimmers auf eine Ausgabe der gesammelten Werke Sigmund Freuds. Die Aufschriften auf dem Deckblatt eines jeden Buches besagten, daß sie nicht meinem Vater, sondern meiner Mutter, Karla, gehörten; und jeder Band war von Sigmund Freud selbst signiert. Ich fragte meinen Vater danach, aber er wollte nicht mit mir über meine Mutter sprechen; wir alle sollten sie - wie er meinte - zu vergessen suchen. Ich las diese Bücher von der ersten bis zur letzten Seite und war sehr beeindruckt von ihnen. Als ich die Lektüre des letzten beendet hatte, entschied ich mich, selbst eine Karriere als Psychoanalytiker anzustreben.

Jahre später, 1956, als ich eines Tages auf der Couch meines Lehranalytikers lag und meiner Wut auf meine Mutter Ausdruck verlieh, erzählte ich meinem Analytiker (den ich Dr. P. nennen werde) über die Bände mit Freuds Werken, die ich im Arbeitszimmer meines Vaters gefunden hatte, und daß sie eigentlich meiner Mutter gehört hatten. Irgend etwas an dieser Enthüllung schien ihn zu verletzen. Er unterbrach nicht nur sein Schweigen, sondern er verlor auch, wie sich herausstellen sollte, seine Beherrschung. Tatsächlich murmelte er nur etwas vor sich hin, aber sein Murmeln war ziemlich laut, laut genug, daß ich es hören konnte. „Zu dumm, daß sie sie nie gelesen hat!" war, was ich hörte. Ich nahm erst an, dies bedeute, daß er dachte, sie wäre eine bessere Mutter gewesen, wenn sie sie gelesen hätte. Aber diese kleine Unbeherrschtheit war so uncharakteristisch für ihn, daß ich sie nicht so vorübergehen lassen konnte. Ich sagte ihm, daß ich seine Worte verstanden hätte und mir Gedanken darüber mache, was er gemeint hatte. Ich erhielt keine unmittelbare Antwort. Er schwieg weiter bis er einige Minuten später verkündete, daß die Zeit um sei.

Obwohl ich zwischen den Sitzungen ein wenig über diesen Vorfall nachdachte, schien er mir von geringerer Bedeutung. Ich sollte eines Besseren belehrt werden. Als ich das nächste Mal das Behandlungszimmer Dr. P.s betrat, sagte er mir zu meiner Überraschung, ich solle mich nicht auf die Couch legen, sondern mich lieber ihm gegenüber in einen Sessel setzen. Er erklärte mir dann, er hätte nach einigem quälenden Grübeln entschieden, daß er nicht weiter mein Analytiker bleiben könne. Ich würde mir, so sagte er, einen anderen Lehranalytiker suchen müssen. Der Grund für diese Ent-

Karla, he told me, was not unknown to him. She had been a significant person in his life. Then he told me the following story:

In 1937, during his own psychoanalytic training, while he was looking for a case to use as one of his control cases, Karla Auer, who had just left her husband and children, had appeared in his office, seeking analysis. The life story she presented had intrigued him greatly. She had, it seems, grown up in Vienna in Freud's neighborhood. Freud, she told him, had a niece who lived part of the year in his household. This niece, said Karla, had been her best friend during most of her childhood and adolescence, and as a result Karla had spent some time in the Freud household.

Dr. P. had brought this story to his supervisor, who, also intrigued, had urged him to accept her as one of his control cases. This he had done, and he had listened with growing fascination as Karla told him about her experience with the Freud family during her childhood. Freud's niece, Annabella, was the leader of a group of neighborhood youngsters who met and played in the basement of the Freud home. One of the activities of this group was listening to the psychoanalytic sessions that Freud conducted in his office above them. They were able to hear what transpired through a hot air vent that entered his consultation room beneath the couch. Two kinds of sessions, she told him, particularly fascinated the young eavesdroppers.

Annabella, it seems, was especially interested in those sessions - of which there were many - in which Freud's female patients spoke about their responses to the sexual seductiveness of their fathers. Freud, she said, seemed to be particularly interested in these stories, and therefore they must have some special significance. After each such session she would insist that the group discuss what they had heard in detail.

The other sessions which seized their attention were those Freud held with himself as he conducted his own analysis. Although they could not see him, they could hear him as he paced back and forth

scheidung war, daß er - wie er sagte - seine Objektivität nicht in dem zur Durchführung meiner Analyse nötigen Maße bewahren könne. Er verlöre seine Objektivität, gestand er, immer dann, wenn ich von meiner Mutter sprach. Karla, erzählte er mir, war ihm nicht unbekannt. Sie sei eine bedeutungsvolle Person in seinem Leben gewesen. Dann erzählte er mir folgende Geschichte:

Als er 1937 während seiner psychoanalytischen Ausbildung nach einem Fall suchte, den er als einen seiner Kontrollfälle verwenden konnte, erschien Karla Auer, die gerade ihren Mann und ihre Kinder verlassen hatte, auf der Suche nach einem Analyseplatz in seiner Praxis. Ihre Lebensgeschichte fesselte ihn sehr. Sie war, so schien es, in Wien aufgewachsen, in demselben Viertel, in dem auch Freud lebte. Freud hatte eine Nichte, die einen Teil des Jahres in seinem Haushalt lebte. Diese Nichte, berichtete Karla, war während des größten Teils ihrer Kindheit und Jugend ihre beste Freundin gewesen; und infolgedessen hatte Karla etliche Zeit im Hause Freud verbracht.

Dr. P. hatte diese Geschichte seinem Supervisor berichtet, der ihn, ebenfalls fasziniert, drängte, sie als einen seiner Kontrollfälle zu akzeptieren. Er tat dies und hörte mit wachsender Faszination, was Karla ihm über ihre Kindheitserfahrung mit der Freudschen Familie berichtete. Freuds Nichte Annabella war die Anführerin einer Gruppe von Jugendlichen aus dem Viertel, die sich im Untergeschoß des Freudschen Hauses trafen und spielten. Eine der Beschäftigungen dieser Gruppe war es, durch einen Heißluftschacht, der unter der Couch in sein Behandlungszimmer führte, die psychoanalytischen Sitzungen zu belauschen, die Freud in seinem Arbeitszimmer über ihnen durchführte. Zwei Arten von Sitzungen faszinierten die jungen Lauscher besonders, erzählte sie.

Annabella, so scheint es, war speziell an den Sitzungen interessiert - und es gab viele davon -, in denen Freuds weibliche Patienten über ihre Reaktion auf die verführerischen sexuellen Reize ihrer Väter sprachen. Freud, sagte sie, schien besonders an diesen Geschichten interessiert, und daher mußten sie irgendeine spezielle Bedeutung haben. Nach jeder solchen Sitzung bestand sie darauf, daß die Gruppe im Detail diskutierte, was sie gehört hatten.

Die anderen Sitzungen, welche ihre Aufmerksamkeit gefangen nahmen, waren diejenigen, welche Freud mit sich selbst abhielt, als er seine Selbstanalyse durchführte. Obwohl sie ihn nicht sehen konnten,

from the couch to the analyst's chair. There was, Karla reported, a mystery engendered by these sessions which the young group spent many hours trying to unravel. They observed that Freud frequently admonished himself to remember that his self-analysis could easily be ruined by something which he called counter-transference. The listeners spent many fruitless hours trying to figure out what he meant.

It was, Dr. P. reported, precisely this phenomen of counter-transference which had made Karla memorable in his life. He had, it seems, become caught up in a counter-transference web in his work with her, a web in which he had been joined by his supervisor. He had fallen in love with Karla - or so he thought - and when he shared this with his supervisor, he was told that his feelings were understandable, since Karla was a remarkable woman toward whom the supervisor had developed some familiar feelings sight unseen. (Only later did Dr. P. come to understand that Karla carried an introject of Freud, and that it was this introject that both he and his supervisor had fallen in love with.)

Unable to contain his passion, Dr. P. had severed his professional relationship with Karla and declared his love to her. Karla's response to this was to disappear from his life for the next six months. Dr. P. had not quite recovered his composure when she then reappeared in his office, now looking and dressed like a man, and going by the name of Carl. She announced that, after her initial shock at his declaration of love, she had been forced to face her total lack of response, not only to him, but also to all the other men who had made similar declarations to her, including my father. She had experienced a sudden and shattering insight. She had realized that she had never really been a woman, emotionally or spiritually. She had been a man who loved women, not a woman who loved men, and she was trapped in a woman's body. The very next day she had left for Mexico City, where she had undergone a sex change operation. S/he was, s/he said, planning next to return to Vienna where s/he hoped to become a psychoanalyst her/himself. Freud, s/he said, was within her/him, and s/he wanted to pattern her/his own life accordingly.

konnten sie hören, wie er zwischen Couch und Analytikersessel hin- und herging. Diese Sitzungen, berichtete Karla, gaben ihnen ein Rätsel auf. Mit dem Versuch, es zu entschlüsseln, verbrachte die jugendliche Gruppe viele Stunden. Sie beobachteten, daß Freud sich häufig ermahnte, nur ja nicht zu vergessen, daß diese Selbstanalyse leicht durch etwas ruiniert werden könnte, das er Gegenübertragung nannte. Die Hörer verschwendeten viele fruchtlose Stunden damit, herauszufinden, was er damit meinte.

Genau dieses Phänomen der Gegenübertragung war es, berichtete Dr. P., das Karla für ihn lebenslang unvergeßlich gemacht hatte. Er war, so scheint es, in seiner Arbeit mit ihr in einem Gegenübertragungsgespinst gefangen worden, einem Netz, in dem auch sein Supervisor gefangen schien. Er hatte sich in Karla verliebt - oder dachte es jedenfalls -, und als er dies seinem Supervisor mitteilte, antwortete der, daß seine Gefühle verständlich seien, da Karla eine außergewöhnliche Frau sei, der gegenüber auch er ganz ähnliche Gefühle entwickelt habe, ohne sie je gesehen zu haben. (Erst später gelang es Dr. P. zu verstehen, daß Karla ein Introjekt Freuds trug und daß es dieses Introjekt war, in das beide, er und sein Supervisor, sich verliebt hatten.)

Unfähig seine Leidenschaft im Zaume zu halten, hatte Dr. P. seine professionelle Beziehung zu Karla zerstört und ihr seine Liebe offenbart. Karlas Antwort darauf war, daß sie für die nächsten sechs Monate aus seinem Leben verschwand. Dr. P. hatte seine Fassung noch nicht ganz wiedergewonnen, als sie wieder in seiner Praxis auftauchte, nun wie ein Mann aussehend und gekleidet und unter dem Namen Carl. Sie enthüllte ihm, daß sie sich nach dem anfänglichen Schock auf seine Liebeserklärung hin gezwungen sah, sich das völlige Fehlen jeglicher Reaktion nicht nur ihm gegenüber einzugestehen, sondern auch allen anderen Männern gegenüber - einschließlich meines Vaters -, die ihr ähnliche Erklärungen gemacht hatten. Sie hatte eine plötzliche und niederschmetternde Einsicht. Sie erkannte, daß sie emotional oder geistig nie wirklich eine Frau war. Sie war ein Mann gewesen, der Frauen liebte, nicht eine Frau, die Männer liebte; und sie war gefangen im Körper einer Frau. Gleich am nächsten Tag war sie nach Mexico City abgereist, wo sie sich einer Geschlechtsumwandlung unterzog. Sie/er plane demnächst, sagte sie/er, nach Wien zurückzukehren, wo sie/er hoffe, selbst Psychoanalytiker zu werden. Freud sei in ihr/ihm, sagte sie/er, und sie/er wolle ihr/sein eigenes Leben entsprechend gestalten.

Carl had berated Dr. P. for not having assisted him to understand this matter in the analytic work they had done and questioned Dr. P.'s capacity to become a certified psychoanalyst. Not only that, but he had sent a letter to the President of the American Psychoanalytic Association in which he told his story and raised the same question about Dr. P.'s competence.

I think you can imagine what happened. Dr. P.'s career as a psychoanalyst would undoubtedly have ended, had not his supervisor, an analyst of considerable renoun, come to his aid. In a letter to the certification board he took responsibility for what had happened. He confessed that he had been seduced by the stories of Carl's (Karla's) early contacts with the Freud family, that he had failed to recognize that Carl (Karla) was not a suitable candidate for analysis, and that he had totally underestimated his (her) capacity for acting out. He had, in fact, taken the rap for what had happened.

Nevertheless, Dr. P. told me, these events had prolonged his training analysis and thus his training for at least four years, and had cost him, therefore, at least $40,000. Under these circumstances, he said, he was quite sure I would understand why he lost his objectivity when I talked of my mother.

I began this letter by expressing considerable bitterness toward Carl Auer, but I now have to tell you that after these revelations were made to me by Dr. P. and after some additional analytic work, I felt no bitterness. In fact, I developed considerable admiration for this strange creature who was my mother. Unlike my poor brother, he was certainly not boring, and, unlike my father, while he was strange he did not seem to be crazy. And, one had to admit, he had an astonishing and highly unusual capacity to wreak havoc with those who ventured close to him. Nevertheless, I had no immediate desire to reestablish contact.

My bitterness towards Auer as reflected in my opening comments in this letter unfortunately returned at a later date. In 1959, just as I was finishing my psychoanalytic training, I had taken a job working with street kids in New York City and had discovered that, not only was the reality out of which psychoanalysis had grown unknown to

Carl hatte Dr. P. heftige Vorwürfe gemacht, daß er ihn nicht dabei unterstützt habe, diese Angelegenheit in der analytischen Arbeit, die sie getan hätten, zu verstehen, und er stellte Dr. P.s Fähigkeit, ein offiziell anerkannter Analytiker zu werden, in Frage. Doch als wäre das nicht genug, hatte er darüber hinaus einen Brief an den Präsidenten der Amerikanischen Psychoanalytischen Vereinigung gesandt, in welchem er seine Geschichte erzählte und dieselbe Frage hinsichtlich Dr. P.s Kompetenz aufwarf.

Ich denke, Du kannst Dir vorstellen, was passierte. Dr. P.s Karriere als Psychoanalytiker wäre zweifellos beendet gewesen, wäre ihm nicht sein Supervisor, ein Analytiker mit beträchtlichem Renommee, zur Hilfe gekommen. In einem Brief an den Prüfungsausschuß übernahm er die Verantwortung für die Geschehnisse. Er gestand, daß er durch die Geschichten von Carls (Karlas) frühen Kontakten mit der Freud-Familie verführt worden war, daß er zu erkennen versäumt hatte, daß Carl (Karla) keine geeignete Analysekandidatin war und daß er seine (ihre) Fähigkeit zum Ausagieren vollkommen unterschätzt hatte. Er nahm wirklich alles auf seine Kappe.

Trotzdem hätten diese Ereignisse seine Lehranalyse und damit seine Ausbildung, so erzählte mir Dr. P., um wenigstens vier Jahre verlängert und ihn so mindestens $40.000 gekostet. Unter diesen Umständen könne ich sicherlich verstehen, warum er seine Objektivität verlor, als ich über meine Mutter sprach.

Ich drückte am Anfang dieses Brief beträchtliche Bitterkeit Carl Auer gegenüber aus. Nun muß ich Dir aber sagen, daß ich nach diesen Enthüllungen von Dr. P. und nach einiger zusätzlicher analytischer Arbeit keine Bitterkeit mehr verspürte. In Wirklichkeit entwickelte ich sogar einige Bewunderung für diese merkwürdige Kreatur, die meine Mutter war. Im Gegensatz zu meinem armen Bruder war er sicher nicht langweilig, und anders als mein Vater schien er, obwohl merkwürdig, nicht verrückt zu sein. Und, das muß man zugeben, er hatte eine erstaunliche und sehr ungewöhnliche Fähigkeit, Chaos bei denen zu stiften, die sich ihm näherten. Trotzdem hatte ich kein unmittelbares Bedürfnis, den Kontakt wiederherzustellen.

Meine Bitterkeit Auer gegenüber, wie sie sich in meinen Eröffnungskommentaren in diesem Brief spiegelt, kehrte unglücklicherweise zu einem späteren Zeitpunkt zurück. Gleich als ich meine psychoanalytische Ausbildung 1959 beendet hatte, bekam ich einen Job in New York City und arbeitete mit Straßenkindern; dort entdeck-

these kids, but also that the psychoanalytic formulations and techniques that I had learned were useless in my work with them. I had, as a result, begun to study and work with their families and had become enmeshed in the early days of the family therapy movement. The change in my thinking had prompted me to think once again about my remarkable mother, and I resolved to make an effort to reestablish contact with her (him). I planned a trip to Vienna.

When I arrived there, I looked in the telephone directory for Carl Auer. There were several listings of that name. I called them all, but none turned out to be the person I sought. I then tried to track down her family of origin. No one I talked to could remember Karla Auer. Remembering that Dr. P. had told me that Carl Auer had wanted to become a psychoanalyst, I looked under the listing of psychotherapists next. There was no listing for Carl Auer, but there was a listing for Dr. Carl *von* Auer. I called the number.

Dr. von Auer himself answered the phone. There was nothing familiar about his voice. I told him my name, and where I had come from and, not knowing how else to approach him, I asked if this had any meaning for him. There was a rather long pause, but his answer was no. I then asked him if he had ever known a man by the name of Carl Auer who had come to Vienna back in the 1930s with the intention of becoming a psychoanalyst. There was another long pause. Yes, said Doctor von Auer, he had known of such a person. He had, in fact, become a physician and a psychiatrist, but he had never been accepted for analytic training, and he had returned to the United States many years ago. Where he had gone in the U. S. he did not know. I invited Dr. von Auer to have dinner with me, but he told me that he was sorry that he could not accept my invitation because he was leaving that day for a vacation. So I thanked him and continued on my way.

When I returned to the U. S., although I had little time away from my work, whenever I could I searched for Carl Auer. I first checked

te ich nicht nur, daß die Wirklichkeit, aus der die Psychoanalyse erwachsen war, diesen Kindern unbekannt war, sondern auch, daß die psychoanalytischen Formulierungen und Techniken, die ich erlernt hatte, in meiner Arbeit mit ihnen nutzlos waren. Also begann ich, ihre Familien zu studieren und mit ihnen zu arbeiten; und so wurde ich in die Anfänge der Familientherapiebewegung verwikkelt. Der Wandel in meinem Denken veranlaßte mich, erneut über meine bemerkenswerte Mutter nachzudenken. Ich entschloß mich, den Versuch zu machen, den Kontakt mit ihr (ihm) wiederaufzunehmen. Ich plante eine Reise nach Wien.

Als ich dort ankam, schaute ich im Telefonbuch nach Carl Auer. Es gab einige Eintragungen auf diesen Namen. Ich rief sie alle an, und keiner stellte sich als die Person heraus, nach der ich suchte. Ich versuchte dann, ihre Herkunftsfamilie aufzuspüren. Niemand, mit dem ich sprach, konnte sich an Karla Auer erinnern. Da ich mich erinnerte, daß Dr. P. mir erzählt hatte, daß Carl Auer Psychoanalytiker werden wollte, schaute ich als nächstes unter den Eintragungen der Psychotherapeuten. Es gab keine für Carl Auer, aber eine unter Dr. Carl *von* Auer. Ich wählte die Nummer.

Dr. von Auer selbst nahm den Anruf entgegen. Es gab nichts Vertrautes in seiner Stimme. Ich nannte ihm meinen Namen und woher ich kam, und ich fragte ihn, da ich nicht wußte, wie ich mich ihm sonst annähern sollte, ob dies irgendeine Bedeutung für ihn hätte. Es entstand eine ziemlich lange Pause, aber seine Antwort war nein. Ich fragte ihn dann, ob er je einen Mann mit Namen Carl Auer gekannt hätte, der in den Dreißiger Jahren mit der Absicht, Psychoanalytiker zu werden, nach Wien zurückgekommen sei. Es entstand wiederum eine lange Pause. Ja, sagte Dr. von Auer, er habe solch eine Person gekannt. In der Tat sei er Arzt und Psychiater geworden, sei aber niemals für die psychoanalytische Ausbildung akzeptiert worden. Vor vielen Jahren sei er in die Vereinigten Staaten zurückgekehrt. Wohin er in den Vereinigten Staaten gegangen sei, wisse er nicht. Ich lud Dr. von Auer ein, mit mir zu Abend zu essen, aber er sagte, es tue ihm leid, daß er meine Einladung nicht annehmen könne, da er noch an diesem Tag in Urlaub fahre. So dankte ich ihm und setzte meinen Weg fort.

Als ich in die Vereinigten Staaten zurückkehrte, suchte ich, wann immer ich konnte, nach Carl Auer, auch wenn ich neben meiner

to see if he was a member of any of the organizations to which psychiatrists belong. He was not. Then I explored the membership of organisations for physicians. Here I found two physicians of that name, neither of whom turned out to be my mother. Once, when in Mexico City on business, I sought out the records of her (his) sex change operation, but no one there knew of his current whereabouts. When I travelled to new places, I would routinely look up the name Carl Auer in the local phone directories, and when I found it, I would call and explore. None of my efforts came to fruition. Finally, after several years of this search, I discovered that a physician named Carl Auer who had come from Germany to settle in Louisville, Kentucky, and who, as far as I could tell, was about my mother's age, had been killed in an automobile accident at approximately the time that I had begun my search. I was unable to track down the family of origin of this unfortunate person, but I decided that he (she) must have been my mother, and I abandoned my search.

Before my search ended, however, I began to run across Dr. Carl von Auer's articles in the family therapy literature. At first, I rather liked his work, especially his articles on family role stability, but as I made the epistemological shift from Cartesian/Newtonian mechanistic reductionistic reality to new science/ecosystemic reality, I paid less and less attention to it. Ultimately, I decided that he was a Newtonian reductionist pig, and I no longer bothered to read his work - that is, until he published his seminal book, *An Ecosystemic Exploration of the Family of Sigmund Freud.*

I suspect that you can guess much of the rest of this story. When I saw this book sitting on the shelf in my local bookstore, I had one of those strange experiences of prescience. I knew without opening it what it contained. I searched immediately for his stories of eavesdropping on Freud's sessions, and, of course, I found them with no trouble. Carl von Auer was my mother, after all. Once again he (she) had betrayed me!

Arbeit nur wenig Zeit hatte. Zuerst überprüfte ich, ob er Mitglied einer der psychiatrischen Berufsverbände war. Er war es nicht. Dann durchforschte ich die Mitgliedschaft der Ärzteorganisationen. Hier fand ich zwei Ärzte mit diesem Namen, von denen sich keiner als meine Mutter erwies. Einmal, als ich beruflich in Mexico City weilte, grub ich die Akten ihrer/seiner Geschlechtsumwandlungsoperation aus, aber niemand dort wußte etwas über seinen gegenwärtigen Aufenthaltsort. Wenn ich auf Reisen an irgendeinen neuen Ort kam, schaute ich routinemäßig im örtlichen Telefonbuch nach dem Namen Carl Auer, und wenn ich ihn fand, rief ich dort an und forschte nach. Keine meiner Bemühungen trug Früchte. Endlich, nach einigen Jahren des Suchens, fand ich heraus, daß ein Arzt mit dem Namen Carl Auer, der aus Deutschland gekommen war, um sich in Louisville/Kentucky niederzulassen, und der, soweit ich es sagen konnte, in etwa das Alter meiner Mutter hatte, bei einem Autounfall getötet worden war - ungefähr um die Zeit herum, als ich meine Suche begonnen hatte. Ich war unfähig, die Herkunftsfamilie dieser unglücklichen Person aufzuspüren, daher entschied ich, daß er (sie) meine Mutter gewesen sein mußte, und gab meine Suche auf.

Bevor sie endete, begann ich auf Dr. Carl von Auers Artikel in der Familientherapieliteratur zu stoßen. Zunächst mochte ich seine Arbeit ganz gern, speziell seine Artikel über familiäre Rollenstabilität. Aber als ich den epistemologischen Wechsel von der Cartesianisch-Newtonschen mechanistisch-reduktionistischen Wirklichkeit zur neuen wissenschaftlich-ökosystemischen Wirklichkeit machte, ließ mein Interesse für seine Artikel nach. Letzten Endes beschloß ich, daß er ein Newtonsch-reduktionistisches Schwein sei, und ich machte mir nicht länger die Mühe, seine Arbeiten zu lesen - das heißt, bis er sein grundlegendes Buch „Eine ökosystemische Erkundung der Familie Sigmund Freuds" veröffentlichte.

Ich nehme an, Du kannst Dir den Ausgang dieser Geschichte fast ausmalen. Als ich dieses Buch auf dem Regal meines örtlichen Buchhändlers stehen sah, hatte ich eine dieser merkwürdigen Erfahrungen der Vorahnung. Ich wußte, ohne es zu öffnen, was es enthielt. Ich suchte gleich nach seinen Geschichten des Belauschens von Freuds Sitzungen, und natürlich: Ich fand sie ohne Schwierigkeiten. Um es kurz zu machen: Carl von Auer war doch meine Mutter. Noch einmal hatte er (sie) mich betrogen!

I immediately cancelled all of my appointments and left for Vienna, where I went directly to his (her) office to confront him (her? - Oh Shit! - him). I could not believe my ears when he continued to deny that he had ever known me. When he had me ejected from his office by the police, I must confess that I had murder in my heart. After it was all over, however, this encounter turned out to be much for the best. My quest for my mother was over once and for all. His behavior had destroyed all hope in me for a reunion, and I erased him totally from my life. At first I gained some satisfaction by reading of the furor created by his book, but I soon found that I no longer cared at all about any of it. As far as I know, he never again published in English, so I was not even reminded of him in my reading. As far as I was concerned, he was dead, and indeed, since time was passing and I knew that he would by now be very old, I assumed that he actually was no longer with us.

Now, this! Out of the blue a letter arrives asking me to participate in the establishment of a publishing company that will bear his name, and in the publication of a *festschrift* to him! I cannot believe it!

Okay. I am writing this several days after I wrote the pages above, and I have calmed down considerably. I am now able to think clearly about what I want to do about all this. I cannot ignore it, for obvious reasons. If so many illustrious people in our field see merit in your proposals, Carl von Auer must have done work that I have simply not been aware of, either because it was published in German and not in English, or because I have been psychologically blind to his continuing existence. If that is the case, I owe it to myself and to the field, to familiarize myself with what he has done and to participate in some way in this project. Not only that, but I am developing a growing curiosity. I want to hear what others have to say about my mother. You have revived him for me.

Ich sagte sofort all meine Termine ab und fuhr nach Wien, wo ich direkt in seine (ihre) Praxis ging, um ihn (sie?- oh, Scheiße! - ihn) zu konfrontieren. Ich traute meinen Ohren nicht, als er weiterhin leugnete, mich je gekannt zu haben. Nachdem er mich mit Hilfe der Polizei aus seiner Praxis hinausgeworfen hatte, trug ich - ich muß es gestehen - Mordgedanken in meinem Herzen. Nachdem alles vorüber war, erwies sich dieses Treffen aber doch mehr oder weniger als das Beste. Mein Suchen nach meiner Mutter war ein für alle Mal vorüber. Sein Verhalten hatte alle Hoffnung auf Versöhnung in mir zerstört, und ich löschte ihn vollkommen aus meinem Leben. Zunächst erfuhr ich eine gewisse Befriedigung, als ich las, welches Aufsehen sein Buch erregte. Aber bald bemerkte ich, daß ich mich nicht länger darum scherte. Soviel ich weiß, publizierte er nie mehr auf Englisch, so daß ich nicht einmal beim Lesen an ihn erinnert wurde. Soweit es mich betraf, war er tot, und in der Tat, da die Zeit verging und ich wußte, daß er jetzt sehr alt sein müßte, nahm ich an, daß er wirklich nicht länger unter uns weilte.

Nun dies! Aus heiterem Himmel kommt ein Brief, in dem ich gebeten werde, mich an der Gründung eines Verlages, der seinen Namen tragen soll, und an der Veröffentlichung einer Festschrift für ihn zu beteiligen! Ich kann es nicht fassen!

Okay. Ich schreibe dies einige Tage, nachdem ich die Seiten oben verfaßt habe, und ich habe mich einigermaßen beruhigt. Ich bin nun in der Lage, klar darüber nachzudenken, was ich mit all dem tun will. Aus Gründen, die offensichtlich sind, kann ich es nicht einfach ignorieren. Wenn so viele berühmte Leute in unserem Feld Deinen Vorschlag als angemessen ansehen, muß Carl Auer etwas geleistet haben, dessen ich einfach nicht gewahr geworden bin: Entweder, weil es auf Deutsch veröffentlicht worden ist und nicht auf Englisch, oder weil ich gegenüber seiner fortbestehenden Existenz psychologisch blind war. Wenn das der Fall ist, so schulde ich es mir selbst und dem Feld, mich mit dem, was er getan hat, vertraut zu machen und in irgendeiner Weise an diesem Projekt teilzuhaben. Nicht nur das, ich entwickle auch eine wachsende Neugier. Ich möchte hören, was andere über meine Mutter zu sagen haben. Du hast ihm für mich neues Leben gegeben.

So, would you be kind enough to send me references for his work since the publication of his work on the Freud family, and, if possible, copies or reprints, too. I will write you again, once I have had a chance to catch up on his work.

Also, please be sure to send me whatever others write for you about this person. I must confess I cannot wait to read what comes forth!

With utmost sincerity

E. H. Auer(s)wald

P. S. Talk about synchronicity! Before I had a chance to mail the above, another astonishing revelation came my way. I have been writing a section of my forthcoming book on the epistemological shift in twentieth century science which includes an exploration of the metaphorical significance and usefulness of chaos theory. Today, in the reading I am doing to research this chapter, I ran across the work Carl von Auer has done since the days when he was writing in the family therapy literature - the work which undoubtedly led you to consider him so significant.

Until today, I did not know that he had become a chaos theorist, or that it was he who convinced the United Nations to establish the controversial World Coincidence Control Center. That idea has interested and bemused me ever since it began to receive publicity, and I have often thought that I would like to meet whoever originated it. Perhaps I can love my mother after all. Since, in the reality of the new epistemology, there is no such "thing" as a "personality," I can live with him in this reality and love his ideas!

Würdest Du also so nett sein, mir Literaturangaben seines Werkes seit der Veröffentlichung seiner Arbeit über die Familie Freud und, falls möglich, Exemplare oder Sonderdrucke davon zu senden. Ich werde Dir wieder schreiben, wenn ich die Chance hatte, mich mit seinem Werk vertraut zu machen.

Außerdem, vergiß nicht, mir zu schicken, was andere für Dich über diese Person schreiben. Ich muß gestehen, ich kann es nicht erwarten zu lesen, was dabei herauskommt.

Mit äußerster Aufrichtigkeit

E. H. Auer(s)wald

P.S. Sprich über Synchronizität! Bevor ich die Gelegenheit hatte, den Brief oben zur Post zu geben, traf ich auf eine andere erstaunliche Enthüllung. Ich war damit beschäftigt, ein Kapitel meines gerade entstehenden Buches über den erkenntnistheoretischen Wandel in der Wissenschaft des 20. Jahrhunderts, das auch eine Erörterung der metaphorischen Bedeutung und Nützlichkeit der Chaostheorie enthält, zu schreiben; heute, während der Lektüre, die ich zum Recherchieren dieses Kapitels betreibe, stieß ich auf das Werk, das Carl von Auer vollbracht hat, seit den Tagen, als er in der Familientherapieliteratur geschrieben hat - das Werk, das Dich zweifellos dazu brachte, ihn als so bedeutungsvoll anzusehen.

Bis heute wußte ich nicht, daß er Chaos-Theoretiker wurde oder daß er es war, der die Vereinten Nationen überzeugte, das so umstrittene Welt-Koinzidenz-Kontroll-Zentrum einzurichten. Diese Idee hat mich immer interessiert und verwirrt, seit sie begann, bekannt zu werden. Und ich habe oft gedacht, daß ich denjenigen, der sie hervorgebracht hat, gerne treffen würde. Vielleicht kann ich meine Mutter doch noch lieben. Da es in der Wirklichkeit der neuen Epistemologie ein solches „Ding“ wie „Persönlichkeit“ nicht gibt, kann ich mit ihm in dieser Realität leben und seine Ideen lieben.

Now What?

Auch das noch!

Carl Auer? We Don't Know him and Don't Want to Know him!

Interview with Mara Selvini Palazzoli and Matteo Selvini

WEBER: As you know, we've named our publishing house after Carl Auer. This man - it is said - has been very innovative. We know that he was born in the year 1900 - presumably in Austria or somewhere in the Austrian border area. We also know that Carl Auer was in Italy during his early years and speaks perfect Italian. And we know that you have also met Carl personally. Luigi Boscolo described how Auer made a decisive contribution to the development of circular questioning. Luigi told us about a conference in the early seventies during which the Milan team met Carl Auer. Can you remember this conference?

MARA SELVINI PALAZZOLI: Well, I can't remember anything about it. But as I am always interested in the causes of mental illness, I am now naturally interested to know why you are convinced that I could be interested in Carl Auer. That's a symptom. . . .

WEBER: That's just it. We would like to make a connection between you and this [1]symptom.

MARA SELVINI PALAZZOLI: You want to connect me with this symptom. But why, why . . . ?

SIMON: We are looking for the roots of systemic thinking and systemic therapy. And you are undoubtedly one of its founders. For that reason we just can't believe that you haven't met Carl Auer at some stage, since he is also one of its founding fathers.

Carl Auer? Kennen wir nicht und wollen wir nicht kennen!

Interview mit Mara Selvini-Palazzoli und Matteo Selvini

WEBER: Sie wissen, daß wir unseren Verlag nach Carl Auer genannt haben. Dieser Mann - so sagt man - ist ein sehr innovativer Mensch gewesen. Wir wissen, daß er im Jahr 1900 geboren wurde - vermutlich in Österreich. Wir wissen auch, daß Carl Auer schon in jungen Jahren in Italien war und perfekt Italienisch spricht. Und wir wissen, daß auch Sie Carl Auer kennenlernen konnten. Luigi Boscolo hat uns die Geschichte beschrieben, wie Auer einen ganz entscheidenden Beitrag zur Entwicklung des zirkulären Fragens leistete. Luigi hat uns von einer Konferenz in den frühen Siebziger Jahren erzählt, in welcher das Mailänder Team Carl Auer getroffen hat. Können Sie sich an diese Konferenz erinnern?

MARA SELVINI PALAZZOLI: Also, ich kann mich überhaupt nicht an so etwas erinnern. Aber da ich immer an den Ursachen psychischer Krankheit interessiert bin, interessiert es mich jetzt natürlich zu wissen, warum Sie überzeugt davon sind, daß ich mich für Carl Auer interessieren könnte. Das ist ein Symptom . . .

WEBER: Wir würden Sie eben gerne auch mit diesem Symptom in Verbindung bringen.

MARA SELVINI PALAZZOLI: Sie wollen mich mit diesem Symptom verbinden. Aber warum, warum . . . ?

SIMON: Wir sind auf der Suche nach den Wurzeln systemischen Denkens und systemischer Therapie. Und Sie gehören zweifellos zu deren Begründern. Wir können uns daher einfach nicht vorstellen, daß Sie nicht irgendwann mit Carl Auer zusammengetroffen sind. Denn er ist auch einer der Gründerväter.

Matteo Selvini: The problem is that we are a long way from inventing reality. In order to construct a reality we need something real to start from. The same applies for Carl Auer. We believe that reality is constructed from something that exists and can be established by everyone.

Mara Selvini Palazzoli: ... from something that has an intersubjective truth: *one* truth. Just as everyone would say that this (points to her handbag) is a bag, for example.

So, the complete change we have undergone from the work described in *Paradox and Counter-paradox* to our present work is exact-ly that we are not interested in what the family thinks of itself, and that we are not interested in what stories it tells. Do you understand?

Simon: But that means we have a problem now!

Mara Selvini Palazzoli: What problem?

Simon: Luigi Boscolo maintains that you know Carl Auer. You maintain that you don't know him.

Mara Selvini Palazzoli: In my opinion, Luigi Boscolo somehow thinks I still think like him, but I don't anymore.

Weber: Gianfranco Cecchin also told us about Carl Auer. He said he is convinced that it was Carl Auer who brought psychoanalysis to Italy.

Mara Selvini Palazzoli: I'd like to emphasize once again that I have no interest whatsoever in Carl Auer.

Simon *(Question to Matteo Selvini)*: How do you explain your mother's maintaining that she does not know Carl Auer?

Matteo Selvini: Well, we have a great aversion to inventing things. We have a sensitive mistrust of telling stories, and when we hear that some therapists think one must tell and invent stories. We have a

The mother of an autistic son refused the treatment because she was deeply shocked by the prescription of telling her mother, "For you the therapy we are participating in is secret; I must never tell you anything about it." That was a clear sign that her mother was more important for her than her child. So today, after nine years of work with these families we know right away, in the first session, that the parents are not telling the truth. Why? Because they insist that their only goal is to heal their son. But this is not the truth. In fact, when we give the prescription, they immediately realize that to follow it would break up their game, so they refuse to continue therapy. This is a fact, not a story told by the family. Their real goal is to maintain their game.

Matteo Selvini: And that is similar or comparable to the problem we have with Carl Auer: Our goal is to reveal facts and to discover what the parents are more or less consciously trying to hide. That's why we say that the problem with Carl Auer is similar to that with the families. We are too interested in finding the recurrent phenomena in the diverse family types. That's why we can't invent them; we want to discover them, since otherwise we are not in a position to do therapy. You, on the other hand, assume that the therapist can invent freely. That's how it is.

Mara Selvini Palazzoli: And now comes the difficult point. This does not mean that we think we don't construct. The human mind cannot not construct. Knowledge, even scientific knowledge, advances by means of construction.

The greatest discovery of genetic science, the double helix, is certainly a construction. But it is a construction which is much closer to the facts and can explain a number of phenomena.

Matteo Selvini: So, a story is constructed together with the family, but it is based only on the kind of thing that others can see intersubjectively. That means that practically we want to connect facts in the families, in the systems, that not only we can determine, but others too. By

Matteo Selvini: Das Problem ist, daß wir weit davon entfernt sind, die Realität zu erfinden. Um eine Realität konstruieren zu können, brauchen wir etwas Reales als Ausgangspunkt. Das gilt auch für Carl Auer. Denn wir denken, daß man die Realität mit etwas konstruiert, das existiert und das von allen festgestellt werden kann.

Mara Selvini Palazzoli: . . . mit etwas, das eine intersubjektive Wahrheit hat: *eine* Wahrheit. So wie zum Beispiel alle sagen würden, daß dies (zeigt auf ihre Handtasche) eine Tasche ist.

Also, die vollständige Änderung, die wir seit der in „Paradoxon und Gegenparadoxon" beschriebenen Arbeit zu unserer heutigen Arbeit vollzogen haben, ist gerade, daß es uns nicht interessiert, was die Familie von sich denkt, und daß es uns nicht interessiert, welche Geschichte sie erzählt. Verstehen Sie?

Simon: Aber dann haben wir jetzt ein Problem.

Mara Selvini Palazzoli: Was für ein Problem?

Simon: Luigi Boscolo behauptet, Sie kennen Carl Auer, Sie behaupten, Sie kennen ihn nicht.

Mara Selvini Palazzoli: Meiner Meinung nach kommt das daher, daß Luigi Boscolo irgendwie denkt, daß ich noch so denke, wie er, aber das tue ich nicht mehr.

Weber: Gianfranco Cecchin hat uns auch über Carl Auer berichtet. Er hat gesagt, daß er davon überzeugt ist, daß Carl Auer der Mensch ist, der die Psychoanalyse nach Italien gebracht hat.

Mara Selvini-Pallazoli: Ich möchte noch einmal betonen, daß ich keinerlei Interesse an Carl Auer habe!

Simon *(Frage an Matteo Selvini)*: Wie erklären Sie sich, daß Ihre Mutter behauptet, Carl Auer nicht zu kennen?

Matteo Selvini: Also, wir haben eine große Abneigung gegen Dinge, die erfunden werden sollen. Wir haben ein empfindliches Mißtrauen dagegen, Geschichten zu erzählen, und wenn wir hören, daß manche

sensitive nose, our stomachs rebel against that kind of thing. We have the same feeling towards Carl Auer, and that's why we don't know him.

Mara Selvini Palazzoli: And I'd like to add that this is the attitude of the whole team. It could appear to be paranoic rigidity, but in truth it's not that at the moment. It's a result of the rejection of what we have done before. Let me explain in more detail: For 17 years I was a psychoanalyst and believed in psychoanalysis. Then, after reading Lyman Wynne's work on mental disturbance and family relationships of schizophrenics in 1965, I immediately stopped believing in psychoanalysis and concluded my psychoanalytical work. I am not Joan of Arc, but I could afford to do that, since I was fed anyway. My husband provided for me. I could afford these silly notions, couldn't I?

After having been a psychoanalyst, I now embraced the systemic model and worked with paradoxical methods. I was in a long manic phase, in a delirium of megalomania. Because instead of needing four years to recover from anorexia, four sessions were enough. Do you understand?

I wasn't mad. But it was a natural reaction to the long frustrations of the past 17 years, during which I accompanied my patients undergoing psychoanalytic treatment to hospital on account of relapses. The same applied to psychotics. These successes were a real triumph, even if there was also a feeling of revenge on these patients: "For so many years you've put one over on me, now it's my turn!"

Then this phase passed, because I saw its faults and its limits, and I transferred to an experimental model that consisted in giving an invariant prescription. Whether it was observed, accepted, not observed or not accepted. As a result the story told by the family was not listened to, but reconstructed from the families' reactions to the prescription.

Therapeuten meinen, daß man die Geschichten erzählen und den muß. Wir haben da einen empfindlichen Spürsinn, unser M rebelliert bei solch einer Sache. Auch Carl Auer gegenüber habe das gleiche Gefühl, und deswegen kennen wir ihn nicht.

Mara Selvini Palazzoli: Und ich will hinzufügen, daß dies die tung des gesamten Teams ist. Sie könnte auch als eine parano Rigidität erscheinen, aber in Wahrheit ist sie das im Moment nich ist eine Folge der Ablehnung dessen, was wir vorher gemacht ha Lassen Sie mich dies genauer erklären. Siebzehn Jahre lang wa Psychoanalytikerin und hab an dieses Modell geglaubt. Dann, al 1965 die Arbeit von Lyman Wynne über Denkstörungen Familienbeziehungen von Schizophrenen gelesen habe, habe augenblicklich aufgehört, an die Psychoanalyse zu glauben, habe die psychoanalytische Arbeit abgeschlossen. Ich bin nicht Jea d'Arc, doch ich konnte es mir erlauben, da ich gleichwohl zu es hatte. Mein Mann gab mir zu essen. Ich konnte mir diese Gri erlauben, nicht wahr?

Nachdem ich Psychoanalytikerin gewesen war, umarmte ich r das systemische Modell und arbeitete mit paradoxen Methoden. war in einer langen manischen Phase, in einem Delirium des Größe wahns. Denn anstatt vier Jahre für die Gesundung einer Anorexia brauchen, genügten mir vier Sitzungen. Verstehen Sie ?

Ich war nicht verrückt. Aber es war eine natürliche Reaktion die langen Frustrationen der vergangenen 17 Jahre, in denen meine Patientinnen während der psychoanalytischen Behandlun wegen Rückfällen ins Krankenhaus begleitete. Dasselbe galt Psychotiker. Diese Erfolge waren wahrhaftig ein Triumph, s wenn auch ein Gefühl da war, sich bei diesen Patienten zu re chieren. „Für so viele Jahre habt ihr mich reingelegt, jetzt lege ich rein!"

Dann ist diese Phase vorübergegangen, weil ich die Fehler die Grenzen gesehen habe, und ich bin zu einem Versuchsm übergegangen, welches darin bestand, die unveränderliche schreibung zu geben. Ob sie sie befolgten, akzeptierten, sie befolgten oder nicht akzeptierten. Folglich wurde die von der F erzählte Geschichte nicht angehört, sondern aus ihren Reaktion die Verordnung rekonstruiert.

MATTEO SELVINI: Das Problem ist, daß wir weit davon entfernt sind, die Realität zu erfinden. Um eine Realität konstruieren zu können, brauchen wir etwas Reales als Ausgangspunkt. Das gilt auch für Carl Auer. Denn wir denken, daß man die Realität mit etwas konstruiert, das existiert und das von allen festgestellt werden kann.

MARA SELVINI PALAZZOLI: ... mit etwas, das eine intersubjektive Wahrheit hat: *eine* Wahrheit. So wie zum Beispiel alle sagen würden, daß dies (zeigt auf ihre Handtasche) eine Tasche ist.

Also, die vollständige Änderung, die wir seit der in „Paradoxon und Gegenparadoxon" beschriebenen Arbeit zu unserer heutigen Arbeit vollzogen haben, ist gerade, daß es uns nicht interessiert, was die Familie von sich denkt, und daß es uns nicht interessiert, welche Geschichte sie erzählt. Verstehen Sie?

SIMON: Aber dann haben wir jetzt ein Problem.

MARA SELVINI PALAZZOLI: Was für ein Problem?

SIMON: Luigi Boscolo behauptet, Sie kennen Carl Auer, Sie behaupten, Sie kennen ihn nicht.

MARA SELVINI PALAZZOLI: Meiner Meinung nach kommt das daher, daß Luigi Boscolo irgendwie denkt, daß ich noch so denke, wie er, aber das tue ich nicht mehr.

WEBER: Gianfranco Cecchin hat uns auch über Carl Auer berichtet. Er hat gesagt, daß er davon überzeugt ist, daß Carl Auer der Mensch ist, der die Psychoanalyse nach Italien gebracht hat.

MARA SELVINI-PALLAZOLI: Ich möchte noch einmal betonen, daß ich keinerlei Interesse an Carl Auer habe!

SIMON *(Frage an Matteo Selvini)*: Wie erklären Sie sich, daß Ihre Mutter behauptet, Carl Auer nicht zu kennen?

MATTEO SELVINI: Also, wir haben eine große Abneigung gegen Dinge, die erfunden werden sollen. Wir haben ein empfindliches Mißtrauen dagegen, Geschichten zu erzählen, und wenn wir hören, daß manche

sensitive nose, our stomachs rebel against that kind of thing. We have the same feeling towards Carl Auer, and that's why we don't know him.

MARA SELVINI PALAZZOLI: And I'd like to add that this is the attitude of the whole team. It could appear to be paranoic rigidity, but in truth it's not that at the moment. It's a result of the rejection of what we have done before. Let me explain in more detail: For 17 years I was a psychoanalyst and believed in psychoanalysis. Then, after reading Lyman Wynne's work on mental disturbance and family relationships of schizophrenics in 1965, I immediately stopped believing in psychoanalysis and concluded my psychoanalytical work. I am not Joan of Arc, but I could afford to do that, since I was fed anyway. My husband provided for me. I could afford these silly notions, couldn't I?

After having been a psychoanalyst, I now embraced the systemic model and worked with paradoxical methods. I was in a long manic phase, in a delirium of megalomania. Because instead of needing four years to recover from anorexia, four sessions were enough. Do you understand?

I wasn't mad. But it was a natural reaction to the long frustrations of the past 17 years, during which I accompanied my patients undergoing psychoanalytic treatment to hospital on account of relapses. The same applied to psychotics. These successes were a real triumph, even if there was also a feeling of revenge on these patients: "For so many years you've put one over on me, now it's my turn!"

Then this phase passed, because I saw its faults and its limits, and I transferred to an experimental model that consisted in giving an invariant prescription. Whether it was observed, accepted, not observed or not accepted. As a result the story told by the family was not listened to, but reconstructed from the families' reactions to the prescription.

Therapeuten meinen, daß man die Geschichten erzählen und erfinden muß. Wir haben da einen empfindlichen Spürsinn, unser Magen rebelliert bei solch einer Sache. Auch Carl Auer gegenüber haben wir das gleiche Gefühl, und deswegen kennen wir ihn nicht.

Mara Selvini Palazzoli: Und ich will hinzufügen, daß dies die Haltung des gesamten Teams ist. Sie könnte auch als eine paranoische Rigidität erscheinen, aber in Wahrheit ist sie das im Moment nicht. Sie ist eine Folge der Ablehnung dessen, was wir vorher gemacht haben. Lassen Sie mich dies genauer erklären. Siebzehn Jahre lang war ich Psychoanalytikerin und hab an dieses Modell geglaubt. Dann, als ich 1965 die Arbeit von Lyman Wynne über Denkstörungen und Familienbeziehungen von Schizophrenen gelesen habe, habe ich augenblicklich aufgehört, an die Psychoanalyse zu glauben, und habe die psychoanalytische Arbeit abgeschlossen. Ich bin nicht Jeanne d'Arc, doch ich konnte es mir erlauben, da ich gleichwohl zu essen hatte. Mein Mann gab mir zu essen. Ich konnte mir diese Grillen erlauben, nicht wahr?

Nachdem ich Psychoanalytikerin gewesen war, umarmte ich nun das systemische Modell und arbeitete mit paradoxen Methoden. Ich war in einer langen manischen Phase, in einem Delirium des Größenwahns. Denn anstatt vier Jahre für die Gesundung einer Anorexia zu brauchen, genügten mir vier Sitzungen. Verstehen Sie ?

Ich war nicht verrückt. Aber es war eine natürliche Reaktion auf die langen Frustrationen der vergangenen 17 Jahre, in denen ich meine Patientinnen während der psychoanalytischen Behandlungen wegen Rückfällen ins Krankenhaus begleitete. Dasselbe galt für Psychotiker. Diese Erfolge waren wahrhaftig ein Triumph, selbst wenn auch ein Gefühl da war, sich bei diesen Patienten zu revanchieren. „Für so viele Jahre habt ihr mich reingelegt, jetzt lege ich euch rein!"

Dann ist diese Phase vorübergegangen, weil ich die Fehler und die Grenzen gesehen habe, und ich bin zu einem Versuchsmodell übergegangen, welches darin bestand, die unveränderliche Verschreibung zu geben. Ob sie sie befolgten, akzeptierten, sie nicht befolgten oder nicht akzeptierten. Folglich wurde die von der Familie erzählte Geschichte nicht angehört, sondern aus ihren Reaktionen auf die Verordnung rekonstruiert.

The mother of an autistic son refused the treatment because she was deeply shocked by the prescription of telling her mother, "For you the therapy we are participating in is secret; I must never tell you anything about it." That was a clear sign that her mother was more important for her than her child. So today, after nine years of work with these families we know right away, in the first session, that the parents are not telling the truth. Why? Because they insist that their only goal is to heal their son. But this is not the truth. In fact, when we give the prescription, they immediately realize that to follow it would break up their game, so they refuse to continue therapy. This is a fact, not a story told by the family. Their real goal is to maintain their game.

MATTEO SELVINI: And that is similar or comparable to the problem we have with Carl Auer: Our goal is to reveal facts and to discover what the parents are more or less consciously trying to hide. That's why we say that the problem with Carl Auer is similar to that with the families. We are too interested in finding the recurrent phenomena in the diverse family types. That's why we can't invent them; we want to discover them, since otherwise we are not in a position to do therapy. You, on the other hand, assume that the therapist can invent freely. That's how it is.

MARA SELVINI PALAZZOLI: And now comes the difficult point. This does not mean that we think we don't construct. The human mind cannot not construct. Knowledge, even scientific knowledge, advances by means of construction.

The greatest discovery of genetic science, the double helix, is certainly a construction. But it is a construction which is much closer to the facts and can explain a number of phenomena.

MATTEO SELVINI: So, a story is constructed together with the family, but it is based only on the kind of thing that others can see intersubjectively. That means that practically we want to connect facts in the families, in the systems, that not only we can determine, but others too. By

Die Mutter eines autistischen Sohnes lehnte die Behandlung ab, weil sie durch die Verschreibung, ihrer Mutter zu sagen: „Die Therapie, an der wir teilnehmen, bleibt für dich geheim. Ich darf dir nie etwas darüber sagen", völlig schockiert war. Das war ein klares Zeichen, daß ihre Mutter ihr wichtiger war als ihr Kind. So daß wir heute, nach neun Jahren Arbeit mit dieser Verschreibung, vor Tatsachen stehen. Wir wissen beispielsweise bei manchen Familien mit chronisch Schizophrenen sofort in der ersten Sitzung, daß diese Familie nicht die Wahrheit sagt. Warum? Weil sie beteuern, daß es ihr einziges Ziel sei, den Sohn zu heilen. Das ist aber nicht wahr. Tatsache ist, daß sie sofort, wenn wir die Verschreibung geben, realisieren, daß ihr Spiel, wenn sie der Verschreibung folgten, verdorben ist. Deshalb weigern sie sich, die Therapie fortzusetzen. Dies ist eine Tatsache und keine von der Familie erzählte Geschichte. Ihr wirkliches Ziel ist, das Spiel aufrechtzuerhalten.

Matteo Selvini: Und das ist dann ähnlich oder vergleichbar mit dem Problem, das wir mit Carl Auer haben: Es ist unser Ziel, Tatsachen aufzudecken und herauszufinden, was die Eltern mehr oder weniger bewußt zu verbergen suchen. Deswegen sagen wir, daß es sich bei dem Problem mit Carl Auer so verhält, wie mit den Familien. Wir sind zu sehr daran interessiert, die in den diversen Familientypen wiederkehrenden Phänomene zu finden. Deswegen können wir sie nicht erfinden, wir wollen sie wirklich entdecken, da wir sonst nicht in der Lage sind, Therapie zu machen. Sie nehmen stattdessen an, der Therapeut könne frei erfinden. So ist das.

Mara Selvini Palazzoli: So, nun kommt der schwierige Moment. Das will nicht heißen, daß wir meinen, nicht zu konstruieren. Der menschliche Geist kann nicht nicht konstruieren. Das Wissen, auch das wissenschaftlichste, schreitet durch Konstruktion fort.

Die größte Entdeckung der Wissenschaft, die doppelte Helix, ist sicher eine Konstruktion. Aber es ist eine Konstruktion, die den Tatsachen sehr viel näher ist und viele Phänomene erklären kann.

Matteo Selvini: Also, es wird eine Geschichte gemeinsam mit der Familie konstruiert, aber die wird nur auf die Dinge aufgebaut, die intersubjektiv auch von anderen gesehen werden können. Das heißt, praktisch wollen wir Fakten verbinden, in den Familien, in den

means of our constructions we want to create co-constructions, to build up a story out of intersubjectively perceptible facts.

MARA SELVINI PALAZZOLI: Essentially the task or work we are now doing consists in draughting maps, very specific maps, for forming a hypothesis: If, for example, a family comes with a chronic schizophrenic child, and the child is openly adored by the father, who is very attached to it and gives it a lot of attention, and the mother rejects the child, then beware! In such a case it is usual to find that there has been a previous pseudo-privileged relationship between the mother and this child and that the mother seduced the child and used him as an anti-father but abandoned him when he failed.... Or when a sibling, for example a brother or sister who is himself/herself a psychiatrist or psychologist, or has a prestige of one kind or another in his family, is the one who encourages family therapy, then be careful about making it, because this very sibling can be at the root of the family pathology. These are not only recurring clues for us, but for other therapists too.[1] If they heed it and it forces true, they have the means of doing good therapy. And that's why we are not interested in inventing stories.

WEBER: What you say makes quite clear why Carl Auer is a suspect figure for you.

MARA SELVINI PALAZZOLI: Carl Auer a suspect? No! In my opinion he represents a particular line of thinking that I no longer share.

MATTEO SELVINI: He represents this radical constructivism....

MARA SELVINI PALAZZOLI: ... which in itself is a very positive thing: it's the botch-up some family therapists have made of it that it is so detrimental. They have often used it for therapeutical relativism and nihilism.

Systemen, die nicht nur wir feststellen können, sondern auch andere. Mit unseren Konstruktionen wollen wir Ko-Konstruktionen schaffen, auf intersubjektiven wahrnehmbaren Tatsachen eine Geschichte aufbauen.

Mara Selvini Palazzoli: Im wesentlichen besteht die Aufgabe oder die Arbeit, die wir jetzt machen, darin, daß wir Landkarten, sehr spezifische Landkarten, für die Hypothetisierung entwerfen: Wenn z. B. eine Familie mit einem chronisch schizophrenen Kind kommt, in welcher der Vater das Kind offensichtlich anbetet und die Mutter das Kind ablehnt, dann seid vorsichtig! Dann läßt sich in der Regel feststellen, daß es vorher eine Pseudo-Privilegiertenbeziehung gab zwischen der Mutter und diesem Kind und daß die Mutter das Kind verführte und es als Gegenvater benutzte, es aber fallenließ, als es versagte... Oder wenn Geschwister es sind, z. B. ein Bruder oder eine Schwester, der/die selbst ein Psychiater/in oder Psychologe/in ist oder sonstwie Prestige in der Familie besitzt, die zu einer Familientherapie raten. Dann prüfe genau, ob du eine machen willst, weil gerade dieser Bruder oder diese Schwester der Ursprung der Familienpathologie sein kann. Dieses sind nicht nur für uns wiederkehrende Fingerzeige, sondern für andere Therapeuten auch. Wenn sie darauf achten, und es sich als richtig herausstellt, haben sie ein Mittel, gute Therapie zu machen. Und darum sind wir nicht daran interessiert, Geschichten zu erfinden.

Weber: Aus dem, was Sie gesagt haben, wird auch deutlich, warum Carl Auer für Sie eine suspekte Figur ist.

Mara Selvini Palazzoli: Carl Auer eine suspekte Person? Nein, meiner Meinung nach repräsentiert er eine bestimmte Richtung des Denkens, die ich nicht mehr teile.

Matteo Selvini: Er repräsentiert diesen radikalen Konstruktivismus ...

Mara Selvini Palazzoli: ... der für sich genommen eine sehr positive Sache ist: Es ist die Pfuscherei, welche einige Familientherapeuten daraus gemacht haben, die so schädlich ist. Sie haben ihn häufig für therapeutischen Relativismus und Nihilismus benutzt.

MATTEO SELVINI: . . . and to free themselves from therapeutical responsibility.

WEBER: We thank you for this interview.

[1] Selvini Palazzoli, M.: "The problem of the sibling as the referring person," *Journal of Marital and Family Therapy*, 11, 21-34, 1985.

MATTEO SELVINI: ... und um sich von der therapeutischen Verantwortung zu befreien.

WEBER: Wir danken Ihnen für das Gespräch.

[1] Selvini Palazzoli, M.: „The problem of the sibling as the referring person", *Journal of Marital and Family Therapy*, 11, 21-34, 1985.

Epilogue

Targets on the Truth - Annotated Chronological Table

Do we not frequently experience that wild fantasies prove to be well-founded, and what seem to be facts turn out to be falsities?

In reference to an exact inquiry into the life and work of Carl Auer this volume can only be the starting point for a careful search for tracks. And yet it provides us with a great number of surprising clues and details. Since all the contributors to this acknowledgement and collection of information are scientists, doctors and psycho-therapists of some reputation, their reports can be considered largely as reliable documents and historical sources. In order to present a first rough summary of Carl Auer´s journey through life we have tried to extract all the important „hard" information from the dense personal accounts of the various authors, put them together in the form of a table and to comment on them. Where we were in possession of material that is not directly referred to in this book (e.g. film material), we have also integrated this knowledge in the chronological table.

1900	Up till now we have practically no reliable information about his early childhood and his parental home. Only one thing seems to be clear: he was born in a small village on the Swiss south bank of Lake Constance, which has meanwhile been incorporated into the climatic health resort of Rorschach, and grew up in the second district of Vienna, where Sigmund Freud lived with his family, too. It has been hinted that he is the illegitimate child of an Italian opera singer. Bertha, one of his father's sisters who lived nearby, was the person to whom he related most

Epilog

Die Wahrheit im Visier - Kommentierte Zeittafel

Machen wir nicht immer wieder die Erfahrung, daß wilde Phantasien sich bewahrheiten und scheinbare Fakten sich als Fälschungen erweisen?

Dieser Band kann, was die exaktere Erforschung des Lebens und Wirkens von Carl Auer betrifft, nur Ausgangspunkt für eine sorgfältige Spurensuche sein. Dafür jedoch liefert er schon wahrlich eine Menge erstaunlicher Hinweise und Details. Da alle, die zu dieser Würdigung und Bestandsaufnahme beitrugen, Wissenschaftler, Ärzte und Psychotherapeuten von beträchtlichem Renommee sind, können ihre Ausführungen als verläßliche Dokumente und historische Quellen betrachtet werden. Um einen ersten, ungefähren Abriß des Lebenswegs Carl Auers zu geben, haben wir uns bemüht, aus den dichten persönlichen Schilderungen der verschiedenen Autoren alle wesentlichen „harten" Informationen zu extrahieren, in tabellarischer Form zusammenzustellen und zu kommentieren. Wo uns Material zur Verfügung stand, auf das in diesem Buch nicht direkt Bezug genommen wurde (z.B. Filmdokumente), haben wir auch dieses Wissen in unsere Zeittafel eingearbeitet.

1900 Über seine frühe Kindheit und das Elternhaus liegen bisher so gut wie keine zuverlässigen Nachrichten vor. Nur eines scheint klar zu sein: Geboren in einem kleinen, inzwischen vom Luftkurort Rorschach eingemeindeten Dorf am schweizerischen Südufer des Bodensees, wuchs Auer im 2. Bezirk in Wien, in dem auch Sigmund Freud mit seiner Familie lebte, auf. Es gibt Andeutungen, daß er der uneheliche Sohn einer italienischen Opernsängerin ist. Bertha, eine Schwester des Vaters, die in der Nähe wohnte, war für ihn eine wichtige Bezugsperson. Über

closely. He had contacts with the Freud family through friendship with Freud's niece Annabella. Over and above this there are indications that relations existed between the Auer Family and the Einsteins. The assumptions that Carl Auer is Albert Einstein's first cousin could not be verified to this day. However, Auer's second wife, Jelena, had an intensive interchange with Einstein's wife Milena later.

1910 Started at the same grammar school which Heinz von Foerster was to attend later.

1914 Important personal insights (content unknown, but probably connected with the outbreak of the First World War).

1917 Passed his 'A' levels with mediocre results.

1918 Participation in the First World War (on the Austrian side). Wounded and made prisoner of war in Italy. In captivity he was cell mate to Ludwig Wittgenstein in Monte Cassino.

1922-23 Student and at the same time private tutor; gave the young Heinz von Foerster private Tuition in mathematics, for example.

1924 Marriage to E. Wald. First emigration to the United States of America (Wisconsin). His marriage to E. Wald produced the sons Edgar and Normal Auerswald.

1926-27 Sojourn in Chile. Acquaintance with Mother Maturana.

1927-29 Studied art in Paris (with Fernand Léger among others). Acquaintance with Mother Hoffman at an opening day of the sculptor Ossip Zadkine.

die Freundschaft zu Annabella, einer Nichte Sigmund Freuds, gab es Kontakte zum Hause Freud. Darüberhinaus gibt es Hinweise darauf, daß zwischen der Familie Auer und der Familie Einstein Beziehungen bestanden. Die Vermutung, daß Carl Auer ein Cousin Albert Einsteins sei, ließ sich bislang nicht bestätigen. Auf alle Fälle hatte später Auers zweite Frau Jelena einen intensiven Austausch mit Einsteins Frau Milena.

1910 Einschulung in dasselbe Gymnasiums, das später auch Heinz von Foerster absolvieren sollte.

1914 Wichtige persönliche Erkenntnisse (Inhalt unbekannt, wahrscheinlich aber im Zusammenhang mit dem Beginn des zweiten Weltkrieges).

1917 Bestehen der Maturaprüfung mit mäßigen Leistungen.

1918 Teilnahme am ersten Weltkrieg (auf österreichischer Seite). Verwundung und Kriegsgefangenschaft in Italien. In der Gefangenschaft Zellengenosse Ludwig Wittgensteins in Monte Cassino.

1922 - 23 Student und nebenbei Hauslehrer, der dem kleinen Heinz von Foerster Nachhilfeunterricht in Mathematik erteilt.

1924 Vermählung mit E. Wald. Erstes Auswandern in die Vereinigten Staaten von Amerika (Wisconsin). Aus der Ehe mit E. Wald gehen die Söhne Edgar und Normal Auerswald hervor.

1926 - 27 Aufenthalt in Chile. Bekanntschaft mit Mutter Maturana.

1927 - 29 Studium der Malerei in Paris (unter anderen bei Fernand Léger). Auf einer Vernissage des Bildhauers Ossip Zadkine Bekanntschaft mit Mutter Hoffman.

1929-34	Achieved temporary fame under the name of Leonard Zelig first in the United States, then in Europe.
1934	Return to Vienna, studied psychoanalysis.
1936	Teaching post at the University of Vienna (probably chemistry, at all events continued analytical work). What contact he had to Ludwig von Bertalanffy, who taught biology there at that time, remains obscure.
1936	Separation from E. Wald.
1937-38	Psychoanalysis in the United States.
1938	Operation in Mexico City (sex change?).
1938	Encounter with Ernst von Glasersfeld on a glacier in the Austrian Alps. At this time occupation as editor of left-wing newspaper in Vienna. First acquaintance with his second wife-to-be, Jelena Kuss. This marriage produced two children, Carl-Anton and Nina. After Anschluß of Austria to the German Reich he fled to Switzerland.
1939	Honorary citizen of Appenzell ("Rescuer of Appenzell").
1940-45	Visiting professor at University of Canterbury/New Zealand. Begin of long friendship with Karl Popper.
1942	Vacation in U.S.A. Stayed with Peggy Penn's family in the Penn(!)sylvanian Hills.
1945	Return to Europe. For the first months stayed with the Enderlin family in Switzerland.
1946-47	Teaching post at the Swiss Technical College in Zurich. Then began a time of intensive travel.

1929 - 34	Erregt zunächst in den Vereinigten Staaten, später auch in Europa unter dem Namen Leonard Zelig eine vorübergehende Berühmtheit.
1934	Rückkehr nach Wien, Beschäftigung mit Psychoanalyse.
1936	Lehrauftrag an der Universität Wien (wahrscheinlich Chemie, auf jeden Fall weiterhin analytische Tätigkeit). Wie der Kontakt zu Ludwig von Bertalanffy, der dort zu dieser Zeit Biologie lehrte, war, bleibt unklar.
1936	Trennung von E. Wald.
1937 - 38	Psychoanalyse in den Vereinigten Staaten
1938	Operation in Mexico City (Geschlechtsumwandlung?)
1938	Zusammentreffen mit Ernst von Glasersfeld auf einem Gletscher in den Österreichischen Alpen. In dieser Zeit Beschäftigung als Redakteur einer linken Zeitung in Wien. Erstes Kennenlernen seiner späteren Frau Jelena Kuss. Aus der Ehe gehen die beiden Kinder Carl-Anton und Nina hervor. Nach dem Anschluß Österreichs ans Deutsche Reich Flucht in die Schweiz.
1939	Ehrenbürger von Appenzell („Retter von Appenzell").
1940 - 45	Gastprofessor an der Universität von Canterbury/NZ. Beginn der langen Freundschaft mit Karl Popper.
1942	Semesterferien in den USA. Aufenthalt in der Familie Peggy Penns in den Bergen Penn(!)sylvanias.
1945	Rückkehr nach Europa. In den ersten Monaten Aufenthalt bei Familie Enderlin in der Schweiz.
1946 - 47	Lehrauftrag an der Eidgenössischen Technischen Hochschule in Zürich. Danach Beginn einer intensiven Reisezeit.

1948	Was occupied for several months in the Chestnut Lodge Sanatorium near Washington D.C.
1949	Met André Gide in Paris (there is no proof of a suspected homosexual relationship). Afterwards journey to Haiti where he called himself Charles d'Auer and cultivated intensive contacts to Voodoo priests.
1950	Stayed in Italy. Ernst von Glasersfeld listened to one of his lectures there. In Heidelberg he then held his meanwhile famous Heidelberg lectures. Towards the end of the year Helm Stierlin thinks he met him in the Black Forest, where Auer had gone for a rest. An encounter with Heidegger is probable. We know for certain that the insight that „nothingness is of itself none" was originally Auer's. The second half of this profound piece of writing „. . . and the hole is essentially hole-istic" was not adopted by Heidegger as an integral part of his philosophy.
1951	Return to the U.S.A. In Phoenix/Arizona he met Milton Erickson, of almost the same age, and Jack Daniels, who was twelve at the time. He left practically no tracks for almost two decades, the few facts and clues available are not sufficiently substantiated.
1959	Practiced psychotherapy in Vienna (?)
1969	Separation from wife Jelena.
1976 - 77	Stayed in Milwaukee where a street was named after him.
1978 - 80	Planned a „new town" in Arcosanti in the Arizona desert together with Paolo Soleri and a young Mexican architect.

1948	Mehrmonatiger Arbeitsaufenthalt im Chestnut Lodge Sanatorium in der Nähe von Washington D.C.
1949	Zusammentreffen mit André Gide in Paris (für eine vermutete homosexuelle Beziehung der beiden gibt es keine Belege). Anschließend Reise nach Haiti, wo er sich Charles d'Auer nennt und intensive Kontakte mit Voodoo-Priestern pflegt.
1950	Aufenthalt in Italien. Ernst von Glasersfeld hört dort einen Vortrag von ihm. Anschließend hält er in Heidelberg seine inzwischen berühmten Heidelberger Vorlesungen. Am Ende des Jahres meint Helm Stierlin, ihn im Schwarzwald, wohin Auer sich zur Erholung zurückgezogen hatte, getroffen zu haben. Ein Zusammentreffen mit Heidegger ist wahrscheinlich. Sicher ist, daß die Einsicht „Das Nichts nichtet" ursprünglich von Auer stammt. Die zweite Hälfte dieses gehaltvollen Gedankens „. . . und das Loch locht noch!" wurde allerdings von Heidegger nicht zum Bestandteil seiner Philosophie gemacht.
1951	Rückkehr in die USA. Zusammentreffen mit dem fast gleichaltrigen Milton Erickson und dem damals zwölf Jahre alten Jack Daniels in Phönix/Arizona. Danach verlieren sich für fast zwei Jahrzehnte seine Spuren, die wenigen Daten und Hinweise sind wenig abgesichert und von fraglicher Zuverlässigkeit.
1959	Psychotherapie-Praxis in Wien (?)
1969	Trennung von seiner Frau Jelena.
1976 - 77	Aufenthalt in Milwaukee, wo eine Straße nach ihm benannt wurde.
1978 - 80	Gemeinsam mit Paolo Soleri und einer jungen mexikanischen Architektin Planung einer „neuen Stadt" in Arcosanti, in der Wüste Arizonas.

1980 - 85	Work on chaos theory.
1985	Travelled to Australia and New Zealand to his former place of work. Encountered David Epston.
1985 - 88	Head of the United Nations World Coincidence Control Center (Wocococ).
1988	Journey to Europe. Hiking in the Odenwald near Heidelberg. Meeting with A. Retzer, F.B. Simon and G. Weber on 22nd November, agreement on the arrangements for publishing a *festschrift* in his honour and on setting up a publishing house.
1988 - 90	For the past two years Auer has lived a secluded life on Coney Island as silent partner of an amusement park.

1980 - 85	Studien zur Chaos-Theorie.
1985	Reise nach Australien und Neuseeland zu seinen alten Wirkungsstätten. Zusammentreffen mit David Epston.
1985 - 88	Leiter des World Coincidence Control Centers (Wocococ) der Vereinten Nationen.
1988	Reise nach Europa. Wanderungen im Odenwald bei Heidelberg. Am 22. November Treffen mit A. Retzer, F. B. Simon und G. Weber, Einigung über die Modalitäten der Veröffentlichung einer Festschrift zu seinen Ehren und die Gründung eines Verlages.
1988 - 90	Seit zwei Jahren lebt Auer zurückgezogen auf Coney Island als stiller Teilhaber an einem Vergnügungspark.